D0337810

Making Chastity Sexy

Making Chastity Sexy

*The Rhetoric of Evangelical
Abstinence Campaigns*

Christine J. Gardner

UNIVERSITY OF CALIFORNIA PRESS
Berkeley · Los Angeles · London

University of California Press, one of the most distinguished university presses in the United States,
enriches lives around the world by advancing scholarship in the humanities, social sciences, and natural
sciences. Its activities are supported by the UC Press
Foundation and by philanthropic contributions from
individuals and institutions. For more information,
visit www.ucpress.edu.

University of California Press
Berkeley and Los Angeles, California

University of California Press, Ltd.
London, England

Library of Congress Cataloging-in-Publication Data

Gardner, Christine J. (Christine Joy), 1969–
   Making chastity sexy : the rhetoric of evangelical
abstinence campaigns / Christine J. Gardner.
      p.   cm.
   Includes bibliographical references and index.
   ISBN 978-0-520-26727-5 (cloth : alk. paper)
   ISBN 978-0-520-26728-2 (pbk. : alk. paper)
   1. Sexual abstinence—Religious aspects—
Christianity.   2. Sexual abstinence—Study and teach-
ing—United States.   3. Teenagers—Sexual behav-
ior—United States.   4. Sex instruction for teenagers—
Religious aspects—Christianity.   I. Title.
   HQ63.G35 2011
   261.8'35708350973—dc22   2010052677

Manufactured in the United States of America

20 19 18 17 16 15 14 13 12 11
10 9 8 7 6 5 4 3 2 1

In keeping with a commitment to support
environmentally responsible and sustainable printing
practices, UC Press has printed this book on Rolland
Enviro100, a 100% post-consumer fiber paper that
is FSC certified, deinked, processed chlorine-free, and
manufactured with renewable biogas energy. It is
acid-free and EcoLogo certified.

To my parents,
Dave and Becky LeShana,
with love

Contents

Acknowledgments

Research projects—like abstinence pledges—are most successful when undertaken in community. I owe a debt of gratitude to the community of colleagues, friends, and family that has supported me through this process.

First, I owe my thanks to the leaders and participants of the evangelical sexual abstinence campaigns. This study would not have been possible without the assistance of the many individuals, organizations, and churches that allowed me access to their programs and to their lives. I am grateful to Dannah Gresh of Pure Freedom, Denny Pattyn of Silver Ring Thing, and Jimmy Hester and Richard Ross of True Love Waits for supporting this study. Their genuine care and concern for young people is evident in all they do. I consider it a privilege to have had the opportunity to observe their work. Special thanks to Debbie Dortzbach and the Kenya and Rwanda country offices of World Relief for granting me access to programs and staff. Seeing abstinence in the context of HIV/AIDS has profoundly shaped my thinking. The World Relief staff members I met are truly living and working on the front line, bringing tangible hope and help where it is desperately needed. I am humbled by their dedication. I am particularly grateful to the many young people I interviewed, both in the United States and in Rwanda. Their stories are the heart of this project. Only some of their stories are included here, but all their stories have enriched and informed my perspective. Regardless of their view of my analysis, I trust my interview subjects will sense the respect with which I approached their work and their stories. I have tried to faithfully share their stories here, just as they candidly shared their stories with me.

Numerous individuals supported this project from its early beginnings. I am deeply grateful for the wise counsel and direction of David Zarefsky. His rhetorical insight and attention to detail is unparalleled. I consider myself fortunate to have worked with him as an adviser when this project began as a dissertation. Tom Goodnight and Jim Ettema read initial drafts and offered helpful advice. Angela Ray went far beyond the call of duty. Her careful edits have made this a much better book, and her support has made me a better scholar. I am especially grateful to my mentor Wendy Griswold for prompting me to expand my inquiry into Africa. Her encouragement—both personally and professionally—infuses this project. Her trenchant comments, inquisitive mind, dynamic teaching, and vibrant scholarship continue to inspire me.

My work has benefited from the opportunity to present portions of this project at various conferences and workshops. I have presented chapters of this work at conferences hosted by the National Communication Association, the Religious Communication Association, and the Rhetoric Society of America. I am grateful to Robert Wuthnow and the members of the Religion and Public Life Workshop at Princeton University for their supportive and insightful critiques. Many thanks to my colleagues in the Faith and Learning Program at Wheaton College who read and responded to early chapters. I am indebted to the members of the Culture and Society Workshop at Northwestern University for being my intellectual home throughout the development of this study. The insightful suggestions and careful edits of many resulted in the best parts of this book; any shortcomings that remain are mine.

I am grateful for the financial assistance I have received in support of this project. The G. W. Aldeen Memorial Fund, Faculty Development Grant, and Junior Faculty Teaching Award at Wheaton College provided time and money for research travel. Funding from the Harvey Fellows program of the Mustard Seed Foundation and a dissertation year fellowship from Northwestern University supported an early draft of the research.

Friends and colleagues have supported me along the journey. There are too many to list here, but I will attempt to name a few: Alan Jacobs, Roger Lundin, Jim Mathisen, Martin Medhurst, Tim Morgan, and John Wilson each offered their wisdom and advice over meals and coffee during early stages of this project. Liz Benacka, Dan Fitzmier, Leslie Harris, Randy Iden, Chris Lundberg, Brett Ommen, Cindy Koenig Richards, Ebony Utley, and Sara VanderHaagen helped me refine my thinking. Jerry Herbert and Wendy Murray knew the right words to say at the right time. Credit goes to Tim Larsen for the title. Many other friends—Duane Grobman, Michael and Rebecca Lindsay, John and Ute Monson, Eric and Afarin Morgan, Rick and Kristen Page, Don and Patrice Penney, and Dan and Amy Trier, to name a few—have offered encouragement and provided welcomed diversions along the way. Reed Malcolm at University of California Press believed in the project from the beginning, and Emily Park guided the editorial process with attention and skill. Special thanks go to Polly Kummel for her smart and careful edits. Sincere thanks go to my colleagues in the Communication Department at Wheaton College for their support and encouragement: Ken Chase, Lynn Cooper, Sharon Crouch, Roy Joseph, Emily Langan, Mark Lewis, Joonhee Park, Read Schuchardt, Rebecca Sietman, and Michael Stauffer. I am especially grateful to the students in my classes on Communication Criticism, Rhetoric of AIDS, and Theology of the Body. Their intellectual passion and social activism invigorated my ideas.

My family undergirds my work and deserves my heartfelt thanks. My three siblings and their spouses—Debbie and Jeff Rickey, Jim and Jeanine Le Shana, and Cathy and Dave McIntyre—along with my ten nieces and nephews (and two nieces-in-law, a nephew-in-law, two grand-nephews, and a grand-niece) have provided a constant source of love and encouragement throughout this process. My heart is filled with gratitude for my parents, Dave and Becky Le Shana. They have never wavered in their support of me and my vocational calling. Their constant prayers have strengthened me during many difficult seasons, and their gifts of chocolate always arrived at the right moment to lift my spirits. I am blessed to be their daughter.

Attempting to acknowledge the contributions of my husband, Brian, to this project is like trying to thank my right lung for my breath—its function is somehow both ordinary and extraordinary, rendering the mere thought of its absence ludicrous because it is so central to my daily existence. Through kindness of heart and gentleness of spirit, Brian has supported and encouraged all my scholarly endeavors. He has patiently listened and offered insightful questions as I have overtaken dinner conversations and long-distance phone calls to verbally work through major sections of the project. He even got on a plane and went with me to Africa. Thank you, Brian, for sharing this journey with me. And to Daniel, who arrived two days after the first draft was complete, your cheesy grins and belly chuckles have transformed my world. Thank you for a season of two-hour morning naps so Mama could get her work done. You are the gift for which I am most undeserving and utterly grateful.

Abstinence, AIDS, and Evangelicals

An Introduction

The walls pulsated with the rhythmic thump-thump-thump of a song from the popular recording artist Usher. Strobe lights flashed across three large screens on the stage. Green lasers probed the darkness, and fake fog felt its way across the floor as eight hundred hormonal teenagers poured into the room. Nothing says rock concert quite like lasers and fake fog, except that this was a sexual abstinence event hosted by Silver Ring Thing in the chapel of an east coast Christian college. "Sanctified, Not Skank-tified," according to one girl's T-shirt.

My research on the rhetoric of the evangelical sexual abstinence campaigns had brought me to the event, and I was feeling, frankly, a bit disoriented. My own adolescent sex education was a hazy memory, but I'm sure the gist of it was "don't do it." I think I would have remembered if green lasers had been involved.

Josh, the twentysomething national program director for Silver Ring Thing, was wearing jeans and a black T-shirt, carrying a cordless microphone, and pacing the stage.[1] "I'm here to talk about how great sex can be," he said, as the crowd hooted and cheered its agreement. Then Josh led the teens in an unusual abstinence cheer: "Sex is great!" The audience repeated the cheer three times, each time gaining in intensity: "Sex is great!" Where were the tearful testimonies of sweaty Saturday nights, I wondered? "Sex is great!" Not even a gross-out slide show of sexually transmitted diseases? On the last cheer Josh followed with a clincher: "Sex is great . . . and it *is* great, in the context of marriage."

Josh, who had been married for four and a half years, held out his left hand as a camera captured a close-up of his wedding ring, which was projected on the screens with the words "License to Practice." A strain from the "Hallelujah Chorus" played over the speakers.

Chastity is getting a makeover. Surrounded by a sex-saturated society, millions of young people are pledging to remain virgins until their wedding night. But how, exactly, are evangelical Christians convincing young people to say no when society says yes?

The strobe lights and sex talk of the Silver Ring Thing event were my introduction to the contemporary evangelical sexual abstinence movement. For the next five years I would travel around the country, as well as across the Atlantic Ocean, attending abstinence events and talking with young people and evangelical leaders alike about abstinence. That nearly half of all American teens have had sex is no surprise.[2] I wanted to know how and why some teens were bucking the status quo and waiting to have sex.

Sexual abstinence has become a significant—and controversial—worldwide public issue in recent years, most notably through the passage of federal legislation that requires sexual abstinence education in U.S. public schools. The controversy centers on what is, and is not, being taught. Comprehensive sex education programs teach that abstinence and contraception use are both viable options for teenagers. "Abstinence-plus" programs talk about contraception use but promote abstinence as the best choice for teenagers. Abstinence-only programs (also called "abstinence-until-marriage" programs by advocates) emphasize that abstinence is the only 100 percent effective way to eliminate the possibility of unwanted pregnancy and sexually transmitted diseases; contraception use is discussed in terms of its ineffectiveness or it is not discussed at all.[3] Despite controversy, abstinence education has received support from the highest levels: during his tenure in office President George W. Bush was a staunch advocate for government support of abstinence education both in the United States and in African countries.[4] The times may be changing, however: President Barack Obama slashed all funding for abstinence-only programs from his 2010 federal budget.[5]

Since the passage of the Welfare Reform Act in 1996, which in part aims to help reduce teen pregnancy, more than $1.5 billion in federal funding has supported abstinence-only education in the United States. Abstinence advocates point to drops in teen pregnancy and abortion rates as indications of program effectiveness. U.S. teen pregnancy rates dropped 34 percent between 1991 and 2005. Teen abortion rates dropped 39 percent between 1990 and 1999. But a 2009 report from the Centers for Disease Control suggests that the tide may be turning: The birthrate for teenagers aged fifteen to nineteen jumped 3 percent in 2006.[6] Comprehensive sex education advocates are quick to blame the spike in pregnancies on more than a decade of government-sponsored abstinence education programs. Abstinence proponents argue that this trend supports the need for increased funding for abstinence programs, since a majority of schools teach comprehensive sex education and receive four times the funding that abstinence programs do.[7]

Internationally, the President's Emergency Plan for AIDS Relief (PEPFAR), first announced in 2003, provided $15 billion over five years to fight HIV/AIDS in sub-Saharan Africa and the Caribbean. In July 2008 PEPFAR funding for HIV/AIDS more than doubled, to $39 billion for an additional five years. Abstinence education remains a central part of PEPFAR, although the reappropriation legislation stipulates only "balanced funding" of prevention activities instead of the former mandate that sent one-third of AIDS monies to abstinence efforts. In Africa, abstinence is the first step in the "ABC" (abstinence, be faithful, use a condom) approach to stopping the spread of HIV/AIDS. In Uganda, for example, some credit abstinence with playing a significant role in reducing the spread of HIV.[8] Prevalence rates sharply declined between 1990 and 2007 in Uganda, from about 15 percent to about 5 percent.[9] Condom use became a contributing factor only in the mid-1990s, after rates had already begun to decline.[10] Incidence of premarital sex declined during the 1990s, with a two-year delay in the onset of sexual activity among fifteen- to twenty-four-year-old Ugandans by 1997.[11] With evidence of the effectiveness of abstinence at reducing HIV transmission, abstinence supporters are boldly promoting the practice in other sub-Saharan African countries.

At the center of the promotion of sexual abstinence in both the United States and African countries are evangelical Christians. While the debate continues to rage about sex education in U.S. public schools, U.S. evangelicals have created an abstinence movement outside the public school structure that encourages young people to pledge their commitment to wait to have sex until marriage. For evangelicals, sexual abstinence is about more than just sex; it has political, as well as moral and religious, implications. Sexual abstinence is positioned, in part, as a solution to the problem of abortion. Evangelicals, who are largely prolife, have failed in their attempts to overturn the legalization of abortion.[12] Sexual abstinence education, along with other reproduction-related issues, such as banning late-term (or "partial-birth") abortion and mandating the use of ultrasound technology, is a strategy to reduce teenage pregnancies and the need for abortions.[13] Evangelicals' involvement in the AIDS crisis in sub-Saharan Africa represents a growing concern for issues of social justice—poverty, gender inequality, environmental degradation, as well as HIV/AIDS—that expand the prolife agenda beyond opposition to abortion. In sub-Saharan Africa the debate is about condom use versus behavior change as part of AIDS prevention. An undercurrent throughout the evangelical sexual abstinence campaigns, whether in the United States or in sub-Saharan Africa, is an impulse toward evangelism: implicit in the campaigns is the belief that committing to delay sex until marriage makes the most sense if one makes a religious commitment to follow Jesus Christ and his teachings.[14] The campaigns acknowledge that, without a new life in Christ, a life of abstinence is more difficult to follow.

Evangelicals have been criticized by comprehensive sex education supporters on precisely this point—that the abstinence campaigns are more about religious and moral indoctrination than results-based sex education. Do the pledge programs keep teenagers from having sex outside marriage? Yes and no. Or, as one of the lead researchers on a study of abstinence programs puts it, "The truth is that pledges seem to delay sex for some kids some of the time."[15] According to the frequently cited National Longitudinal Study of Adolescent Health, the evangelical sexual abstinence campaigns have been moderately effective. The study credits the Southern Baptist Convention, the largest evangelical denomination in the United States, with launching the contemporary sexual abstinence movement. The nationally representative study draws on data collected from surveys of more than 90,000 junior high and high school students attending 141 schools, in-home interviews with more than 20,000 youth (and nearly 15,000 additional follow-up interviews), along with parent interviews and school administrator surveys. The study, cited by abstinence supporters and detractors alike, concludes that teens who pledge abstinence are "much less likely" to have sexual intercourse than nonpledgers. The impact of the pledge on delaying sexual debut is "substantial and robust," however the abstinence pledge delays sexual debut among fifteen- and sixteen-year-olds by only eighteen months (which is a third longer than those who do not make a pledge). Also, those who pledge are less likely to use contraception when they have their first sexual experience.[16] A 2009 study published in *Pediatrics* uses the same data to compare pledgers and nonpledgers who share similar characteristics such as church attendance and religiosity. After five years the pledgers were just as likely to have had sex as nonpledgers.[17]

Not all the studies show the ineffectiveness of abstinence education, however. A 2008 study by the Rand Corporation published in the *Journal of Adolescent Health* determined that virginity pledges are helping young people wait to have sex. In a nationally representative survey of young people aged twelve to seventeen conducted in three waves over three years, researchers compared pledgers and nonpledgers who shared similar characteristics such as religiosity. They found that 42 percent of those who did not make a pledge had sex within three years, whereas only 34 percent of pledgers reported having had sex during the same period.[18]

So what accounts for the differences between the studies, and what does it tell us about the effectiveness of abstinence pledges? Age may make a difference. Abstinence pledges seem to be more effective among younger teens. The *Journal of Adolescent Health* study, which found the pledges to be effective, looks at a younger population, the youngest of whom were twelve years old when they made an abstinence pledge and the oldest of whom were twenty at the end of the three-year study. The *Pediatrics* study, in contrast, considered pledgers as young as sixteen and followed them for five years until they were twenty or older. By the time the pledgers reach the age of twenty-one, they are just as likely to have had sex as those who did not pledge abstinence. As the Rand Corporation researcher Steven Martino points out, abstinence pledges may not last until marriage, but perhaps they are better understood as influencing adolescence, the developmental stage before adulthood. Even with a limited period of effectiveness, the abstinence pledge could still have "significant health benefits," he reported.[19]

These large quantitative studies provide a broad overview of the state of abstinence pledges (along with inconsistent and inconclusive results when compared with each other), but in general they do not go far beyond the statistics to the stories of individuals who are pledging abstinence. If most teens eventually have sex, why do they bother committing to abstinence in the first place? Quantitative studies tend to reduce the complexities of sexual behavior to black-and-white categories of "abstinent" or "sexually active," ignoring the range of sexual activity that may be acceptable even to abstinent teens. My goal here is to provide a "thick description" of *how* virginity pledge events such as those in the evangelical sexual abstinence campaigns are persuading young people to wait to have sex and how young people are negotiating their sexuality while remaining abstinent.[20] This is a study of rhetoric, the words and symbols used to construct our understanding of reality. I examine the rhetoric used in the abstinence events as well as the rhetoric used by abstinent young people to describe their pledges. For my U.S. case studies I turn to the oldest of the contemporary evangelical sexual abstinence campaigns, True Love Waits, and consider two of the more recent campaigns, Silver Ring Thing and Pure Freedom. The three campaigns represent a diversity of approaches in abstinence persuasion.

STADIUMS, STROBE LIGHTS, AND TEA PARTIES: THREE ABSTINENCE CASE STUDIES

True Love Waits

True Love Waits is widely credited with launching the contemporary evangelical sexual abstinence movement. It is perhaps most known for its stadium-filled rallies and public displays of signed abstinence pledge cards.

A ministry of LifeWay, the publishing arm of the Southern Baptist Convention, True Love Waits was begun in 1993 by Jimmy Hester, senior director of student ministry publishing for LifeWay, and Richard Ross, professor of student ministry at Southwestern Baptist Theological Seminary. The idea grew out of a Christian sex education project on which Hester and Ross worked together at LifeWay in Nashville in 1987. Ross, who at the time was also working as a youth pastor at Tulip Grove Baptist Church in Hermitage, Tennessee, came up with the name True Love Waits during a brainstorming session for an abstinence campaign in 1992. The following year fifty-three youths at his church took the first abstinence pledges.

Ross asked the pledgers if they would share their abstinence commitment with the thousand Southern Baptist youth ministers who would be in Nashville a few months later for a conference he was organizing. Ross later recounted the emotional power of the testimony of a teenage boy and girl who were dating: "And then [in] one of the most important sentences in the history of True Love Waits, this guy and girl said, 'And we think there are teenagers in every one of your youth groups who are ready to do the very same thing.' The youth ministers jumped up.

Somebody looked at their watch, for ten minutes the youth ministers wept and cheered at the same time. They were clapping and crying together. It was such a moving moment." The youth ministers returned to their churches and told their youth groups, and, with the help of broad media attention, the True Love Waits campaign grew.

A typical True Love Waits abstinence event is like a large church youth rally. Events feature guest speakers and evangelists, testimonials from young people who have pledged abstinence, and miniconcerts from contemporary Christian recording artists. The events culminate with an appeal to the attendees to commit to sexual abstinence, demonstrated by the signing of the True Love Waits abstinence pledge card: "Believing that true love waits, I make a commitment to God, myself, my family, my friends, my future mate, and my future children to be sexually abstinent from this day until the day I enter a biblical marriage relationship." Although True Love Waits seems to have slowed its promotion of large sports arena events in recent years, it continues to offer resources—including a curriculum, devotional guides, clip art, jewelry, and a script for an abstinence commitment service—on its Web site for entrepreneurial churches and youth leaders to plan their own events.

A distinctive feature of the True Love Waits campaign is its emphasis on dramatic displays of vast numbers of pledge cards representing the groundswell of teenage commitments. The first national display of signed pledge cards occurred on the National Mall in 2004, with 210,000 cards and twenty-five thousand youth in attendance. In 1996 supporters stacked 340,000 signed pledge cards from the floor to the roof of the Georgia Dome in Atlanta. In 1999 more than fifteen hundred youth carried 100,000 signed pledge cards in a prayer walk across the Golden Gate Bridge. On Valentine's Day 2002, 82,411 youth signed pledge cards on the True Love Waits Web site. At the 2004 Summer Olympics in Athens, the group displayed 460,000 signed pledge cards from twenty countries. Although the organization partners with more than ninety "cooperating ministries" and does not keep strict records on partners' activities, the group estimates more than 2.5 million young people have signed abstinence commitments since the inception of True Love Waits.[21]

While True Love Waits is focused on the United States, it also has a presence in sub-Saharan Africa, most notably, Uganda, where First Lady Janet Museveni credits the group with helping to reduce that country's HIV transmission rates.[22] In 2007 True Love Waits announced a $950,000 expansion of its abstinence programs in sub-Saharan Africa to include Botswana, Lesotho, South Africa, Swaziland, Tanzania, and Zambia.[23]

Silver Ring Thing

Like True Love Waits, Silver Ring Thing uses popular music to attract teens, but the venues are smaller, holding a few hundred youth compared with the thousands who attend True Love Waits rallies. The form and content of teen vernacular are a defining part of the Silver Ring Thing program. According to the group's Web site, "By featuring awesome lighting and video systems, hilarious skits, concert sound systems, high-energy music, TV's, computers, and a faith-based abstinence message, students become interested in the message being offered to them about their sex lives." Silver Ring Thing events have been described as part rave, part *Saturday Night Live,* and part Saturday night revival.[24]

Attendees typically pay about ten dollars for admission and another twenty dollars for a ring, a Silver Ring Thing Sexual Abstinence Study Bible, and follow-up materials.[25] Behind the scenes and on stage, the events are run mostly by older teens and young adults, most of whom first learned about Silver Ring Thing by attending an event and making a pledge. The campaign estimates that more than 450,000 young people have heard the message of abstinence and more than 150,000 young people have made pledges through Silver Ring Thing events since 1995.[26]

Denny Pattyn and his wife, Amy, created Silver Ring Thing in 1996 in response to their belief that the incidence of teen pregnancy was increasing.[27] The Pattyns moved the program from Arizona to Pennsylvania in 2000, in part to expand the program to the national level. Silver Ring Thing has been affiliated with the John Guest Evangelistic Team, a ministry organization located at the evangelical Christ Church at Grove Farm near Pittsburgh.[28] The group expanded its reach internationally with Silver Ring Thing events in the United Kingdom in 2004 and South Africa in 2005.

Of the three U.S.-focused groups included in this study, Silver Ring Thing is the only evangelical abstinence organization to have received federal funds for its abstinence education. The group received more than $1 million in government money between 2003 and 2006. As a consequence of accepting the funds, the organization attempted to separate its religious and secular messages. At Silver Ring Thing events, before an intermission during which attendees would collect their rings, audience members were told that they could return to the main event location for an explicitly Christian call to abstinence or go to a nearby alternative site to continue abstinence instruction without religious overtones. Additionally, Silver Ring Thing offered a religion-free abstinence program for public school assemblies, and this program served as a promotion for the weekend club-style event. In May 2005 the American Civil Liberties Union claimed that Silver Ring Thing had not gone far enough in separating its abstinence education from its Christian evangelism. In a lawsuit filed in federal court against the Department of Health and Human Services, the ACLU asserted that Silver Ring Thing was using "taxpayer dollars to promote religious content, instruction and indoctrination." In a 2006 settlement the government agreed to stop funding Silver Ring Thing in its current form.[29] Now supported solely by private funds, the group has eliminated the religion-free venue option, leading all attendees through a pledge of abstinence combined with an evangelistic altar call.[30]

Pure Freedom

Pure Freedom was founded in 1996 by Dannah Gresh, a former marketing consultant and corporate trainer, out of a desire to teach young girls how to live a life of sexual purity. Gresh confessed to her husband after five years of marriage that she had had premarital sex with a boyfriend as a teenager. The weight of the guilt of years of silence, and the accompanying forgiveness and relief she found when she confessed her sin, prompted Gresh to start a ministry for teenage girls to teach them how to live pure lives.[31] Within weeks of telling her husband, Gresh was leading her first retreat for a dozen teenage girls at her church. According to the group's Web site, the stated mission of the organization is to "equip men and women of all ages to live a vibrant life of purity, to experience healing from past impurity if it exists in their lives and to experience a vibrant passionate marriage which portrays the love Christ has for his Bride the church." Gresh sees her ministry as an improvement on the True Love Waits message: in a 2005 interview she told a reporter, "Bob [Gresh] and I started it eight years ago because, while we love what True Love Waits does to increase abstinence awareness, we felt kids needed some practical skills to avoid the pain of sexual sin."[32]

Pure Freedom primarily focuses on teenage girls through overnight slumber-party-style purity retreats or its one-day Mother/Daughter

Summits held at churches. Both events feature the "Truth or Bare Fashion Show," in which event participants model modest teenage fashions, and a tea party, after which participants are allowed to keep the china teacups. The daughters' retreat is intended to encourage participants to "embrace God's plan for modesty and purity, through interactive teaching and object based lessons." The goal of the mother-daughter event is "to provide a forum for mothers to pursue an open line of communication with their teenaged daughters especially in the area of sexuality." Dannah Gresh's husband, Bob, also leads a retreat for teenage boys, which the organization's Web site describes as "a radical, high contact event which includes sports-themed teaching." Topics covered for the boys include "masturbation, pornography, mental virginity, responsibility to protect a girl's emotions and envisioning a godly wife." In contrast, girls cover such topics as "self-esteem, modesty, emotional healing, refusal skills and envisioning a godly husband."[33]

Dannah Gresh and her supporting facilitators lead more than fifty Pure Freedom events across the country each year. According to the organization's Web site, more than twenty thousand churches worldwide have used Pure Freedom's curriculum to hold a purity retreat. One of the newest events for Pure Freedom is the "Secret Keeper Girl Tour" for girls aged eight to twelve and their mothers. The upbeat two-hour events blend worship with teaching and stories about modesty, self-esteem, and body image. The "Yada! Yada! Youth Event" is a larger coed retreat featuring the entire Pure Freedom teaching team, including its own worship band. In the summer of 2004 the Gresh family traveled to Zambia at the invitation of the director of a crisis pregnancy center there to train a group to teach abstinence education to a thousand students in local public schools. Gresh has since written an abstinence curriculum for the government schools of Zambia, reaching more than seventy-five thousand students.[34]

Sex Is Great

My study of True Love Waits, Silver Ring Thing, and Pure Freedom began in 2004, and I conducted the bulk of my field research in 2004–2005 and 2008–2009. I focused my analysis on the rhetoric of producers and receivers of the campaigns, both the organizational leaders who were crafting the arguments for abstinence and the young people at whom the arguments were aimed.[35] In total, I conducted sixty-five in-depth, open-ended interviews with evangelical leaders, staff members, abstinence educators, and young people who have attended abstinence events.[36] I conducted most interviews in person at a location of the respondent's choosing, including churches, offices, college campuses, high schools, coffee shops, and sports arenas. I also traveled to ten abstinence events hosted by the three organizations in eight U.S. cities (or, in some cases, their greater metropolitan areas): Boston; Chicago; Dallas; Grand Rapids, Michigan; Harrisburg, Pennsylvania; Milwaukee, Wisconsin; Nashville; and Pittsburgh.[37] I analyzed sexual abstinence curricula, books, leaders' kits, Web sites, press releases, news articles, CDs, DVDs, pledge declarations, and purity rings in order to understand the abstinence message.[38] My research also took me to sub-Saharan Africa, where I traveled to Kenya and Rwanda to interview staff members of World Relief, the international relief and development arm of the National Association of Evangelicals. I conducted group interviews with members of four church-based abstinence youth clubs organized by World Relief in Kigali, Rwanda. In addition to my formal research, numerous casual discussions—both in and out of class—about abstinence and sexuality with evangelical students at Wheaton College in Illinois, where I serve as a faculty member, undoubtedly have informed my analysis.[39]

While sociological in nature, this is a study in rhetoric: How do the words, symbols, and visual images used by the evangelical sexual abstinence campaigns construct the movement?[40] What, and how, does abstinence mean?[41] Not just what does abstinence mean in a definitional sense, but how does the word function to construct meaning for the individuals who use it?[42] Does the way that evangelical young people talk about abstinence match the arguments of the campaigns? In other words, do the arguments for abstinence resonate with young people? If so, how?[43] Are there occasions when the arguments for abstinence are not persuasive to young people? And what happens when the same abstinence arguments are exported from the United States to a different cultural context such as sub-Saharan Africa? What is the significance of these constructions of abstinence for evangelicalism as a whole? To answer these questions, I conducted a qualitative, rhetorical analysis of my interview data and participant-observation field notes, focusing on key words, visual images, narrative structures, repetitive themes, tropes, and metaphors.[44]

This book follows two main narratives. The first is the narrative of the contemporary evangelical sexual abstinence campaigns—how and why they were started, how the leaders of the campaigns are persuading young people to wait to have sex, and how the abstinent young people are receiving (or in some cases modifying) the message. This narrative largely takes place in the United States, but I follow the narrative to Kenya and Rwanda to see what the cross-cultural permutations of evangelical sexual abstinence rhetoric can tell us about American evangelicals' understandings of Africa and AIDS, as well as the construction of American evangelicals' own subcultural identity.

The second narrative is intimately intertwined with the first: I am interested in a broader story of what happens when private religious beliefs are articulated in the public sphere and the role of rhetorical agency in this move. The evangelical sexual abstinence campaigns illustrate this shift from private to public, as private arguments about religion, reproduction, and sexuality become public arguments about sexual behavior. Rhetorical agency constitutes the ability to act or the power to choose as it is constructed in rhetoric.[45] How does rhetorical agency function to persuade individuals that they have the power to control their sexual behavior and choose abstinence? Power is an underlying theme connecting the two narratives, as the chapters that follow will show, whether personal power through the control of one's body and sexual desires, gender power through the control of men through female modesty, or collective power through the identity of Americans as saviors and Africans as victims in the context of HIV/AIDS.

Both narratives—evangelicals and sexual abstinence and religion in the public sphere—are drawn from an examination of rhetoric. I am less concerned with mapping the terrain of sexual (or sexually abstinent) practices among teenagers than discovering how teens talk about their sexuality and abstinence. Rhetoric is more than hot air and hyperbole. Aristotle defined rhetoric as the means of persuasion. More broadly, rhetoric consists of the symbols we use—both words and images—to shape our understanding of reality. In this book I do not aim for a definitive or representative study of teens and sexuality; others have accomplished this elsewhere.[46] Instead, I take a narrow but detailed look at the specific rhetorical arguments and strategies persuading young people to say no to sex.[47]

What I found in my analysis of these case studies surprised me: for campaigns whose focus is abstinence, there is an awful lot of talk about sex. In popular culture, sex is used to sell everything from automobiles to cell phones to deodorant; apparently, sex is also now being used to sell pledges to not have sex. As I argue in the chapters that follow,

American evangelicals are persuading teenagers to avoid sex by making abstinence "sexy." Evangelicals are using sex to "sell" abstinence, shifting from a negative focus on "just say no" to sex before marriage to a positive focus on "just say yes" to great sex within marriage. Sex—along with marriage—is presented as the reward for abstinence, which I suggest presents potential problems for the campaigns and evangelicalism as a whole. Overall, the evangelical abstinence campaigns do not address the challenges of singleness (What if I never get married? Where, then, is my reward for my abstinence?) or homosexuality (What if marriage is not an option?). They also present a limited and distorted view that marriage is all about self-fulfilling sex.

The campaigns use a variety of rhetorical tools to craft this simultaneously pro-sex and proabstinence argument, including club-style events, testimonials from attractive peers, a positive framing of abstinence as "purity," and a retelling of the fairy-tale narrative that instills a romantic vision of sex and marriage through the construction of traditional gender roles. At the core of each of these rhetorical strategies is an appeal to the teenager as an autonomous, choice-making individual who will make decisions in his or her own self-interest. From the standpoint of persuasion, this is a challenge for the campaigns, considering that abstinence is essentially about prohibition and self-denial. The ability of the campaigns to turn something negative into something positive, using the very object of denial—sex—as a reward is, it seems to me, rhetorical genius.

The fourth case study—World Relief and its abstinence education work in Kenya and Rwanda—underscores this American "what's-in-it-for-me" approach in contrast. In Rwanda, the young people with whom I spoke gave very different reasons for why they are committing to abstinence. Avoiding HIV/AIDS seems like a logical reason, but Rwandan young people told me that they saw their bodies as temples of the Lord and themselves as the caretakers—a more deeply theological response than I heard from my American evangelical respondents.

IN THE WORLD, BUT NOT OF IT: EVANGELICALS AND THE RHETORIC OF CHOICE

Evangelicals have long held a tenuous relationship with secular culture, making their discourse a fascinating case in which to study the changing nature of religious language in the public sphere. One claim of this study is that in the case of the sexual abstinence campaigns, American evangelicals appear to be borrowing a central argument of secular society: they are recasting an essentially feminist argument of "my body, my choice" and persuading teenagers that they are choice-making individuals who can control their bodies and wait for sex.[48] This is a curious rhetorical approach, given that evangelicals are both proabstinence and antiabortion, spreading abstinence education as one strategy for reducing the need for abortion. Evangelical prolife activists are growing increasingly savvy in their public discourse. In a 1999 *New York Times* editorial entitled "The New Abortion Rhetoric," then-presidential hopeful George W. Bush (a self-identified evangelical Christian) is noted for his positive focus on a "reverence for life" agenda instead of a negative focus on overturning legalized abortion. The editorial ends with the observation that while the extreme positions of those opposed to abortion rights have made things "easy" for supporters of choice in the past, prolife forces will "use much subtler strategies this time around."[49] Evangelicals' use of sexual abstinence campaigns to chip away at legalized abortion may be a not-unexpected rhetorical strategy. In the present case, however, prolife evangelicals are adopting the rhetoric of their opponents to make their argument.[50]

To push the "odd bedfellows" example a bit further, both evangelicals and feminists can be considered "subaltern counterpublics," groups that have been marginalized or excluded from the public sphere.[51] American evangelicals, like feminist groups, have formed parallel discursive arenas in opposition to the public sphere: radio and television stations, publishing companies, and colleges and universities. For example, instead of CNN, evangelicals may watch Pat Robertson's CBN (the Christian Broadcasting Network). Instead of reading *Time* or *Newsweek,* they have *Christianity Today.* Instead of Harvard University, they might attend Baylor University or Wheaton College. This separatist impulse is a hallmark of American evangelicalism's fundamentalist origins.[52]

Because of their positions as counterpublics, American feminists and American evangelicals provide a useful, if unusual, comparison: both have crafted a public stance of opposition or victimization from which they have attempted to liberate private concerns into the public.[53] In her critique of the public sphere, Nancy Fraser highlights the irony that "a discourse of publicity touting accessibility, rationality, and the suspension of status hierarchies is itself deployed as a strategy of distinction."[54] In a similar fashion, evangelicals craft a discourse of publicity touting victimization and marginalization, which is itself deployed as a strategy of persuasive power. A *Newsweek* poll, conducted by Princeton Survey Research Associates International in November 2005, suggests that 54 percent of American adults self-identify as a born-again or evangelical Christian.[55] Evangelicals may constitute a majority of Americans, but their discourse constructs them as marginalized. For example, so-called values voters (of which evangelicals were a significant part) made significant political gains in the 2004 elections, although evangelicals maintained a position of victimization, labeled as "victim politics" by some.[56] The formation of a counterpublic such as the one shaped by American evangelicals implies a necessary oppression and victimization, which provides power when speaking from the margins of society.

In addition to their constructed positions as marginalized, feminists and evangelicals share two private concerns that both counterpublics have worked to liberate into the public sphere: sexuality and reproduction.[57] The public sphere manifestations of those private concerns are different for both counterpublics: for feminists the public manifestation is abortion; for evangelicals it is sexual abstinence. Whereas feminist concerns with abortion and evangelical concerns with abstinence may be dyadic opposites, the two counterpublics have a critical element in common: once their private concerns of sexuality and reproduction are liberated into the public sphere, both abortion and abstinence assume the goal of justice for the individual, not justice for the common good.[58] The refrain "my body, my choice," whether the choice is for abortion rights or sexual abstinence, reflects a language of individualism, which some scholars suggest contributes to the general erosion of public life.[59] American evangelicals have encouraged the liberation of private issues such as chastity, marital fidelity, sexuality, prayer, and the free practice of religion into public issues such as sexual abstinence, homosexuality "recovery" programs, late-term abortion bans, prayer in schools, and school vouchers.[60] As evangelicals' private religious rhetoric enters the public sphere on issues like sexual abstinence, it necessarily takes on the language of the public sphere. The rhetoric of choice, based on the primary language of individualism, is the primary language of the public sphere.[61]

In a nation founded on principles of religious freedom, it is not far-fetched to assume that religious symbols, beliefs, and rituals can function as cultural resources for framing public life. However, the language of individualism suggests that public life no longer has any unifying foundations.[62] Religious language and symbolism may reach only a narrow segment of the population. For example, the beliefs that Americans are God's chosen people or that homosexuality is sinful would be unintelligible to citizens with varying conceptions of God or who are unfamiliar with the Bible. In fact, the shared foundation of liberal society seems to be the commitment to diversity and pluralism: we are committed to unity through our differences. Part of that diversity includes an allowance for civil religion, as seen in a long tradition of public religious language in U.S. history, from John Winthrop's "city on a hill" to "in God we trust" on our dollar bills to public appeals to God's assistance in presidential inaugural addresses.[63]

Some scholars argue that explicitly religious arguments should not be used in the public sphere because they would polarize debate.[64] Biblical allusions and personal religious testimonies can be shared in public but only if they are descriptive and not persuasive or audience directed.[65] Religious arguments—considered conversation stoppers—must assume the cloak of secular language if they are to appear in the public sphere.[66]

Others argue that the respect for diversity in our pluralist society gives religious arguments a place in the public sphere.[67] Restraints should be placed not on the content of religious reasons but on the manner in which those reasons are presented. Nicholas Wolterstorff advocates the position that religious arguments display civility, encourage obedience to the law, and support justice, not personal self-interest.[68] From the standpoint of rhetorical studies, this view places rhetorical agency in the hands (and mouth) of the rhetor. In this way, religious arguments are cultural resources that a rhetor may draw upon for persuasion.

Conversely, Rhys Williams acknowledges that when private religious language enters the public sphere, it necessarily becomes less sectarian. He locates the agency for this shift not in the religious rhetor but in the audience: "Once religious language crosses social boundaries, its interpretations, meanings, and impact are open to variation and contestation. . . . Those who originate cultural messages cannot control them completely, nor control who else may choose to adopt and use them."[69] The very nature of public life as consisting of various publics, made up of individuals who employ tools of debate and reason, places a check on the power of a single rhetor. Accessibility is a key characteristic of language in the public sphere. Religious rhetoric that does not achieve resonance with its audience will not make for effective public discourse.

The relationship between religion and the public sphere is not unidirectional. What, then, is the impact of the public sphere on religion?

If religious arguments in public necessarily adopt the form of public discourse, do they retain their religious distinctiveness? In other words, does the existence of religious arguments in the public sphere contribute to the secularization of religion?

Secularization theory suggests that religions become increasingly secular as they come in contact with modernity. James Davison Hunter outlines this view in his study of American evangelicalism. He identifies various accommodations or concessions to secular modernity, such as the rationalization and standardization of spirituality into codes and laws; increasing civility through the removal of evangelicalism's more offensive aspects such as an emphasis on evil and hell; and privatization of spirituality into a "psychological Christocentrism" that places the individual at the center of religious transformation.[70]

Recent scholarship counters the secularization thesis, suggesting that pluralism offers more choices for potential adherents instead of necessarily diminishing each religion.[71] The larger debate about secularization is more nuanced, however, than merely a zero-sum game. In his chronology of secularism, Charles Taylor suggests that religion has contributed to its own secularization, notably through the Protestant Reformation and its focus on the individual. Yet religion itself appears undiminished by the forces of the modern age, as our post-9/11 world witnesses the spread of Islam and Christianity around the globe. Religion has not remained in the private sphere.[72]

Engagement in the public sphere, instead of being a presumed evil among some religionists, could serve to sharpen religious distinctiveness. Christian Smith offers a "subcultural identity" theory of religious strength in his study of American evangelicals. He suggests that evangelicals (the in-group) define themselves in relation to secular culture (the out-group). He goes on to suggest that engagement with secular culture, not isolation, is the source of evangelicalism's strength: "American evangelicalism, we contend, is strong not because it is shielded against but because it is—or at least perceives itself to be—embattled with forces that seem to oppose or threaten it. Indeed, evangelicalism, we suggest, *thrives* on distinction, engagement, tension, conflict, and threat."[73] Yet this engagement could have a lasting negative impact on religion.[74] Closer to the center of the secularization of religion debates, however, is an acknowledgment that the public sphere and religion, through active engagement, mutually modify each other.[75]

Although persuasive efficacy is a standard measure for public rhetoric, it is important to offer a caveat that some public religious rhetoric may exist not so much to persuade an audience as to demonstrate a rhetor's ethos. American evangelicals provide an interesting case study for this because evangelizing, or sharing religious beliefs in order to persuade an individual to convert, constitutes the identity of what it means to be an evangelical. Public religious rhetoric becomes not so much a tool for persuasion as a lived expression of individual and group identity. To take a contemporary example, evangelicals may try to persuade non-Christians that abortion is wrong by quoting the Bible. This religious argument may be ineffective at persuading non-Christians, but it may be effective at renewing the symbolic boundaries between evangelicals and nonevangelicals, thus affirming in-group identity.

Some religious rhetoric may exclude large portions of the public, resulting in low resonance and a reinforcement of the symbolic boundary between the secular out-group and the religious in-group. On the other hand, religious rhetoric that adopts the language of the public may achieve greater resonance and effectiveness at mobilizing collective action, but it may also blur symbolic boundaries, resulting in weakened religious identity. As the theologian Stanley Hauerwas writes, success in the public sphere may result in making the "church less than the church": "The problem is that when Christians in America take as their fundamental task to make America work, then we lose our ability to survive *as church*. We do so because in the interest of serving America, the church unwittingly becomes governed by the story of America. . . . That is a story meant to make our God at home in America."[76] The price of becoming popular may be that the church becomes less prophetic.

Following the New Testament injunction to "be in the world, but not of it," evangelicals straddle the line between secular accommodation and religious distinction. Based on my analysis of the evangelical sexual abstinence campaigns, evangelicals are co-opting forms of secular culture to make chastity sexy. The individualistic what's-in-it-for-me approach may resonate with today's teenagers, promising great sex and future marriage as the reward for abstinence, but the persuasiveness of that argument subtly shifts the nature of evangelicalism away from sacrifice and suffering to self-gratification.

PLAN OF THE BOOK

My analysis begins with an examination of key arguments of the abstinence campaigns. Chapter 1 considers the incongruity of the positive, benefits-oriented rhetoric of a campaign that is all about a prohibition.

The message focuses on a positive call to a lifestyle of purity instead of a negative prohibition implied by the term *abstinence*. The campaign rhetoric is reconfiguring virginity too, constructing it as a choice that can be found after it has been lost. To a public audience, abstinence is portrayed as the healthy choice. I consider the impact of this shifting rhetoric—from prohibition to admonition—on attempts to control adolescent sexuality, as well as how it defines the contours of evangelicalism as a whole. Evangelicals use rhetorical agency as a strategy of persuasion, constructing their audience as teenagers who have the power to control their bodies.

Chapter 2 focuses on the use of sex to sell the abstinence message. From attractive Christian celebrities as spokespersons to the sale of panties printed with chastity slogans, the abstinence movement harnesses the power of sex to make chastity appealing to the Lindsay Lohan generation. The positive message of great sex portrays traditional marriage as the goal of abstinence. Virginity pledges and purity rings mimic the wedding ceremony. The "great sex" message focuses on bodies and embodiment, just as personal testimonies become embodied arguments to channel positive peer pressure and to persuade young people to commit to abstinence.

Another key argument in the evangelical sexual abstinence campaigns is that delaying sexual gratification today means a greater prize of true love and romance tomorrow. One way that this theme is communicated is through the use of the fairy-tale narrative, complete with beautiful princesses in distress, valiant princes on horseback, and evil forces that threaten to steal the princesses' virginity. In chapter 3, I analyze how the fairy-tale narrative both supports and subverts traditional gender roles. Young women may be waiting for their princes, but they are also taught that modestly covering their bodies exerts power and control over lustful young men. The young men, in turn, are actively pursuing and protecting their princesses, but they are also trapped and emasculated by their seemingly uncontrollable hormonal urges.

For American evangelical youth the commitment to abstinence means no sex, but it does not mean the absence of sexual activity. The message of the abstinence campaigns is resonating with evangelical young people, but the teens are largely on their own when it comes to figuring out how to live out their abstinence commitments in an overly sexualized society. In chapter 4, I look at how American evangelical teenagers are negotiating the gray area between sex and no sex. Although all the respondents have pledged to practice abstinence, they regularly make choices as to what constitutes appropriate physical intimacy within the context of the abstinence pledge. Young people choose to limit their choices in acts of self-control, creating boundaries of sexual activity. Whereas a diversity of appropriate boundaries exists, young people seem to agree on an execution of the concept of purity in which respecting others trumps self-gratification. Abstinent teens use their personal agency to discipline their sexuality and choose to surround themselves with communities of support. Positive peer pressure can reinforce the abstinence message, but it also can lead to rebellion within the peer group. Going along with the crowd can sometimes weaken the abstinence commitment by masking a false pledge.

Millions of young people have pledged abstinence, but that does not mean that they are all virgins. What happens to the happily-ever-after of the fairy tale of abstinence if the prince or princess did not wait for true love? Or, worse, what if the prince or princess never shows up? What, then, happens to the reward for abstinence? The abstinence campaigns offer a message of second virginity for those with sexually active pasts who want to renew a commitment to abstinence, but often young people are left to deal with the pain of their own fractured fairy tales. Chapter 5 tells the stories of young people who have committed to abstinence but are also managing the pain of past sexual relationships, the challenges of forgiving a partner who did not wait, and the silent suffering and loneliness of singleness and homosexuality in a heterosexual world.

In chapter 6, I follow the American evangelical sexual abstinence rhetoric to sub-Saharan Africa to explore the differences between the American and African cases. Does a pledge of abstinence make sense next to the specter of HIV/AIDS? The abstinence message in Kenya and Rwanda largely borrows the rhetoric of the abstinence campaigns in the United States, with a stronger emphasis on the fear of AIDS. Surprisingly, Rwandan youth express less fear of acquiring HIV/AIDS than fear of displeasing God. The sub-Saharan African and American cases offer some striking differences: American evangelicals offer a positive focus on purity and emphasize that pleasing God has tangible benefits for the individual. In contrast, Kenyan and Rwandan young people emphasize that pleasing God is an end in itself. For evangelicals in the United States, sin is an individual problem; in the context of sub-Saharan Africa, sin is viewed as a structural problem. There are gender differences, too: in the United States, the campaigns portray females as possessing power over their bodies; in sub-Saharan Africa, Kenyan and

Rwandan young people portray females as bearing responsibility for their bodies.

The condom has become a site of contestation among evangelicals in their promotion of abstinence in the United States and sub-Saharan Africa. In the United States, a key criticism of comprehensive sex-education programs by abstinence-until-marriage advocates is that providing details about condoms and how to use them dilutes the message of abstinence and implies that teenagers have no choice but to be sexually active. According to critics, the rhetoric of condom education constructs youth as possessing limited agency over their bodies and reduces the credibility of educators who promote both abstinence and condoms. U.S. abstinence advocates insist that the condom is a tool for promiscuity. In Kenya and Rwanda, however, evangelicals tend to view the condom as a necessary part of AIDS prevention efforts. In chapter 7, I explore competing conceptions of personal sin and structural sin and consider whether the abstinence pledge is a fitting rhetorical response.

The "sex is great" message is certainly persuasive, but it makes abstinence all about sex. As I suggest in the chapters that follow, this poses potential problems for both young people and evangelicalism. In chapter 8, I conclude by suggesting that religious rhetoric achieves greater accessibility and resonance when it adopts the language of the public, but it may lose its transcendence in the process.

CHAPTER I

From *Abstinence* to *Purity*

The Changing Tropes of Chastity

There is nothing like a pregnant teenage daughter of an anti–comprehensive sex education politician to thrust sexual abstinence into the national spotlight. Within days of the 2008 selection of the relatively unknown Alaska governor Sarah Palin to be the running mate of John McCain, the Republican candidate for president, the campaign announced that the governor's seventeen-year-old unwed daughter, Bristol, was pregnant.

Two months after giving birth to her son, Tripp, Bristol Palin decided to claim some of the spotlight to tell her own story. In one of the more awkward television interviews in recent memory, the Fox News personality Greta Van Susteren tossed softball questions to the then eighteen-year-old Palin, who answered with a disarming teenage frankness. There is plenty here to cheer about for advocates of choice and those who oppose abstinence education as the sole means of sex education. In response to a question about whether Bristol's antiabortion mother forced her to keep the baby, she replied, "It was my choice to have the baby. It doesn't matter what my mom's views are on it, it was my decision, and I wish people would have realized that, too."[1] In an echo of the feminist battle cry of "my body, my choice" for a new generation, Bristol asserted burgeoning adolescent agency to insist that the decision to keep the baby was her own.[2] Yet with heartbreaking candor she emphasized repeatedly during the interview that she wished motherhood would have happened ten years later. Like any new mother,

Bristol marveled at her son's smiles and coos. She also acknowledged that motherhood was turning out to be different than she thought it would be: "Well, it's not just the baby that's hard. It's just, like, I'm not living for myself anymore."

Bristol Palin echoed her mother's prolife stance, affirming that teens should wait to get pregnant (and presumably wait to have sex) "because it's so much easier if you're married and if you have a house and a career and—it's just so much easier." But what set the blogosphere abuzz was Bristol's apparently contradictory acknowledgment that abstinence is unrealistic for teenagers: "I think abstinence is, like—like, the—I don't know how to put it—like, the main—everyone should be abstinent or whatever, but it's not realistic at all," she told Van Susteren, awkwardly pushing back her hair as she struggled for words. As Bristol went on to say, abstinence is unrealistic because having sex is more accepted among teenagers. So of course abstinence seems unrealistic if everyone around you is having sex outside marriage. Everybody's doing it, or at least that's what everybody thinks.

In her adolescent vernacular Bristol Palin restated an essential argument of the evangelical sexual abstinence campaigns: that today's culture of sex portrays abstinence as an unrealistic option for teenagers. This claim is supported by scientific studies, which are significantly influencing the use of federal funds for abstinence education in public schools. But evangelicals have a loftier aim in the abstinence campaigns than scientifically proven effectiveness. As Albert Mohler, president of Southern Baptist Theological Seminary, has written, "The real issue for Christian teenagers and their parents is not to debate whether sexual abstinence before marriage is realistic or not. The larger and more important issue is that sexual abstinence until marriage is the biblical expectation and command. Once this is realized, the responsibility of all concerned is to ensure that expectations and structures are in place so that abstinence *is* realistic."[3]

The contemporary American evangelical sexual abstinence campaigns began in the early 1990s as a reaction to what was perceived as a hypersexualized culture in which abstinence is viewed as unrealistic and teenagers are assumed to have no choice but to have sex. Against this societal depiction of teenagers as hormone-driven automatons, the evangelical abstinence campaigns portray teenagers as choice-making agents with the power to control their own bodies. American evangelicals construct sexual abstinence as a choice.

Key words such as *choice, choose, decision,* and *decide* fill abstinence books and events. The focus of the message is that teenagers do not have to succumb to hormonal urges, peer pressure, or the dictates of a sex-saturated culture; they can choose not to have sex. Abstinence events are structured to make a case in support of abstinence, then to conclude by giving participating teenagers an opportunity to choose abstinence until marriage and to declare their choice publicly by signing and submitting a pledge card (True Love Waits); standing and accepting a pearl necklace (Pure Freedom); or receiving a Bible and donning a ring, signing a covenant, and standing and reading the covenant aloud (Silver Ring Thing).

The contemporary evangelical sexual abstinence campaigns began in response to what evangelical leaders regarded as a "condom culture" in which teens were expected to be sexually active. The abstinence campaigns seek to expand sexual behavior choices by offering abstinence as a viable alternative to promiscuity. Far from being merely one option among many, abstinence is portrayed as the correct choice for teens. Abstinence is recast as a positive call to a life of purity. In addition, the movement defines virginity in a manner that enhances the agency of teens: it claims that virginity is a gift that teens have the agency to lose, find, take, and give. Obedience to God is downplayed as the health benefits of abstinence are emphasized.

The rhetoric of abstinence goes beyond trying to convince teenagers not to have sex. It also shapes the identity of the evangelical community as a whole. The evangelical abstinence campaigns function to both control the liminality of teenagers and underscore the symbolic boundaries between evangelicals and secular society.[4] The sociologist Christian Smith argues that American evangelicals are thriving because they see themselves as embattled. They define themselves oppositionally: to be an evangelical (part of the in-group) is not to be part of secular society (the out-group). Yet evangelicals are not modern-day monastics, separate from the rest of society. Smith says that evangelicals thrive on "distinction, engagement, tension, [and] conflict" with secular society.[5] This engagement has shaped the rhetoric of evangelicals. The abstinence campaigns themselves display a form of liminality or border crossing. The campaigns seek to reinforce symbolic boundaries, but they also seek legitimacy and persuasive power through the reclamation of rhetorical forms used by secular society.

CONTEXT OF NO CHOICE

According to the cofounders of True Love Waits, the largest and oldest of the evangelical sexual abstinence campaigns, the prevailing cultural attitude in the early 1990s was that true love couldn't wait. Richard Ross and Jimmy Hester insisted that it could. "The overarching message of adults to teenagers was, 'We do not believe you can control your sexuality,'" recalls Ross, a professor of student ministry at Southwestern Baptist Theological Seminary. "The surgeon general of the United States looked square in the cameras in 1993 and said the American teenager is incapable of controlling his or her sexuality."

The mass distribution of condoms in public schools in the early 1990s signaled to evangelical leaders that society assumed that teenagers had no choice but to be sexually active. "We know you are going to have sex anyway," the government-funded programs seemed to say, "so when you do, at least use a condom." Hester, director of student ministry publishing for LifeWay, the publishing arm of the Southern Baptist Convention, saw this as a culture of promiscuity. He recalls, "The perception of students was, at least what we were hearing, the perception of students was that everybody is sexually active, that adults expect us to be that way, and so they're providing us these options to keep us safe in that. . . . Whether that was true or not, that was what they were hearing. And so the expectation was there."

Some evangelical sexual abstinence leaders single out groups like Planned Parenthood for their harshest critique, charging that the organization assumes that "nobody really does abstinence."[6] Instead, abstinence leaders say that Planned Parenthood promotes recreational sex through its condom distribution, based on a faulty assumption that teens lack agency to control their sexuality. Kristi Hayes, director of government relations for the Abstinence Clearinghouse, a government-funded umbrella organization serving more than thirty-six hundred abstinence affiliates, says, "A lot of things that people will try to get you to believe is every teenager is having sex, so we've got to give them condoms. Every teenager. And that's not true."

Planned Parenthood, however, is not alone in being blamed for promoting unbridled sexual activity. Evangelical sexual abstinence leaders frequently castigate mass media—and MTV in particular—for assuming teenagers have no choice but to be sexually active. A history of the True Love Waits campaign describes the sex-saturated culture: "In the early

1990s, teenagers were being bombarded with sexual messages from advertisers, television producers, movie makers, fashion designers, and media channels of every form. This led to a common belief among teenagers that everyone was having sex—especially their peers."[7] Joe McGarry, a program director for Silver Ring Thing, says he tries to "find a way to communicate that maybe life isn't like a Nelly video." Paraphrasing the popular MTV recording artist, McGarry says, "I've been around a lot and I've been in very many hot places. Just because 'it's getting hot in here,' it doesn't necessarily mean we're all 'taking off all our clothes.'" Denny Pattyn, the founder of Silver Ring Thing, tells his teenage audience that adults have created the sex-obsessed culture that teens now are forced to live in: "Forgive us, we adults, who have done this to you. . . . I challenge you to be the generation of change."[8]

The evangelical abstinence message is positioned as an expansion of choice (adding the option not to have sex) as well as the affirmation of teen agency to make the right choice in the context of a culture that asserts the absence of teen choice. The symbolic boundary is clear: sexualized "MTV culture" is the out-group. Avoiding sex is characteristic of the in-group. The argument for abstinence is a refashioning of the protofeminist argument of "my body, my choice."

Part of what makes abstinence sexy is the campaigns' construction of its audience as autonomous, choice-making individuals who have the ability to control their bodies and wait for sex. Here, agency is symbolically constructed through rhetoric. This is a necessary step in the process of persuasion: teenagers must be rhetorically constructed as agents with the power to choose before they can be persuaded to choose abstinence. Agency is offered as reclamation of power: evangelicals adopt the persona of victim, claiming that society is telling teens that bodies are uncontrollable and that sex is inevitable, a position from which agency must be reclaimed and restored. The role of the victim is a powerful stance in persuasion. Making oneself weak in order to (re)claim agency offers a narrative of overcoming and triumph that is absent from a normative understanding of agency. If the possession of agency is the status quo, then self-identification as an agent contains little transformative power. The claim of agency from a self-proclaimed stance of victim (the ultimate nonagent or absence of agency) rhetorically constructs a type of rebirth that is more powerful than mere agency. Portraying the rest of society as hypersexualized and evangelicals as marginalized creates rhetorical space for evangelicals to reclaim power and to motivate a generation of young people to make the right choices with their bodies.

RIGHT AND WRONG CHOICES

There may be an expansion of choice in the rhetoric of the abstinence campaigns, but there is clearly one right or correct choice, and that is to choose sexual abstinence until marriage. Sexual activity and sexual abstinence both may be available options for American teenagers, but the evangelical abstinence campaigns are clear that choosing to wait is the best option. Instead of merely stating the prohibition and expecting teens to obey, evangelical leaders appeal to the adolescents' budding sense of self-determination while at the same time presenting compelling arguments for what the leaders feel is the best choice. By focusing on the power to choose instead of merely the one best choice of abstinence, evangelical leaders affirm teens' developing sense of agency, changing a negative proposition of "Stop" or "Do not" into "I will" or "I choose."

Mary Douglas contends, following Emile Durkheim, that "holiness and impurity are at opposite poles." Dirt, or impurity, is "matter out of place."[9] For the abstinence campaigns, sexuality manifested in the body of a teenager—in that liminal state between childhood and adulthood—is matter out of place and must be managed. Yet, as the previous examples suggest, social control takes place as a liberal call to choose. The invitation to choose to wait to have sex reinforces symbolic boundaries between evangelicals and the rest of society, but the invitation itself crosses that symbolic boundary to reappropriate the rhetoric of choice.

Consequences is a key word repeated in books, at events, and among campaign leaders. All three highlight the negative consequences of making the wrong choice, nonmarital sex.[10] Pure Freedom makes a distinction between "poor choices" and "wise, head-defined choices." Poor choices such as sexual activity have negative consequences, including emotional stress, unwanted pregnancy, and sexually transmitted diseases.[11] Kristi Hayes of Abstinence Clearinghouse says that she hopes to see students she works with make "right choices": "I've worked with students before who were not able to save themselves, made wrong choices, and they're living with that consequence. I've also seen those who have decided to wait and have incredible marriages and don't have to carry some of those consequences." The abstinence message points out negative consequences of making the wrong decision, but overall the campaigns focus more on the positive consequences of making the right decision, for abstinence. By placing a higher value on one choice, choice rhetoric appears to be a false construction. Although the campaigns may present one correct choice, the power of choice rhetoric is displayed in the construction of the teenage audience as choice-making individuals.

Of course, the loophole in the construction of this argument is that the audience may claim its agency and make the "wrong choice," for sexual activity. Here the burden of proof lies in the evangelical leaders' ability to present the one right choice of abstinence as the best and most appealing choice for teenagers to make. One way that the evangelical abstinence campaigns do this is to turn an essentially negative prohibition into a positive choice by focusing on a call to purity.

FROM PROHIBITION TO ADMONITION: PURITY AS THE POSITIVE CHOICE

A key rhetorical construction of the evangelical sexual abstinence campaigns is a shift from a negative focus of "just say no" to sex before marriage to a positive focus of "just say yes" to sex within marriage. Although "to abstain from" is essentially negative—a call to prohibition—evangelicals place more emphasis on the positive aspects of waiting for sex within marriage. The evangelical sexual abstinence message rhetorically transforms a negative message of "abstain from" to a positive message of "wait for." Trumpeting the positive benefits of sexual intercourse does not attract much disagreement from a teenage audience, but that may be precisely the point: the positive transformation of abstinence begins with the presumption held by the campaigns' primary audience (teenagers) that sex is good, establishing the positive ethos of the rhetors, instead of perpetuating a negative stereotype of dour-faced, puritanical disciplinarians who insist that sex is bad.

The origin of the contemporary evangelical sexual abstinence campaigns is located in a desire to shift from a negative to a positive focus. The True Love Waits cofounders frequently use the word *positive* in describing the campaign. In his description of how True Love Waits was formed out of an interdepartmental committee at LifeWay to create Christian sex education materials, Ross says, "Increasingly, we were feeling there ought to be some kind of positive message, some kind of positive challenge to young people related to their sexual expression." Hester recounts that there seemed to be a number of negative public campaigns in the early 1990s, like the "Just Say No" campaign (which began in the 1980s) to combat drug abuse. It was in that context that Hester says the LifeWay committee was brainstorming names for its abstinence campaign: "We were just trying to think of different names and different thoughts, trying to find something that was positive, not negative in nature. . . . There were a lot of negative themes going around to students, and we thought there needed to be something positive." "True Love Waits" answered the question of why teenagers should wait to have sex, instead of just telling them not to have sex. Hester says that teenagers have told him that they like the name because of its positive focus.

Pure Freedom also was formed out of a motivation for a positive focus. Dannah Gresh, founder of Pure Freedom, says that when she and her husband began their abstinence ministry in 1996, they had an intense disdain for the word *abstinence:* "We said there's got to be another word. Abstinence is like 'Protestant.' It's like such a negative word. Like yes, we are the protesters; yes, we are the abstainers. It's such an awful word. Really, it is."

FROM ABSTINENCE TO PURITY

A primary way that the evangelical sexual abstinence campaigns maintain a positive construction of an essentially negative proposition is in the rhetorical shift from *abstinence* to *purity.*[12] Although the positive construction of abstinence focuses on waiting for great sex within marriage, the behavior of waiting is passive. The rhetorical shift from abstinence to purity provides a positive and active behavior for youth to pursue.[13]

A focus on purity allows the campaigns to issue a positive active call to pursue purity, instead of dwelling on a list of specific don'ts that qualify as abstinence: "Abstinence is about not having sex. Purity and sexual integrity is about waiting to have it right," writes Dannah Gresh's husband, Bob, in his book for teenage boys, *Who Moved the Goalpost?*[14] This quotation appears next to a photo of a smiling teenage boy with the caption, "Fun sex is blessed by God," connecting the focus on purity with a positive view of sex. Apart from the context of purity, the "blessing of God" on "fun sex" could appear to be an invitation for nonmarital sex. Instead, the call to purity challenges youth to wait to have sex "right." Purity also extends to behaviors beyond just sex. According to the *Silver Ring Thing Sexual Abstinence Study Bible,* "Purity is a way of life. It has to do with the way you dress, the

way you act, what you think, and what you say. Purity is not about
what *you can not do* but rather about treasuring *who you are*."[15]
Instead of emphasizing prohibitions in dress, thought, action, and
speech, purity emphasizes the positive freedom to "treasure who
you are."

Some campaign leaders talk about purity as an inward process or
motivation that influences behavioral choices. Jimmy Hester relates
purity to a state of mind: "Purity then speaks to your thoughts, which
could lead to the behavior, or your attitudes in other things." Suzy
Weibel, a Pure Freedom retreat facilitator, describes purity in terms of
identity, in contrast to the behavioral focus of abstinence. For her, purity
is about being rather than doing: "I think abstinence is a definition of
a conscious choice that a person makes, and I think purity needs to
become more of a person's identity, who the person is. So abstinence
is probably behavior related, whereas purity is identity related."

If purity encompasses a wider range of abstinent behaviors than
merely sexual abstinence, one could abstain from nonmarital sex and
not be living a pure life, as Pure Freedom's Dannah Gresh, points out:
"Well, you can abstain from sex and not be pure, I think. Purity is more
all encompassing. It's about your thought life. It's about your emotional
life. It's about everything, whereas abstinence is obviously a lot more
about the technicality of sex." In the context of purity, sexual abstinence
becomes a moral decision, part of a broader call to a morally pure
lifestyle.

The emphasis of the evangelical sexual abstinence campaigns on
purity is a relatively recent rhetorical construction in the campaigns'
views on abstinence. The evolution of the wording of the True Love
Waits pledge offers an example of the abstinence-to-purity transformation. The original True Love Waits pledge says, "Believing that *true
love waits,* I make a commitment to God, myself, my family, those I
date, my future mate, and my future children to be sexually pure until
the day I enter a covenant marriage relationship."[16] The wording of the
pledge reflects the campaign's original focus on abstinence until marriage but unintentionally denigrates traditional marriage by suggesting
that the commitment to purity lasts only until marriage begins. One
True Love Waits staff member challenged the use of "sexually pure,"
questioning why sex within a monogamous, faithful marriage relationship would not also be considered pure. The pledge was soon reworded:
"To be *sexually abstinent* from this day until the day I enter a biblical
marriage relationship."[17]

The most significant rewording of the pledge, according to campaign staff, occurred in 2003 in response to the increasing popularity of the word *purity* in sexual abstinence circles: the word kept "popping up," according to cofounder Jimmy Hester. He also says that the rewording was an attempt to define abstinence, but the change actually allowed the campaign to avoid specific do's and don'ts of what it means to be abstinent. As of 2003, the True Love Waits pledge read, "Believing that true love waits, I make a commitment to God, myself, my family, my friends, my future mate, and my future children to a lifetime of purity including sexual abstinence from this day until the day I enter a biblical marriage relationship."[18] Hester points to the sexual scandal involving President Bill Clinton and Monica Lewinsky, an intern, as inadvertently raising the purity issue. "Our former president helped with that in some ways because [of] the whole oral sex issue," Hester recalls. " 'Is this sex? Is this not sex? What do we mean by abstinence?' We get that question a lot. 'How far do you go before you say you're abstinent? Is it sexual intercourse? Is that where you draw the line?' And so I think the purity issue came up."

This shift from abstinence to purity has the practical result of eliminating the need for evangelical abstinence campaigns to explicitly define what constitutes sex. Instead of being forced to make lists of acceptable and unacceptable sexual activity, the campaigns can focus on purity, thus subsuming sexual activity under the general category of lifestyle choices that are pleasing to God. Purity, then, involves more than mere sexual abstinence: it involves what movies one watches, what clothes one wears, and the people with whom one associates. The passive stance of waiting for true love becomes an active choice. Purity becomes a general call to enact the spiritual decision of a Christian to follow Christ as a physical decision of Christlike lifestyle behavior, not unlike the sentiment proposed by the popular Christian catchphrase "What would Jesus do?"

In its books and events, Pure Freedom emphasizes that "purity is a process."[19] At one of Pure Freedom's mother-daughter events in the Chicago area in 2004, Dannah Gresh pointed to a vertical black line projected on a screen in front of attendees. She said that this line represents a misguided definition of purity: anything to the left of the line, even if it is close to the line, is purity, and anything that crosses the line is impurity. She said that many girls come close to the line by dressing provocatively, acting "boy crazy," and engaging in physical exploration but technically are still virgins. "We think that virginity is purity," she told the attendees. "But virginity doesn't equal purity." Another slide was projected on the screen—a spiral line and a small ugly cartoon face with horns—which Gresh told the attendees is God's definition of purity. Citing Bible verses, she said that individuals are not born pure, but they can become pure through the gift of Christ's salvation. Expect that temptations and lust (the horned figure) will come, but as one chooses to obey God, one continues on the spiral path and becomes pure. This portrayal of purity allows for a rhetorical reconstruction of virginity while avoiding a legalistic list of do's and don'ts regarding sexually abstinent behavior.

VIRGINITY LOST, FOUND, TAKEN, AND GIVEN

A primary example of this portrayal of teenagers as choice-making individuals is found in the rhetorical construction of "second virginity," also called renewed virginity, or revirginization. True Love Waits, Silver Ring Thing, and Pure Freedom all contain a message of second virginity. Although physical virginity ceases to exist after a person engages in sexual intercourse, the evangelical sexual abstinence campaigns construct virginity as essentially rhetorical, using language to reconstruct symbolically a physical state of being.

Second virginity is portrayed as a positive outcome of the spiritual act of repentance and forgiveness of sexual sin. It allows sexually active teens to choose virginity again. As Josh McDowell writes in his book, *Why True Love Waits,* "No one can regain his or her physical virginity. That's lost forever. But I really believe that one's spiritual and emotional virginity can be regained."[20] The second virginity message acknowledges that some audience members already may have chosen a sexually active lifestyle, but the choice for sexual abstinence is always an option. The significance of this message is that it does not exclude anyone from the potential audience: the choice for abstinence is always an option, regardless of previous choices.

The theological basis for second virginity relies on God's forgiving nature. As the popular contemporary Christian recording artist and True Love Waits spokesperson Rebecca St. James sings in her song "Wait for Me," "Now I know you may have made mistakes / But there's forgiveness, and a second chance. So wait for me."[21] The current version of the True Love Waits pledge declares sexual abstinence "from this day until I enter a biblical marriage relationship," and this phrasing allows sexually active pledgers to be free from their past and start over, living sexually abstinent lives. Silver Ring Thing events offer an evangelical altar call for the forgiveness of sins before the purity ring ceremony: "I don't know why you came, but only God can make sure you leave here with your sins forgiven. You need to let God wipe that slate clean. Then you put on the ring," Denny Pattyn, Silver Ring Thing founder, told a 2004 crowd in the Boston area, with Bible in hand.[22]

The concept of second virginity allows evangelical leaders to share the abstinence message with the largest possible teen audience, both sexually active and abstinent teens. But the concept also could function as a "get out of jail free" card for teens who are looking for a way to make an abstinence pledge after they first have enjoyed a sexually active life. Silver Ring Thing's McGarry recalls hearing of such conversion stories when he was a teenager: "They got to have their cake and eat it, too. They lived this life of fun, but then they got to have God at the end." McGarry says he followed that example, and although he was raised in a Christian family, he began engaging in sexual activity at age sixteen.

Rebecca St. James denies that forgiveness and second virginity encourage carefree sexual behavior. During a break from her performance at a True Love Waits rally in Dallas in 2004, St. James told me, "That's why, whenever I talk about this, I talk about the consequences, you know, STDs [sexually transmitted diseases], AIDS, pregnancy outside of marriage, emotional consequences, and I kind of lay out there. . . . So I don't think anybody would walk away from hearing me talk about it and going, 'Oh, well, I'm just going to have sex because I can get forgiven.' I think they know there are consequences of your actions." McGarry too says he now tries to warn teenage boys of the consequences of nonmarital sex: "I'll very intentionally say, 'Listen, if I could go back and do everything over, I would do everything differently. You don't want the issues I have with my marriage.'" But he also acknowledges the appeal of second virginity to teenagers who feel invincible and are unconcerned with threats of emotional consequences.

In private interviews and public testimonials, sexual debut is frequently referred to as the occasion when one "lost" one's virginity. This is an interesting rhetorical construction of limited agency, considering that in almost all cases the sexual debut is between consenting individuals. It is as if one unintentionally misplaced one's virginity, even though one knowingly consented to giving it up.[23] The concept of being spiritually lost is familiar in the evangelical context, with New Testament parables of a lost sheep, a lost coin, and a prodigal son all suggesting the redemptive act of Jesus as saving the lost through his crucifixion and resurrection. Being spiritually lost allows the possibility of being spiritually found in and by Jesus. In a similar way, the popular rhetorical construction of losing one's virginity supports the evangelical concept of second virginity in that it relies on the power of God's forgiveness to "find" it again.

The exception to this rhetorical construction of sexual debut as lost virginity is in situations of rape or sexual abuse. In these cases the sexual activity is described as one's virginity being "taken away." Virginity that is taken away is not lost. Thus a victim of sexual abuse does not need to renew his or her virginity since it was never lost.[24] True Love Waits makes the distinction between consensual sex and nonconsensual abuse in *When True Love Doesn't Wait*: "If you consented to the sexual acts, then you can receive a second virginity. . . . Virginity has to be given away, not taken. If you were forced to have sex, you did not lose your virginity."[25] The distinction places blame for the abuse on the abuser: "This concept is invaluable for several reasons. It places responsibility where it belongs, assists with your recovery, and may keep any other teenagers from being mistreated as you were. Virginity is more of a mind-set and an attitude of purity than it is a physical feature," one book counsels.[26] Claiming virginity as more attitudinal than physical creates space for the rhetorical construction of a second virginity where what was lost becomes found. In the case of sexual abuse, virginity was never lost.

Central to the distinction between consensual nonmarital sex/lost virginity/found second virginity and nonconsensual sex/maintained virginity/found recovery is the rhetorical construction of virginity as a gift. The gift of physical virginity can be taken in sexual abuse, but it is meant to be given to one's spouse on one's wedding night. Virginity as a gift strengthens one's agency and ability to choose when and to whom to give it. Virginity that is lost does not suggest an active choice to give it away. By describing virginity as a gift, the evangelical abstinence message that sex is meant only for marriage empowers virgin teens to choose when and to whom to give their gift. In this way, consensual marital sex consists of a mutual giving and receiving of gifts of virginity.[27]

Although second virginity is portrayed as an acceptable option, the gift of first-time virginity is portrayed as possessing higher value. Choosing to be sexually abstinent as a teenager endows the gift of virginity with increased value, which is portrayed as a significant gift to one's future spouse. An important part of the evangelical sexual abstinence campaigns is the use of various material symbols to represent the spiritual gift of virginity, which, when given to a future spouse, becomes both a material and a representational gift. The purity ring is perhaps the most popular symbol. The purity ring symbolizes the gift of virginity and the commitment to preserve the gift until one's wedding day, as I discuss in chapter 2. The use of the purity ring demonstrates the agency of teens to control their sexuality and give it away in marriage, as well as the positive focus on the evangelical abstinence movement to emphasize the benefits of the good marriage over the negative consequences of nonmarital sex.

ABSTINENCE AS A HEALTHY CHOICE

The rhetorical shift from abstinence to purity among evangelical sexual abstinence campaigns is perhaps not surprising, given biblical admonitions to live a pure and sin-free life. Here the rhetoric of purity is an example of audience-centered persuasion, using religiously inflected rhetoric to appeal to a primarily religious audience. What is perhaps more unexpected is that evangelical leaders position the abstinence campaign as a health campaign, not a spiritual revival.[28] Whereas the abstinence events assume the form of youth revival meetings or Bible studies or church retreats, complete with altar calls, their content uses religious language to promote healthy lifestyle habits. Here spirituality is in service to public policy, as abstinence educators emphasize the practical health implications of choosing abstinence, namely, a reduction in teenage pregnancies (and the subsequent need for abortions) and the transmission of STDs, both of which have societal impact in welfare and public health policy. Abstinence is promoted as the "100 percent effective" way to stop unwanted pregnancies and STDs, regardless of whether one believes in Jesus Christ or not. Although evangelical leaders believe that abstinence is God's design for human sexual behavior, they say they promote it because it works.

It's a savvy argumentation structure that begins with a moral and religious commitment and ends with a pragmatic and secular outcome. The commitment to sexual abstinence may be made to God, but the benefit of abstinence is received by the individual and society at large. Evangelical leaders demonstrate astute attention to tailoring their message for particular audiences, including an understanding that "God-talk" is not particularly persuasive in the public sphere. Instead, they focus on the effectiveness of abstinence at solving social ills such as unwanted pregnancy (and corresponding problems of welfare dependency and abortion) and the transmission of STDs. Abstinence becomes the ultimate solution for abortion, dismissing the current stasis of debate about when life begins by offering fail-safe prevention for unwanted pregnancy. To their public audience, evangelical leaders downplay the commandments of God and emphasize the pragmatic fact that abstinence works.

This bifurcated argument reveals the evangelical abstinence campaigns' double position of appealing to the church and secular society. Evangelical abstinence educators use the rhetoric of health instead of the rhetoric of religion in order to convince the public audience that abstinence education is effective. In doing so, evangelicals open the possibility of a back-door channel for evangelization: if abstinence works and abstinence is part of God's plan for humanity, then God and his plan must work.

According to the evangelical leaders, abstinence works because it promotes a healthy lifestyle that benefits children, families, and society. In response to a question about the most effective argument for abstinence, Kristi Hayes of Abstinence Clearinghouse offered a health-focused response: "It's *the* one-hundred-percent way to keep your kids healthy. Why in the world wouldn't we want our kids to be a hundred percent healthy? Why wouldn't we give them that choice?" The choice, as she describes it, is to be healthy or not. Hayes defines nonmarital sex as unhealthy because it can lead to unwanted pregnancy, STDs, and emotional distress. Teen health is her focus: "I think the main issue is the students' health. That is what we're focused on. . . . I think it's about keeping teens healthy," she says.

Concerned Women for America's Wendy Wright describes the healthy lifestyle that comes from sexual abstinence as benefiting more than just the individual: "So when you've got a healthy lifestyle, then you're on a better track to having a healthier marriage, healthier family life, healthier career, because you're not obsessed with all these personal problems. So it leads to better individual lives and then also better family lives, and family being the foundation of society, it helps all society. . . . And so if you can promote self-control and discipline and a mind-set that is focused on healthy living through abstinence, that can have an effect in other areas of your life." According to Wright, abstinence is a foundational building block of a healthy society, not just a key element in adolescent health.

Although all the abstinence events included in this study contained a type of altar call or an evangelical plea for individuals to accept Jesus Christ as their savior, interview respondents insist that religious conversion is not the main focus of the abstinence events. Hester of True Love Waits insists that encouraging conversion is "not the purpose of it. That's almost been a serendipity thing. . . . We've had students in rallies and other places who, in our case, have come to know Jesus Christ because of the message, but that wasn't necessarily the intent of the message." He goes on to describe the intent of the message as encouraging young people to make a pledge to remain sexually abstinent until marriage: "But they realize, 'Okay, if I'm going to make that commitment, it says something about my spirit and my faith, and I need to make this commitment also.'"

Religious conversion may not be the explicit focus of the abstinence campaigns, but crafting a broad message that appeals to Christians and non-Christians alike is central to the campaigns' public aims. Silver Ring Thing's emphasis on the forms of popular secular culture is a strategy to boost Silver Ring Thing's ethos with its teenage audience. "We have to earn the right to be heard," says founder Denny Pattyn. "I'm focusing on the guy in the backseat who didn't want to come tonight."[29] Pattyn boasts that the first half of the Silver Ring Thing show is intentionally focused on humor, "not pity laughs, but really funny," in order to engage the attention of the proverbial guy in the back row. Pattyn emphasizes the lack of Christian jargon as a positive example of the broad appeal of Silver Ring Thing's message.

Some interview respondents portray religious faith as a supplement to the abstinence commitment, providing abstinence pledgers with a transcendent reason for maintaining a healthy lifestyle. In this sense, religious conversion is a secondary, not primary, aim of the abstinence events. Silver Ring Thing's Joe McGarry says that his organization's focus is on abstinence commitments, not religious commitments. "When we talk about success of shows, we talk about rings on fingers and then faith commitments, . . . so obviously it's not a primary metric of success. And yet if you don't want to hear about God at all, hey, more power to you. . . . We are most concerned about your future and the future of our next generation." McGarry goes on to refute those who may say that Silver Ring Thing uses abstinence merely as a tool for religious conversion: "So that's one of the things some folks say, 'Yeah, but isn't it really just . . . What's the word? . . . Just telling people . . . trying to convert people and you're just wrapping it up in sexual education?' I say, 'Well, no. It's about health.' We believe that faith is the best way to do that, and so for those who haven't made a faith commitment, we offer that opportunity." McGarry asserts that a faith commitment assists in maintaining an abstinence commitment, but he denies that abstinence is merely a front for a covert conversion agenda. Abstinence Clearinghouse's Hayes also denies that one has to be a Christian to make an abstinence pledge. "No one says you have to be a Christian to be abstinent or you have to do this," Hayes says. "It is the message of how do we help our teens stay healthy and make the right choices, and this is how we do it, whether you're faith based or not." Health is the primary focus of the abstinence message, but religious commitment can help when temptation is strong by providing a transcendent authority that one aspires to please.

Some evangelical leaders describe a strategic decision to use a health-focused portrayal of the evangelical abstinence movement when speaking to a nonevangelical or secular audience. Janice Crouse of Concerned Women for America says, "When I talk to a secular group, I usually frame it in terms of women's well-being. What is best for women. What is best for children." When Hester is interviewed on secular radio stations, he recounts how the interviewer often tries to get him to talk about Christian hot-button topics such as abortion or homosexuality in order to expose him for being more concerned about issues of faith than the social issue itself: "They want to pin you as a flaming evangelical Christian person. And so the way to defuse that real quick is to say, 'Okay, let's don't talk about anything related to faith. Let's just talk about the commonsense reality of sexual abstinence.' Well, then, when you start talking about health issues and social issues and those kind of things, it changes the whole tenor of the conversation, and they realize they can't do that. . . . They can't just pin it on as a faith issue because it's bigger than that. It really is bigger than that." Hester's response reveals a strategic choice to discuss abstinence rationally in terms of health with a secular audience that is accustomed to treating "flaming evangelical Christians" as an irrational sideshow. Focusing on the rational effectiveness of abstinence allows Hester to portray abstinence as a social issue, not a religious issue, with implications for Christians and non-Christians alike. The health focus serves to broaden the potential audience for the abstinence message while improving the image of evangelicals as rational, socially conscious individuals.

Concerned Women for America's Wright approaches abstinence from a women's health standpoint and talks about the effectiveness of abstinence as abortion prevention. Wright says that she avoids overtly religious arguments when talking to members of Congress because "it's the old thing of speak to your audience. So you use language that the person you're trying to persuade will understand and relate to." In an extended example of a related morality-based health issue, Wright recounts how in her testimony at a Food and Drug Administration hearing on a type of "morning-after" pill, she presented her case against the drug based not on a religious conviction regarding the sanctity of life but as a threat to women's health. She pointed out the inadequacies of medical studies to evaluate the hormone's impact on female adolescents, as well as the health complications that could arise if women were allowed to purchase this high dose of hormones over the counter, when low doses in the form of birth control pills still require a doctor's prescription. Wright says that when she presented similar arguments during a radio program with Sam Donaldson, callers to the program agreed with her that the drug should not be available over the counter. She says that this is in contrast to the support the drug receives when someone argues that it will reduce the number of abortions. By changing the stasis of the argument from abortion to women's health, Wright was able to make a more persuasive case.

Wright goes on to discuss how abstinence is a health preventative for both abortion and AIDS. She sees abortion as a treatment for unwanted pregnancy and argues that abstinence renders abortion unnecessary. The significance of her argument is that she portrays abstinence as a healthy lifestyle behavior that prevents unwanted effects like pregnancy and AIDS. "And so [abortion rights supporters] often treat it as these kids are going to [have sex] anyway: 'It's better that she have the abortion than be burdened with a baby,' " Wright says. "And we can point out that, no, we shouldn't be encouraging that behavior in the first place, and that would alleviate them from having to face that terrible decision."

Regarding AIDS, Wright argues that it is unpopular to offer behavioral change as a preventative measure against the disease: "And so the message is, 'Don't tell us to change our lifestyle or to change our behavior, but be there to clean up our mess afterwards. We want you to pay for our drugs. We want society, others to take care of us, but we don't want to be responsible for our behavior.' " The only preventative measure that is discussed, according to Wright, is the use of condoms, which she deems less effective than abstinence. Instead of viewing the condom as a medical device to prevent disease, she suggests that the condom is a tool for promiscuity. Abstinence, in contrast, is the best prevention because it is the most effective.

The physical body is a symbol of the social body.[30] Attempts to control the physical body suggest "the desire to control or protect specific institutions and groups within that society."[31] The evangelical sexual abstinence campaigns aim at social control through the control of teenage sexuality, underscoring the symbolic boundary between evangelicals and the rest of secular (and, they would claim, sexualized) society. Whereas the evangelical sexual abstinence rhetoric attempts to manage the liminality of teenagers, it also performs a type of liminality, appropriating feminist arguments of choice, focusing on positive calls to purity, rhetorically constructing virginity, and promoting health benefits for the individual, all for ostensibly religious ends.

A critical view of this focus on practical benefits suggests that the rhetorical border-crossing reframes evangelical rhetoric as focused on the individual, reducing its transcendence. A more positive view suggests that this what's-in-it-for-me rhetoric can strengthen religiosity by broadening appeal and demonstrating effectiveness through rational measures. In essence, God is effective when his biblical admonitions are supported by medical research, are backed by federal funding, and result in tangible benefits for the individual. God is hip when he is accompanied by attractive celebrities, loud music, and laser light shows, as I explain in the next chapter.

CHAPTER 2

Of Purity Rings and Pop Stars

Using Sex to Sell Abstinence

MTV is not the first place one would expect to find the message of abstinence. On the other hand, an abstinence event is not the first place one would expect to find the message of great sex.

A week after the high-octane Silver Ring Thing event in the Boston area in 2004, the message that sex is great traveled from a college chapel to a more sexualized venue. A video clip of Josh and the "sex is great" chant, along with interviews with Silver Ring Thing staff and volunteers, appeared on the program "Sex, Votes, and Higher Power," part of MTV's *Choose or Lose* series to encourage teenage voting. The program was hosted by the pop artist Christina Aguilera, whose popular album *Stripped* and its debut single "Dirrty" contribute to her overtly sexual persona.

Segments of Aguilera's interview of two Silver Ring Thing staff members were spliced between clips from movies and music videos of couples in the heat of passion. The pop star, dressed in a relatively demure but tight sweater, blazer, and miniskirt, probed Gordo, twenty-two, and Julie, nineteen, a couple, about their dating habits. Aguilera's sexually explicit language contrasted with the couple's conservative boundaries for physical intimacy:

> *Gordo:* We'll kiss, we'll hang out, we'll hold hands, we'll hug and stuff, but we don't want to let it go any further than that.
>
> *Christina Aguilera:* Touchy-feely over clothes, then, is one step closer—

G: Yes, definitely.

CA: Dry-humping—

G: Yeah.

CA: Sorry.

G: No, that's fine. You start doing that, then it's real easy to, "Well, maybe you can take off that, well, maybe you can do that." We don't want to take it there at all.

Aguilera continued the interview by asking if the couple felt that sex is only for the purpose of procreation, to which they responded no. Following a video clip from the Silver Ring Thing about great sex, Aguilera asked if they thought it possible they could have a bad sex life:

Christina Aguilera: I mean, could the sex be bad because it's something you've never tried? According to the partner—?

Gordo: If you see a donut and it looks good, it's probably going to be good.

CA: Really? Because I've had some rotten ones, you know? You never know. You've got to test out the car before you buy it, right?

MTV and "sex is great"? Christina Aguilera and the music of Usher? The evangelical Christian sexual abstinence campaigns are using some unlikely bedfellows to help break down negative stereotypes of "just say no" and transform the movement into "just say yes . . . but wait."

Regarding issues of sex, popular wisdom portrays American evangelicals as righteous moralists who are more concerned with disciplining the body than with having a good time. Religious conservatives believe that "sex is inherently dirty and wrong," according to Gloria Feldt, president of the Planned Parenthood Federation of America and author of *The War on Choice: The Right-Wing Attack on Women's Rights and How to Fight Back*. This conservative ideology is based on fear, Feldt writes, "fear that the ancient tradition of male-dominated marriage will come crumbling down, fear that women will have more power." As the title of her book suggests, Feldt believes that the religious right, which generally includes evangelical Christians, is fighting to limit women's choice. In a chapter on abstinence education, Feldt portrays school-based abstinence programs as offering an "appallingly backward, almost medieval view of the world" in their focus on virginity before marriage and justified punishment in the form of unwanted pregnancy, disease, and death for those who engage in the sin of nonmarital sex.[1] Contrary to Feldt's portrayal, evangelicals are embracing the joy of sex and spreading the good news to teenagers that sex is great—within the context of marriage. A prime example of the shift from a negative prohibition to a call to a positive lifestyle is that evangelicals are using sex to sell abstinence (see chapter 1).

And yet Feldt's charge that evangelicals view sex as dirty is not far off base. Evangelicals view nonmarital sex—like dirt itself—as matter out of place; the proper place is within marriage.[2] In chapter 1, I discussed the function of the evangelical abstinence message in controlling the liminality of teenagers and underscoring the symbolic boundaries between evangelicals and secular society. At the same time, the form of the campaigns themselves displays a type of liminality or boundary crossing. The campaigns seek to reinforce symbolic boundaries, but they seek both legitimacy and persuasive power through the reclamation of secular rhetorical forms. The message may be to control sexual urges (or, more positively, to "choose purity"), but the medium is all about sex. The rhetorical strategies of the campaigns borrow secular forms to make abstinence appealing to young people. The campaigns also aim to make evangelicalism appealing to the rest of society.

THE APPEAL OF POP CULTURE

Walking into a Silver Ring Thing event is like walking into a scrubbed-up rock concert or hip club. Loud music thumps in your chest and rings in your ears, but the crowd consists of throngs of suburban young people, many of whom look as though they've stepped off the pages of an American Eagle catalog. No smoking or body piercings here. The main difference, though, is that the venue is a church, not an arena. As I entered the foyer of a large midwestern evangelical church, I was greeted by a middle-aged woman with a generous smile who was standing near one of about eight round tables. She asked if she could get my ring size. In the middle of the tables were stands displaying the two different styles of silver rings—wider bands for guys and thinner ones for girls. The event was free, but the ring cost $20. I passed on the ring and was given a plastic wrist band. All around the foyer were clusters of high school students—mostly white, a few African American, in a sea of headbands and flip-flops for the girls and T-shirts and baseball caps for the guys.

I made my way through the crowd and paused at the souvenir table selling the usual concert mix of T-shirts, hats, buttons, and stickers. The products were familiar, but the messages were certainly unusual.

"How to Have the Best Sex Ever," shouted one provocative T-shirt. The white letters stood out against the black background. The word *sex* was in red, with the organization's Web site printed in small lettering below. "Safe Sex?" asked another, above the ominous image of a red skull and crossbones. Small print below read, "Warning: No condom can protect 100% against pregnancy, AIDS, or any STD." Buttons proudly announced, "I'm waiting" or "No ice, no dice," featuring a picture of a diamond engagement ring. A sticker with red crabs asked, "You want 'em?" There was even a glossy 8 x 10 black-and-white photo for sale of the attractive Silver Ring Thing crew. Before and after the show I noticed a number of young people with the photo, seeking autographs of team members, who seemed happy to oblige.

The sanctuary was completely dark except for strobe lights and spotlights on the stage. The overall effect was 1980s industrial: The stage was set with four large metal oil drums, open shelving with pipes and tools, and the image of gears projected on the wall. A large media screen occupied each corner, and two crash dummies (with clothing) stood guard. Before the show began, a guy and girl from the Silver Ring Thing team invited audience members to come up on stage and demonstrate cheesy dance moves, like the electric slide and Michael Jackson's dance from the *Thriller* video. The crowd was on its feet, cheering on friends. The leaders threw T-shirts into the crowd. A smartly produced introduction to the show involved a male leader interacting with scenes from *Transformers,* the previous summer's popcorn hit. As the film showed asteroids preparing to hit Earth, the four metal cans on stage shot fountains of fire in a flaming burst. More loud music and strobe lights followed. The show had begun.

A significant part of the appeal of evangelical abstinence campaigns like Silver Ring Thing is that they look and feel like a concert or club, not church. The sobering message of the consequences of nonmarital sex is packaged to make it more palatable to a teenage audience. Silver Ring Thing events are replete with humor and teenage pop culture references. A regular feature is the use of original parodies of familiar commercials. There is "STD Harmony": in a twist on dating service ads, a guy playfully twirls a young woman around as they announce that one has syphilis and the other has herpes. In a parody of the Mac/PC commercials, two men stand side by side and introduce themselves with "Hi, I'm waiting" and "I'm not waiting." In one version Not Waiting is holding two crying babies. In a send-up of the Apple ad mocking the problem-plagued PC Vista operating system, Not Waiting is sitting on a pallet with other sick men who are also Not Waiting and who now all have sexually transmitted diseases. Between the commercials, two team leaders dressed as out-of-touch junior high music teachers perform a version of the popular *Saturday Night Live* music teachers skit that features Will Ferrell and Ana Gasteyer. Placing a sign over the keyboard that reads "Mr. and Mrs. Nelson present Sex Stops Here," the two offer off-key harmony to familiar pop refrains, including "I Like Big Butts," "You Can't Touch This," and even the "Oompa Loompa" song from *Willy Wonka and the Chocolate Factory*. The quality of the performance is reminiscent of a church youth group talent show, but the performers give it their all and the crowd erupts with laughter and applause.

The organizers of abstinence campaigns castigate popular media for spreading a culture of sex, but at the same time they also reappropriate the forms of popular media such as movies, television shows, and music to appeal to their teenage audience. Mark Regnerus, in his study of sex and religion among American young people, argues that popular media have a powerful role in teaching young people about sex. Sexually explicit television programs, teenage movies, and Web sites are within easy reach of most teenagers, rendering serious debate about sex education in public schools irrelevant, according to Regnerus.[3] Mass media are persuasive teachers of sex ed. Can they also teach abstinence? The abstinence campaigns are testing that idea, borrowing common media forms—pop music, commercials, sketch comedy, and blockbuster movies—to communicate a different kind of message about sex.

At a True Love Waits rally in Dallas, ten thousand teenagers filled a sports arena, waiting for the concert to begin. A beach ball substituted for a blown-up condom was tossed around the crowd. A group started a chant, which echoed across the arena: "We love Jesus, yes we do! We love Jesus, how 'bout you?" Out in the hallways teenagers purchased standard event fare like nachos and candy, while a basket of pink plastic models of ten-week-old fetuses sat nearby at a display sponsored by a local crisis pregnancy center. Finally, the popular Christian contemporary artist Rebecca St. James took the stage. With her long brown hair cascading over her shoulders in loose curls and wearing a modest yellow and black minidress over jeans and boots, St. James worked the beat—and the crowd—with a minimum of gyrations. Changing moods, she led the crowd in an a cappella version of the worship chorus "Awesome God" before telling the cheering teenagers, "I'm still a virgin. I'm saving sex for marriage."

While the abstinence message is presented in myriad ways, including weekend retreats, Bible studies, church youth group meetings, pledge ceremonies, fashion shows, and tea parties, the largest abstinence events simulate a common teenage public event: the stadium rock concert. Abstinence events often feature popular Christian contemporary artists, such as Rebecca St. James, BarlowGirl, or Salvador, complete with screaming fans, strobe lights, and ear-popping acoustics. Based on standards of beauty featured in current teen magazines and television programs, all the artists can be considered physically attractive. Here, the abstinence organizations use sex to sell abstinence by presenting their message through sexy (albeit modestly dressed) celebrity spokespersons. The celebrity status (as well as physical appearance) of the artists elevates their ethos among the teenage audience, making their abstinence message easier to hear than most of their song lyrics.

Popular culture presents a particular dilemma for evangelicals. Are media forms such as television, movies, concerts, and the Internet tools for evangelism or tools of the devil? Evangelicals are known for their entrepreneurial spirit, as they are among the first to incorporate new elements of popular culture, sanctifying them for the holy purposes of spreading the gospel message.[4] Whether one looks to the high dramatics of frontier camp meetings during the Second Great Awakening, the fiery radio preaching of the early twentieth century, or the technical stage productions of televangelists, evangelicals have been quick to adopt many of the new communication technologies for the purpose of reaching a wider audience.[5]

In a move that exemplifies the tension between the positive and negative effects of the forms of popular culture, Denny Pattyn, Silver Ring Thing founder, apologized to the teenage audience at an event in the Boston area for what he sees as his generation's creation of a culture of sex. In the same sentence in which he excoriated the influence of MTV (a popular target among all the abstinence organizations examined in this study), Pattyn encouraged the audience to watch MTV for the upcoming show on abstinence hosted by Christina Aguilera. He acknowledged the contradiction in his announcement but justified tuning in to the media leader of the sex culture because of the show's message on abstinence. His message seemed to be that secular forms of popular media are to be avoided unless they are sanctified with an evangelical message. The sheer popularity of a media outlet like MTV packs a certain appeal to evangelicals because of its broad reach among an unchurched demographic. Getting the message of abstinence on MTV is like beating the devil at his own game. But the message itself has morphed to match the form: abstinence is now all about sex.

At a Silver Ring Thing event in the Chicago area in 2009, Chaz, a team leader, took the stage to give the "sex is great" talk. Movie clips from edgy youth comedies like *Superstar, Napoleon Dynamite,* and *Anchorman* punctuated his talk. He told the crowd that this wasn't the kind of sex talk where the leaders claim that if you have sex you will "burn in fire and leprechauns will tickle you." Chaz didn't have to try hard to exude an aura of cool. He was wearing a white sports cap backward, long baggy jeans shorts, black high tops, and a white wrist band on his left wrist. In style and attitude Chaz was channeling the urban culture of the moment. With a charismatic blend of self-confidence and cool, Chaz was the kind of guy the guys in the audience want to be and the kind of guy the young women wanted to date. "So who was checking out the girls when you came in here tonight?" he taunted the crowd. Chaz spoke of how great sex is and how normal it is—"If none of us had sex, none of us would be here"—of course, in the context of marriage. He talked about virginity as the best gift you can give your spouse. He used the extended analogy of Christmas morning: if you have already opened your gifts and then rewrapped them and placed them back under the tree, they aren't that special on Christmas morning because you didn't wait. The new sexy abstinence message is not about the absence of sex; it is about waiting for great sex in marriage.

THE PROMISE OF A GOOD MARRIAGE AND GREAT SEX

At a girls-only breakout session at the Pure Freedom mother-daughter retreat, the organization's founder and the retreat leader, Dannah Gresh, asked the girls to close their eyes and dream of their wedding day. She passed a microphone around the church sanctuary and asked the mostly junior-high- and high-school-age teens to share their dreams. Kim wants a big wedding. Katie has selected pink and white for her colors, while Abby wants yellow and white. Brianna envisions a wedding in a garden, but Chantal dreams of exchanging vows on a beach at sunset. Sophia's dream of releasing doves when she and her beloved say "I do" was received with giggles of approval from the other girls. Gresh read the story of her own wedding day—"we were the prince and princess of the ball"—and asked the teens to take a piece of paper and write down their dreams, asking for God's direction during the "next hard years of waiting."[6]

The young women were waiting for their prince (more on this in chapter 3) and planning for their wedding day. The focus on the perfect wedding incorporates the romanticized view of the fairy-tale narrative and, more significantly, serves as a tangible symbol for the campaigns' goal of the good marriage. For evangelicals, sex can legitimately take place only within the context of the marriage relationship, so marriage becomes not only the goal but also the implied reward for the abstinence commitment.

Marriage is an explicit part of the abstinence pledges. The Silver Ring Thing pledge says that the abstinence ring will be given to one's spouse on one's wedding day. The True Love Waits pledge implies that marriage is the goal of abstinence: the commitment is made to "God, myself, my family, my friends" as well as to "my future mate, and my future children." The commitment extends "until the day I enter a biblical marriage relationship."[7] Even the name of the organization implies that "true love" is possible; it's just not possible right now. If a person waits for true love, it will wait for the person.

In my interviews with abstinent young people, I repeatedly heard the marriage argument as a common reason for their commitment. Both young men and young women said that they committed to abstinence in their teenage years so that they could ensure a good marriage in the future. Without my prompting, most people with whom I spoke claimed that they would like to be married someday. They told me that the goal of abstinence is not as much to avoid negative consequences like pregnancy or disease as to have a good marriage.

These young people described waiting to have sex as "saving" oneself for marriage. What is saved is their virginity, which they describe as a gift given to their spouse in marriage.[8] Rebecca Blithefield, twenty-one, described sex as a gift of love that can bring pain if given away too soon.[9] "It's just a sweet thing to save like a precious gift to give to someone that you love," she says. "And for one thing I think it's important to emphasize that these kinds of things rip up your heart if you do give yourself away. Your life is more than just having sex." The connection here is that saving oneself for marriage involves saving one's gift of virginity.

Instead of focusing on the negative consequences of diseases, Rachel Hollister, twenty-six and married, cites the appealing focus on the positive benefits of marriage as the reason to remain abstinent: "I think it's really compelling to talk about the potential of what a marriage could be and how the lack of committing to something like making an abstinence stand will affect their future." Kevin Brooks, twenty-two, says that he is "really happy" that he is abstinent so that he can "save himself" for marriage. He says that he and his friends have always valued abstinence and never viewed virginity as a stigma.[10]

I ask Kevin what he thinks is the most persuasive message in support of abstinence. He replies, "Just the fact that you care enough for the person who you love that you're going to save yourself until you get married, I think, is the most compelling thing." He also includes the avoidance of sexually transmitted diseases in his response, but he mentions disease in the context of marriage, not personal health: "I've heard that you won't have any sexually transmitted diseases if you remain pure until your wedding night, and that's one really good thing to know that both of you have been honest with each other and haven't been doing anything before." According to the logic of his argument, disease avoidance helps to ensure a good marriage.

The reward for abstinence is not just marriage but a good marriage, which is defined as great sex with no emotional baggage from other sexual relationships. A regular feature of the Silver Ring Thing events is a type of emotional baggage dating game. The stated point of the game is to dismantle the myth that having sex outside marriage has no consequences. The team leader selects three young women from the audience to join him onstage. One young man, who has been preselected from the audience, comes out onstage wearing a silly get-up, including an industrial apron and safety goggles. He is clearly ill at ease, but he warms to the audience's laughter. He is given two pieces of plywood that, when held together, form a red heart. The team leader tells him that he is going to go on a date with each young woman. With each one they take things a little too far, the team leader says, and eventually break up. To demonstrate this, the young man awkwardly stands with each young woman in the middle of the stage for their "date" while the refrain from a popular love song plays over the sound system. The team leader returns to the stage wearing a hockey mask and carrying a chain saw (in a nod to the Jason character in the slasher hit *Friday the Thirteenth*). Placing half of the plywood heart in a vise grip, he proceeds to saw it into three pieces, which he then burns in one of the flaming barrels. He gives the destroyed piece of the young man's heart to each of the ex-girlfriends. In a skit intended to debunk the myth that having sex has no consequences, it is curious that the only consequence that is highlighted is the emotional risk of giving your heart to too many people.[11]

Young evangelicals clearly have internalized this message. Jennifer Bartell, nineteen and engaged to be married, describes freedom from regret as one of the most compelling reasons for abstinence. "I think it would be the regret that a person can feel when they've compromised themselves and others just for a few moments of pleasure," she says. "I can't imagine having different loves, then trying to say I love you. It seems so wishy-washy." Jennifer is willing to forgo "different loves" for the one true love that she is waiting for in marriage.

For those who have not experienced such emotional baggage them-selves, many can cite cautionary tales of friends who have. Rachel Hollister talks about two friends whose previous sexual experience damaged their marriages. In one case both partners had had sexual relationships with other people before their wedding. Rachel says the newlyweds "didn't really trust one another." She goes on to describe her marriage, saying that she and her husband were both virgins when they married, so they have memories of having sex only with each other. In contrast, her friend carried emotional sexual memories into her mar-riage, which created problems. The problem, Rachel says, is "like the trust factor and then memories of old relationships and comparing their current mate to someone they dated when they were a freshman in high school. Just all kinds of memories that would be stirred up that just caused problems."

Whereas the abstinence campaigns may talk about the emotional baggage of previous sexual relationships as a threat to a good marriage, young people I interviewed also talked about a different kind of emo-tional baggage, what many of them referred to as the problem of "flip-ping the switch." I was told a story of a friend whose fiancé wanted to have sex before marriage. The young woman kept trying to push him away because she felt it was wrong. After they were married, she con-tinued to push away her husband and his sexual advances because of the emotional pattern she had set during their engagement. Somewhere in her psyche she still felt that sex was wrong, and the sexual relation-ship with her husband suffered. The emotional challenge of "flipping the switch" refers to the wedding ceremony where one "flips the switch" from believing that sex is sinful one minute to celebrating it the next. Arguably, the abstinence campaigns' focus on great sex in marriage aims at bridging this divide. Yet the argument implies that sex outside marriage is not great, an argument that conflates the damaging consequences of nonmarital sex with the inherent goodness of the sex act itself.[12]

Great sex in marriage is promised to those who wait.[13] Sex is no longer a taboo to be avoided but the prize to be earned. It is the "revenge of the church ladies," as Dannah Gresh told the young women at a Pure Freedom event, quoting a *USA Today* article about a University of Chicago study that reported that married, church-going women have the best sex.[14] Abstaining from sex now is described in terms that make it seem like a secure investment account with a guaranteed high rate of return, something that will make sex even better during marriage. Abstaining from nonmarital sex is characterized not as "no sex" but as an investment for future "great sex." Abstinence is portrayed as more than just delayed gratification; it is a promise of sex in marriage that is better than if one had not waited to have sex. Marriage, then, becomes the goal of sexual abstinence.

But what is the proper role of sex within marriage? This is a glaring omission in the campaigns' "great sex" discussion. The logic goes this way: If sexually promiscuous behavior before marriage brings sexually damaging emotional baggage in marriage, then the avoidance of sexually promiscuous behavior before marriage will necessarily bring rewarding and fulfilling sex in marriage. The structure of the argument makes marriage all about sex. But the aim of the campaigns is not to develop healthy marriages; the aim is to keep teenagers from having sex. Instead of elevating sex as something worth waiting for, which is a goal of the campaigns, the campaigns' rhetoric reduces sex to a persuasive tool to sell abstinence. Sex is used to sell all manner of consumer goods, from automobiles to beer to toothpaste. Abstinence, it appears, is no different.

"WITH THIS RING, I THEE WAIT": THE POWER OF THE PURITY RING

"I never take it off," Nora Williams claims emphatically. She thrusts her left hand in my direction and wiggles her fingers as if she is showing off a new engagement ring. "Like, I actually have a suntan line. I know where it is. I take a shower with it, sleep with it. It's almost becoming a part of who I am, you know, like it's just a part of my body now, it's a part of who I will always be."

Nora, a twenty-year-old college student, has been wearing her silver ring for four years. I met her at a Silver Ring Thing event. She is proud of her ring, pointing out its unusual lettering since Silver Ring Thing now uses a different design: "It's kind of cool. There are only a couple of us that have that." More than just a reminder of her continuing commitment to abstinence, Nora's ring serves as a reminder of the gift that she is saving for her future husband: "It reminds me of how exciting it's going to be to finally meet that person and be able to tell them, 'Look what I did for you,' because sometimes saying 'I love you' isn't enough. Sometimes you need to show it, and I think this is an awesome way to show your future husband or wife how much you really do love them, and you didn't even know who they were. I think that's the most important thing that it means to me right now, is that I'll be able to give somebody a really awesome gift." Nora has summarized for me the two primary roles of the symbol of the purity ring: it functions as a reminder to the wearer of her commitment to abstinence, but it also functions as the material manifestation of the symbolic gift of her virginity for her future spouse. Purity rings play a significant role in the evangelical abstinence campaigns' promotion of the goal of the good marriage. The ring and corresponding pledge ceremony foreshadow the wedding ring and wedding ceremony. In this way, the use of the purity ring trains young people for a traditional wedding and marriage.

Silver Ring Thing, as the name suggests, is centered on the use of a ring to represent the gift of virginity.[15] The Silver Ring Thing covenant, which is printed on the first page of the *Silver Ring Thing Sexual Abstinence Study Bible* and pledged aloud at the end of each Silver Ring Thing event, reads: "In signing this covenant before God Almighty, I agree to wear a silver ring as a sign of my pledge to abstain from sexual behavior that is inconsistent with Biblical standards. On my wedding day, I will present my silver ring to my spouse, representing my faithful commitment to the marriage covenant." This pledge is unique in that it includes both a commitment to abstain from sex before marriage—to choose to hold on to the gift of virginity— and to give the gift of virginity and its symbol, the silver ring, to one's future spouse. The symbol of the abstinence ring elides with the symbol of the marriage ring in that the former represents abstinence from nonmarital sex and the latter represents, in part, abstinence from extramarital sex.

True Love Waits makes explicit the connection between the purity ring and the marriage ring. Its curriculum provides instructions for a "ring ceremony," which foreshadows a marriage ceremony, placing a parent and child in the roles of bride and groom: "A True Love Waits Ring Ceremony is a special picture of the commitment to sexual purity shared between a parent and his or her teenage son or daughter. . . . In it a parent presents a ring to his or her teenager to wear as a symbol of that teenager's commitment to purity." The leader guides the teenagers, parents, and congregation through a scripted ceremony that includes purity pledges for all. The leader concludes the ceremony by reminding the students that their ring is a reminder of their purity commitment and that "it was given to you by someone who loves you and supports you in this commitment." The ring itself is a gift from the teenager's parents as a sign of their support of the decision to be sexually abstinent. The gift of the ring is passed from the parent to the child and eventually to the future spouse: "On your wedding night you are to give this ring to your spouse as a celebration of promises given and promises kept."[16]

For Jake Weber, eighteen, his silver ring is a promise to himself that he will have a better marriage than his parents had. "[My ring] means that someday I'm going to have a really kickin' marriage," he tells me. Jake has never met his real father. His mother married when he was in the third grade, and his stepfather was involved with drugs and "all sorts of stuff," according to Jake. "To me, this ring means that, you know, I'm starting out now to lay the foundation for the best possible marriage." For Jake the ring does not so much represent his gift of virginity to his future wife as it represents a gift to himself of future happiness in marriage because he chose to remain abstinent now.

Nineteen-year-old college student Katie Peterson has not removed her silver ring since she put it on at a Silver Ring Thing event more than three years ago. She points out that her sister takes hers off when she plays volleyball and when she showers, but Katie insists, "My ring has never actually been off my finger, ever." Like Nora Williams, Katie Peterson uses her ring as a material manifestation of her commitment to remain sexually abstinent: "It's kind of a reminder, you know, and Silver Ring Thing is a huge part of my life. It really changed my life, and so it's kind of like making my commitment known and, like, actually, like, physical."

Katie sees her ring as binding her to a community of other ring wearers who are also choosing sexual abstinence. Instead of describing her ring as representing a gift to a future spouse, Katie says that her ring represents a commitment to her peers to uphold the standards of a sexually abstinent lifestyle. Here she describes what she thinks of when she looks at her ring:

> [I] definitely [think] about my commitment, and how much I want to stay pure, not only for myself, but to support the twenty-five thousand other people that have a ring on, too. At the end of our show, we actually have a part where we tell people if you find yourself in a situation where you are going to violate your commitment, you know, stop, really think about it, and if you feel you cannot wait, we ask people to take their ring off and flush it down the toilet out of respect for everyone else who is wearing the ring and keeping that commitment and staying pure. So, I'm kind of like, You know what? I'm not going to mess it up for everyone else. I'm not going to, like, wear my ring, and say, Yeah, I'm staying pure and, you know, have sex every weekend on the side, because that's not . . . It's a commitment that I've made and I'm going to stick to it, you know? And sometimes it's really hard.

Katie's description of throwing the ring into the toilet dramatically illustrates the significance of the ring as a symbol of an active commitment to sexual abstinence, not a symbol of a one-time decision in the past. Awareness of a large community of ring wearers offers positive peer pressure for maintaining the abstinence pledge and implied negative peer pressure if the ring is removed and the abstinence pledge broken. Both Nora Williams and Jake Weber describe their rings in terms of marriage: Nora's ring is a gift to her future spouse, and Jake's ring is a gift to himself of the promise of future marital happiness. However, for Katie Peterson her ring is a gift to her peers in that she will uphold the integrity of what it means to be a ring wearer.

Rings are not the only symbols of purity used in the abstinence campaigns. At Pure Freedom retreats, young women receive a necklace with a pearl on a clear string. "And I just still have mine and have had it since eighth grade. I wear it, and I'm planning on giving it to my husband when we get married, if I get married," laughs Jodi Simmons, twenty. Like those who wear purity rings, Jodi sees her pearl necklace as a reminder of her commitment to God and her future husband "just to remain abstinent and to remain pure, physically and emotionally and just mentally even, to do everything I can with the Lord's strength to remain pure for my husband and so that I've saved that for him and only him."

The purity ring functions as a material manifestation of the abstinence commitment and the gift of one's virginity to one's future spouse. For some it may function more as a souvenir, like a T-shirt from a rock concert. Krista Willette, twenty-one, made a pledge of abstinence in junior high and tries to renew it each year. Instead of one ring or neck-lace as a reminder of her pledge, Krista has amassed a small collection of purity paraphernalia: "Yes, I have a silver band. It was like a wedding band that says *purity*. I've gotten tons," she acknowledges. "I have another ring with a rose on it. I have a necklace that says 'True Love Waits.' I have earrings my dad gave me at a ceremony. I have seven, eight commitment cards taped up in my room." Krista's purity jewelry establishes her as a member of a community of abstinent young people. When she wears her jewelry, it also makes public her abstinence com-mitment and promotes it to others.

Not all the young people with whom I spoke are persuaded by the power of the purity ring. Jonathan Ebersol, nineteen, says that he never really got into True Love Waits, although his friends did. "They'd buy the ring, or they'd buy . . . I don't know," he says. "I always thought it was kind of stupid where you had to buy something to signify what you believe. Somebody's making money off them, I guess." Jonathan sees the purity ring as a commodity, a marketing ploy to take his money. He does not feel the need to have a physical reminder of his commitment.

Colin Smith too never got into the hoopla of large abstinence events, but when he and his friends made a pledge to be abstinent, he bought himself a six-dollar ring at a street fair. He wore it on his right hand until he became engaged to his girlfriend and then moved the ring to his left hand as a sign of his increased commitment. He planned to give it to his fiancée on their wedding day, but he lost it while the two were moving hay in a barn. "So it was literally looking for a needle in a haystack," Colin laughs. "But I'm going to get another one."

EVERYBODY'S DOING IT: PUBLIC TESTIMONY AS EMBODIED ARGUMENT

A significant rhetorical form used by the abstinence organizations to make chastity sexy is public testimony. Well-known celebrities and unknown teenagers and adults alike share their personal stories of living a sexually abstinent life or living a life of second virginity following a period of sexual activity. Abstinence organizations rely on winsome personal testimonies to convey the message that abstinence works and is a realistic lifestyle choice for teenagers.

Between musical sets at a True Love Waits rally, Rebecca St. James told the crowd how she made an abstinence pledge as a high school student at a similar True Love Waits event. She recalled her reaction to the rally: "I just thought, this is so awesome. I'm so taken by the fact that these young people [are] just taking a stand for God. And I knew that . . . [I wanted] to make that same commitment. So I did that day, and I just said, 'God, I want to wait and make that commitment to my future husband, as well.'" The Christian pop star explained to the arena filled with teenagers that she was still a virgin and that "God's way is best," since abstinence means avoiding AIDS, pregnancy, and emotional stress. She encouraged the crowd to follow her example: "God knew what he was saying when he said waiting is for our good. And so I just want to encourage you, you know, let's stand together on this issue, let's be involved, let's be radical for God, let's commit to his way and celebrate the fact that there is so much freedom within God's boundaries for us."[17]

St. James's abstinence message is not particularly unique or compelling. What makes testimonies like hers attractive to young people who are considering abstinence is that St. James is attractive. As a young successful pop star with long brown hair and the latest fashions, she is not the kind of young woman who would want for boyfriends. Beyond the circle of Christian pop stars, the evangelical abstinence campaigns are getting a boost from other attractive celebrities. The Jonas Brothers, a trio of good-looking brothers who have achieved pop stardom through the Disney Channel, all wear purity rings. The American Idol winner Jordin Sparks does, too.[18] Since abstinence deals with subverting or redirecting sexuality, it is not appealing if its only spokespersons are physically unattractive. It is easy for someone to pledge sexual abstinence if the opportunity for sex is nonexistent. On the other hand, if people as popular and beautiful as Rebecca St. James or the Jonas Brothers or Jordin Sparks can pledge abstinence, so the argument goes, then perhaps I can pledge abstinence, too.

Silver Ring Thing features peer testimonies at its events. At a Boston-area event in 2004 a pretty high school student with long auburn hair and a short skirt told the crowd that she attended her first Silver Ring Thing event two years earlier because she knew a cool girl who had attended. She had been wearing her purity ring ever since. "Look around you," she told the audience. "If you make this commitment tonight, you are not alone." She assured the young women in the audience, "If you put on this ring tonight, there are guys who will fall in love with you." Another young woman shared her testimony, saying that she had "made some mistakes in the past," but she had been wearing her purity ring for two months. "It's so much hotter when a guy wants to wait 'til marriage," she told the young men. "I can't tell you what to decide," she said, "[but] I hope you make a decision to respect yourself because it's so cool." The next testimony came from a high school sophomore who had been wearing a purity ring for three years. He warned the crowd, "You need to keep your eyes in check, not just your hands." He acknowledged that "it's tough, but I'm doing it, so you can, too."

The sharing of testimonies from both celebrities and ordinary teenagers is a regular feature of abstinence events. However, spontaneous testimonies from event attendees assume the same form and function as planned testimonies. At the close of a girls-only Pure Freedom event, attendees are encouraged to share publicly what they have learned. At two separate Pure Freedom events, testimonies included a junior in high school who shared that she was keeping herself pure and had a journal with hearts on it to write to her future husband; a young woman who talked about the "purity party" she had for her fifteenth birthday, complete with white dress, a ring, and her pastor; a seventeen-year-old who said that she and her boyfriend had decided to stay pure; and two sisters who lost their virginity and became pregnant. One miscarried; the other announced her pregnancy to the group: "I pray God not to take my baby, but it hurts. . . . I never should have opened my legs," she said between sobs.

The testimonies of celebrities and teenagers alike serve as embodied arguments in support of abstinence. Embodied argument can be defined as an argument displayed in physical form.[19] The story alone is not enough to create identification; the power of the body in which the story is ascribed is what bridges the gap between rhetor and audience.[20] (In the case of abstinence T-shirts, rings, fake tattoos, and so on, the story is actually inscribed *on* the body.) Indeed, the gap between rhetor and audience, producer and receiver, becomes blurred as teenage audience members stand and publicly testify to the decision for abstinence that they have just made. Personal testimony uses a striking physicality that trumps logical arguments and appeals to positive peer pressure by providing a physical argument that abstinence works. More than supporting evidence, the personal testimony delivered in public also functions as an enthymematic argument: *if I can wait, so can you.* The attractive bodies of the testifiers function as grounds for the claim that abstinence is sexy, making the abstinence pledge attractive in the process. In this way, personal testimony physically embodies the argument that abstinence works as teens attempt to persuade an audience of peers that they have the agency to make the same choice.

The use of personal testimonies as embodied arguments is not a new rhetorical strategy for social action.[21] In campaigns promoting abstinence from alcohol, for example, the temperance movement of the mid-1800s relied on the testimonies of former drunkards to describe in detail the debauchery of their past lives to encourage other men to give up the "demon rum." Up to this point in the temperance movement, the focus had been on moderate drinkers and those who had yet begun to drink; the drunkard was considered beyond help.[22]

The Washington Temperance Society, founded in 1840 after some tavern-going friends attended a temperance lecture at a nearby church as a joke and became convinced to quit drinking, turned its focus on the drunkard. A distinctive feature of the organization was the use of personal testimonies of "reformed drunkards," as they called themselves, to appeal to other heavy drinkers. Attendance grew so rapidly at weekly meetings that the group soon had to have its own hall.[23] Personal testimonies ended with a call to audience members to sign a pledge of abstinence: "I looked and felt as bad as you do. . . . Look at me now . . . healthy, happy and respectable . . . good clothes . . . money in my pocket. All comfortable and happy at home; no more rags and starvation *there,* to buy silk shawls and bonnets for the tavern-keepers' wives and daughters. . . . Come and sign the pledge, *as I did,* and you'll be a happy man. Keep the pledge and all will come right again!"[24]

The rhetorical strategy here, as in the evangelical sexual abstinence campaigns, is for the testifier to establish common ground with the audience: *I used to be like you.* Next, the testifier offers (sometimes sordid) details of the wretchedness of the former life in order to heighten the contrast with the glories of the present life of abstinence, whether from alcohol or nonmarital sex. Finally, the embodied presence of the testifier signifies (and sometimes the testifier explicitly states) that the audience can also live a life of similar happiness—*you can be like me*—if a pledge of abstinence is made. Reason-laden logical arguments are not as compelling as narrative-driven embodied arguments: personal experience functions as indisputable warrant.

The use of multiple public testimonies combines to create positive peer pressure for teenagers to commit to abstinence. In this way, abstinence organizations are reclaiming the "everybody's doing it" perception of teen sexual activity and using it for their own purposes. Both cofounders of True Love Waits cite the perception that everyone is having sex as a motivating factor in starting their abstinence campaign. Although the decision for abstinence may be personal, it does not necessarily have to be private. True Love Waits wants to make the abstinence decision public so that young people do not feel alone in their decision. Jimmy Hester recalls a young girl who claimed that she was the only virgin in her high school. Richard Ross says that when True Love Waits was founded, a few teens were making this "very private decision toward abstinence but with a sense that there's hardly any of us doing this." Ross says that young people need to feel part of something larger than themselves: "The students choosing abstinence needed to feel a part of something big, they need[ed] to feel a part of a movement, they needed to feel there's this massive group in my generation that's living the same way, which is tremendously empowering. And one of the values of rallies today is it reaffirms to young people that they are a part of something very large, that they are actually statistically now in the majority rather than the minority." Hester notes that news outlets no longer contact True Love Waits as often as they once did, which he sees as a sign that the abstinence campaign has become a mainstream movement. A flurry of news articles across the country in 1993 helped launch True Love Waits because the idea was new and different. Almost twenty years later, Hester says, "Instead of us being different we've now become kind of the norm and so we're not news anymore." By making it seem as if everyone's doing it, abstinence campaigns attempt to persuade teens to jump on the bandwagon.

VIRGINITY, THE SEQUEL

Part of the broad appeal of the evangelical abstinence events is that they are not just for the abstinent. Each organization in this study places an emphasis on a message of renewed or second virginity.[25] Although all the young people whom I interviewed agree that sexual enjoyment in the present is not worth risking a bad marriage in the future, they acknowledge that a sexually active teen can still look forward to a good marriage if he or she commits to abstinence now. In an apparent contradiction, the respondents claim that a good marriage can be achieved whether one has had nonmarital sex or not. Second virginity is available to those who have had nonmarital sex but want to reclaim their virginity and commit to a sexually abstinent lifestyle. Based on a theology of God's forgiveness, individuals who have engaged in nonmarital sex are able to repent of their behavior as sin before God and receive forgiveness and the opportunity to start with a clean slate. Although the events uphold abstinence as the standard, they go out of their way to make sure that sexually active teens do not feel ostracized. Abstinence events may affirm virgins in their lifestyle choice, but the events are arguably aimed more at sexually active teens to encourage them to stop their risky behaviors. The most persuasive form of the second virginity message is the public testimony.

A regular feature of the Silver Ring Thing events is a segment called Starting Over, featuring testimonies of young people who had been sexually active before committing to abstinence. On this particular night Lily appeared to be nervous. She walked out on stage following a funny commercial spoof and tentatively began to tell her story. Bleached blond hair, heavy black eyeliner and a faint weariness around her eyes made her appear older than twenty-three. Lily began, dry mouthed, by telling the audience that she was raised in a Christian home and had struggled with eating disorders and personal insecurities. She had a sexual relationship with her high school boyfriend and was involved with the party scene, including drugs and alcohol. A few times she was scared that she was pregnant. Once she passed out at a party and woke up and realized that she had been raped. During her senior year her boyfriend asked her to marry him. Lily said yes, although he was verbally abusive and was in trouble with the police. Before they could plan a wedding, her boyfriend moved in with another girl whom he had gotten pregnant. He hadn't told Lily.

The testimony lacked a clear ending or moral, as if Lily was still trying to discover it. As I later learned, this was Lily's first time sharing her testimony after serving as part of the Silver Ring Thing traveling team for three consecutive years. The emotional pain had been too raw. Implicitly, Lily's story assured the audience that God's grace can save anyone, no matter what she or he has done, and the young person can begin again as a virgin. Yet the emotional consequences of Lily's past behavior, which were clearly on display, served as a cautionary tale for virgins in the audience who may have thought that God's grace is a free ticket to sexual promiscuity.

After Lily shared her story that night, another young woman told the audience how she made a pledge of abstinence at a Silver Ring Thing event. She exchanged purity rings with her spouse on their wedding day two years earlier. Now she was pregnant with their first child. Her story followed the traditional narrative of a virgin who stays a virgin until her wedding night. Whereas this may be the aim of the

abstinence campaigns—to keep teenagers virgins until they are married—
the young woman's story lacked the emotional punch of Lily's story of
reckless promiscuity. In part, this is because conversion narratives resonate with evangelicals. Evangelical theology includes the concept of
being born again, in which accepting Christ's forgiveness and salvation
allows one to start over with a new life. Evangelical culture is filled
with dramatic conversion narratives of individuals who were mired in
sin of various kinds—drugs, sex, pornography, embezzlement, murder—
and experienced a changed life because of Christ's salvation.[26] A testimony of second virginity holds dramatic power and the possibility of
reaching the broadest possible audience—both virgins and nonvirgins—
with the message of abstinence.

Abstinence events are sexy because they include a lot of talk about sex.
Second virginity testimonies have the added benefit of being prurient.
Testimonies of teenage sex are much more dramatic and titillating than
bland tales of lifelong virginity. Although the evangelical young people
I met may not be having sex, they certainly talk a lot about it. The
campaigns themselves help spur this sex talk in both form and content.
The campaigns borrow the forms of concerts and comedy clubs from
the secular sexualized culture. The message of abstinence focuses on
great sex in marriage. Its spokespersons are popular celebrities and
attractive teenagers, and public testimonies focus on salacious tales of
sexually promiscuous pasts.

This positive, even sexy, portrayal of abstinence is more than a mere
spoonful of sugar to conceal the unsavory medicine of prohibited sex:
it is a fundamental shift from a solely God-centered approach to a
self-centered approach to behavioral change. Although purity may be
a God-centered approach to abstinence in that purity is described
as a lifestyle standard created by God, the underlying reason offered
for pursuing purity is that it is a lifestyle that is most beneficial
(and pleasurable) to the individual. The argument proceeds this way:
a life of purity, including sexual abstinence until marriage, is God's plan,
and God's plan is the best plan for young people, resulting in great
marital sex in the future and the absence of unintended consequences
such as pregnancy or STDs in the present. God's plan is best not just
because it is God's plan, but because it has great benefits for the
individual.

This does not mean that the evangelical abstinence campaigns
have necessarily substituted the spiritual for the sexy. God-centered

arguments are still central to the campaigns' claims, but they are presented using the forms of popular secular culture to appeal to teenagers' sense of autonomous agency. In this way, the effectiveness argument is geared not only to a secular public audience but also to a presumably religious audience that is steeped in secular culture, one that can quote Christina Aguilera or *Anchorman* as readily as the Bible.

CHAPTER 3

"Someday My Prince Will Come"

The Fairy-tale Narrative and Female Power

Abby Jenkins dreamed of her future husband. Even as an eighth-grader, she knew what she wanted and wrote down a list of qualities she believed essential in the man she would someday marry. But no one at her middle school or, later, her high school or even her church met her standards. "So I chose not to date anyone," she said, "because I knew I needed to hold out for that incredible prince that God had for me one day."

In college Abby met a cute guy named Dylan, who one day asked her out on a date. Abby initially declined, because she wasn't sure that Dylan matched her standards for a future mate. But as she and Dylan spent more time together, they became best friends: "God really showed me every day how Dylan met my standards. And I soon realized that he was the prince that I had prayed for.

"That's when my True Love Waits commitment had really come into action," Abby told the teenage girls who had filled the Dallas sports arena. Abby and Dylan dated for about two and a half years, during which time they maintained high moral standards of purity. "We set high standards and boundaries for our physical relationship, and we committed to God that we were going to remain pure until marriage."

Abby's dreams were coming true:

One day Dylan took me on a romantic storybook carriage ride, and it was filled with roses and poems and all these sweet things, and I ended up in the middle of the wilderness on a blanket full of roses with my eyes blindfolded. And when I opened them, my prince Dylan came riding out on a horse through the woods and jumped off and asked me to be his wife. He was the prince that I had waited my entire life for and had saved my entire heart for. The night before our wedding, I was able to give to him my True Love Waits ring that I had put on my finger in eighth grade, and I was also able to give him my list of standards and show him how God had been faithful to fill all those standards in him.

The crowd cheered and applauded as Abby recounted her fairy-tale romance. Before leaving the stage, Abby challenged the teenage girls to follow her example and wait for their dreams to come true: "Girls, keep holding on and wait for that incredible prince that God has in store for you."[1]

Abby's story exemplifies one of the prevalent themes of the evangelical sexual abstinence campaigns: choosing to wait is rewarded with true love. Abstinence campaigns such as True Love Waits promote the promise that delaying sexual gratification today means a greater prize of true love and romance tomorrow. One way this theme is communicated is through the use of the fairy-tale narrative, complete with beautiful princesses in distress, rescuing princes on horseback, evil forces that threaten to steal the princesses' virginity, and the promise of a life lived happily ever after.

FAIRY TALES: PERFORMING GENDER

The genre of the fairy tale is widely considered by literary scholars as folklore of morality and patriarchy.[2] From the very first fairy tales, the purpose of the narratives has been didactic, transmitting the meaning of natural and social events like hunting, harvesting, and marriage, establishing a sense of purpose for the community. The transition from an oral tradition to a literary tradition in the late seventeenth century tended to make the tales exclusionary and private, but it did little to change the fairy tale's essential function: French writers like Charles Perrault created a fairy-tale genre to address issues of *civilité*, or "proper behavior and demeanor in all types of situations."[3] Thus a fairy tale about a beautiful princess's being rescued by a valiant prince on a white horse functions less as escapist entertainment and more as a morality tale about gender and sexuality. In this way, the fairy-tale genre is a natural fit for evangelical sexual abstinence campaigns: a tale of a princess and a prince dictates appropriate gender-specific behavior for abstinent youth. When a public testimony of abstinence assumes the form of a fairy tale, such as Abby Jenkins's engagement story, the implied moral of the story equates sexual abstinence with later sexual fulfillment. Sexual abstinence guarantees a happily ever after of marriage and sex.

Stories of princes and princesses and weddings are not typical of traditional fairy tales, which feature themes of sacrifice and patriarchy.[4] Disney has become the modern-day Mother Goose, revising and retelling traditional fairy tales in Technicolor glory.[5] Today, generations raised on Disney films equate the term *fairy tale* with *Cinderella*, *Sleeping Beauty*, and *Beauty and the Beast*. All feature themes of love, romance, and lives lived happily ever after.

Beyond the oral and literary traditions of fairy tales, Disney's cinematic transformation of the stories amounts to a performance of gender: the archetypes of princess and prince are played out in colorful detail, representing for young movie watchers what it means to be a woman or a man, along with specific definitions of sexuality, love, and romance. Thus Abby Jenkins's engagement story not only mimics the narrative structure of a Disneyesque fairy tale, but also suggests an internalization of a specific performance of gender and sexuality. The "romantic storybook carriage ride," roses, poems, and other "sweet things" become indicators of love, along with purity rings and a "list of standards" for the princely male. The scene of the wilderness and the state of being blindfolded, which suggest the appropriate physical scene and psychological characteristic of being a young woman, create the narrative tension fulfilled by the rescuing moment of Dylan's arrival on a horse and his subsequent proposal of marriage, which are communicated as appropriate actions for a young man.

In Disney's *Beauty and the Beast*, the character of Belle is depicted as a bookworm who loves fairy tales, which self-reflexively help her to make sense of her experience when she winds up in the castle of the Beast.[6] Similarly, Disney-style fairy tales help filter and frame the actions and expectations of young women and men. In the context of sexual abstinence, stock characters such as the princess, the prince, and even the frog communicate the gender-based expectations underlying the argument to choose to wait for sex.

THE PRINCESS: WAITING FOR HER PRINCE

The popular Christian recording artist Rebecca St. James's book, *Wait for Me: Rediscovering the Joy of Purity in Romance*, begins with two fairy tales, one of a princess and one of a prince, both told in second person. The first story begins: "You've dreamed the dream many times. . . . You're lost and alone in darkened woods with danger lurking around every corner. You're cold, hungry, and tired."[7] Her protagonist suddenly hears a "large beast" thundering in her direction. She panics and looks for a place to hide. But when the creature reaches her, she finds that it is a "powerful stallion carrying a tall, dark, and handsome rider":

> All fear vanishes as he dismounts his horse to accompany you out of the forest and safely to your home. Before you know it, you are scooped up into his arms, placed gently on the horse, and expertly taken from the terror of the forest, out into open spaces and the sun's warm rays.
>
> As you ride off into the sunset, you feel like flying and know that not only will life never be the same but this might just be the "happily ever after" of which you have always dreamed.[8]

This fairy tale depicts the princess as lost and in need of rescuing. The man on the horse is capable of providing rescue. The princess cannot choose to be rescued, nor can she choose who rescues her: agency lies with the prince alone. The story ends with a traditional ride into the sunset and a happily ever after. St. James goes on to explain in the first chapter that this is the dream of "true romance": "If you're a girl, perhaps you've grown up with the desire to be rescued by a knight in shining armor. If you're a guy, maybe you've thought about being the knight who rescues his princess. . . . A guy longs to protect; a girl longs to be protected. And that's exactly the way God created us." The dream is fulfilled in the "storybook wedding" in which the princess, now the princess bride, and her prince celebrate their mutual sexual purity.[9]

This abstinence fairy tale follows the narrative arc of many Disney-style fairy tales: The setting for the female protagonist is one of danger and darkness. She is powerless to defend herself from the approaching "large beast" and must be rescued by a "tall, dark, and handsome" man. Although the tale ostensibly centers on the female protagonist, the action of the tale swirls around her in the form of the beast and the male rider. Despite the domination of females in the lead roles in fairy tales, including Disney films, the stories perpetuate a "male myth," according to the German scholar and fairy-tale authority Jack Zipes: "The young women are helpless ornaments in need of protection, and when it comes to the action . . . , they are omitted."[10]

Although the female protagonist in St. James's abstinence fairy tale lacks agency, the princess character in another fairy tale displays a limited, passive agency. In Jennie Bishop's abstinence story, *The Princess and the Kiss: A Story of God's Gift of Purity,* the princess is depicted both as waiting for a husband and as possessing the power to choose one.

The picture book format and pastel illustrations of knights, serfs, turreted castles, a medieval royal family, and illuminated text locate the story as a fairy tale. The story tells of a young princess and the gift of her "first kiss" that was given to her by God on the day she was born. Her parents, the king and queen, take care of the gift until the young princess is grown. "This kiss is yours to keep . . . or to give away, as you see fit. . . . But use wisdom, my daughter," warns the king, "and save your kiss for the man you will marry. Never part with it for the sake of a stranger."[11]

Suitors begin to appear, but the princess turns each one away. She decides that Prince Peacock is too full of himself and would not have room for the princess's kiss; Prince Romance promises an exciting honeymoon, but he might lose interest in her kiss; and Prince Treasurechest offers her riches, but he does not need her kiss since he already has so much money to satisfy him. A two-page illustration depicts a disinterested princess and four suitors, all trying to capture her attention.

Because the choice of a husband lies with the princess in this story, she does not need to be rescued from a dark forest; instead, she has a variety of suitors from among whom to choose, but she opts to wait for the right one. The story suggests that the princess may end up waiting forever. Her other option, if she does not find a man worthy of her kiss, is to "treasure forever" her kiss, as the queen tells her. The correct choice of a husband for the princess turns out to be a commoner who was captivated by her beauty and purity, which "sparkled like diamonds." The only gift he has to offer her is his first kiss, which was given to him by God on the day he was born. The two are married and "lived happily ever after."[12] The story ends with the birth of their first child and the child's gift from God of a first kiss. Sexual purity—here referred to as a "first kiss" and illustrated as a mysterious yellow light—is the sign for the princess of the correct choice of a husband, the one who will allow her to live happily ever after. The princess possesses agency, but it is a passive agency in that she must wait for the man of purity to find her. She has many options for a husband but only one correct choice that will reward her with a lifetime of happiness.

THE PRINCE: FEARLESS WARRIOR AND RESCUER

The second fairy tale at the beginning of St. James's book describes a brave knight who boldly rescues the abducted princess. The story begins: "The call has gone out from the king to find and rescue his only daughter, the princess. She has been abducted by the corrupt Dark Lord, and the king has promised her hand in marriage to whoever can return her safely to her own kingdom."[13]

The knight is depicted with limitless agency through a string of action verbs as he faces the dangerous mission: he must "successfully navigate alligator-infested waters; trek through forests filled with wild creatures, quicksand, and quagmire; and climb a steep seaside cliff that leads to the Dark Lord's fortress." After defeating a "fire-breathing dragon," the knight rescues the princess: "As you sweep her into your arms, she gazes at you with radiant eyes of adoration, knowing you are the true love she has dreamed of. Your heart feels the same."[14]

The role of the brave knight (or honorable prince) is presented as the model for young evangelical men. Versions of the knight can be found in a number of Christian books targeted at young men. Eric Ludy's book *God's Gift to Women: Discovering the Lost Greatness of Masculinity* depicts an armored knight on horseback on the cover. "With its riveting vision of Christ-centered manhood, *God's Gift to Women* shows young men how to become the heroic, selfless knight that every woman dreams about," claims a description on the book cover.

The knight is a rescuer, but he is also a warrior who must do battle with forces that prevent him from reaching the princess, such as the dragon and the Dark Lord's minions. In *The Squire and the Scroll*, the young squire must battle a dragon to rescue the "Lantern of Purest Light," which "an enemy of all truth and beauty" with "leathery wings" stole from the kingdom.[15] The squire is poor but honest, raised by parents with "clean hearts" who "taught their son to guard his pure heart by the words from a simple scroll," which they presented to him as a gift for his journey. The valiant knight with whom the squire is sent on the perilous mission turns to stone when he grabs a sparkling jewel embedded in a cave filled with evil images. The squire knows better than to touch the precious gems: one of the five truths in the scroll instructs him to "let your eyes look straight ahead." The words of the scroll protect the squire on his quest, even transforming into a double-edged sword with which he slays the dragon. The squire rescues the lantern and the knight (along with other knights who previously attempted the quest and were turned to stone). The jewels from the cave now fall from the walls "as treasure to be gathered for the king and his kingdom."[16] The brave squire is rewarded with the king's daughter for his wife and the opportunity to rule the kingdom.

According to this fairy tale, young men must actively battle the forces of the world to rescue and restore their purity. The metaphors are heavily underscored here: the lantern is purity (or virginity), the dragon is Satan (or evil in the world), and the scroll is the Bible. The tempting jewels can be read as pornography or as young women in general (which becomes disturbing at the end of the story, when the jewels drop from the walls of the cave and are brought as treasure to the king). The squire does not rescue the princess: she is the reward for his successful attempt to restore his (and the kingdom's) purity. The princess in *The Princess and the Kiss*, also written by Jennie Bishop, passively waits and chooses to whom she will give her kiss. Here, the squire must journey through a dark forest and cave, avoid quicksand, and slay a dragon: the preservation of the lantern (or kiss) for young men is a battle, not a beauty contest.

The masculine battle metaphor is common in abstinence rhetoric geared to young men. Stephen Arterburn and Fred Stoeker, authors of *Every Young Man's Battle: Strategies for Victory in the Real World of Sexual Temptation,* instruct teenage boys in "setting your defenses" and "developing your battle plan."[17] In 2004 Arterburn addressed approximately five thousand young men at a True Love Waits event in Dallas about the shame and guilt that comes from masturbation and Internet pornography: "Every man has a battle, and you win it or you lose it every day."[18] Robert Daniels, author of *The War Within,* uses his experiences in the navy to frame his personal war with sexual temptation. Chapters include diagrams of battle plans with images of ships, submarines, and fighter jets to symbolize the fight for purity, in which memorized scripture verses are used as weapons. The knight must wage war with sexual temptation before he can rescue the princess.

The battle metaphor also appears in the context of a sports narrative, where the knight is now the sports hero who must do battle both on and off the field in the game of life. *Who Moved the Goalpost? Seven Winning Strategies in the Sexual Integrity Gameplan* uses sports images and analogies such as "adjust your stance," "stay in bounds," "striking out may be your best option," and "guard your future . . . and hers" to communicate a plan to fight sexual temptation.[19] Like a marathon runner, the young man has a clear goal: to successfully reach the finish line—the wedding day—with sexual purity still intact.

The battle metaphor promotes the fight for sexual purity for young men, while defining what it means to be a man. Purity books for young men claim that society—and the church in particular—has stripped men of their God-given masculinity. John Eldredge's popular *Wild at Heart* claims that masculinity has been redefined "into something more sensitive, safe, manageable, and, well, feminine." The evangelical church contributes to this emasculation, he says, by telling men that they should strive to be "Really Nice Guys." He asserts that every man has "a desperate desire for a battle to fight, an adventure to live, and a beauty to rescue." When a schoolyard bully knocks his son down, Eldredge teaches him to hit back. He acknowledges that his advice may seem at odds with the scriptural command to follow Jesus' example and "turn the other cheek," but Eldredge insists that the difference between his son's situation and Jesus' is that Jesus had the power but chose not to use it: "[Not hitting the bully] may look moral, it may look like turning the other cheek, but it is merely *weakness*. You cannot turn a cheek you do not have. Our churches are full of such men."[20]

Eric Ludy's *God's Gift to Women* takes a similar tack, eschewing both the secular model of men as testosterone driven and sex hungry (which Ludy calls the "Brotherhood") and the Christian version, which produces men who are "spineless, afraid, and insecure enough to avoid doing anything *really* bad—but spineless, afraid, and insecure enough to never do anything *really* good, either." Ludy straddles the line between aggressive and wimpy masculinity by calling men to be "warrior-poets" who attack Satan and defend the purity of women while cultivating tenderness. This tenderness, Ludy writes, "is the secret to winning a woman's heart, as well as the secret to cultivating God's heart within *us*."[21]

In the fairy-tale narrative within evangelical purity books for males, the role of the valiant knight (or prince) describes a traditionally masculine hero who battles evil forces and actively seeks to rescue the beautiful damsel. His action depends on the relative inaction of the princess. Whether waiting for rescue locked in a tower or lost in dark woods, or waiting in her parents' castle for the right suitor to come along, the princess displays limited agency in the face of the seemingly limitless agency of the knight or prince to free her. Part of the definition of being a princess is waiting for a prince. Referring both to a familiar refrain from Disney princess films and to the evangelical belief that Jesus Christ will return to the earth to reign, a purple and pink school folder at a Christian bookstore near the True Love Waits headquarters reads, "Someday my prince will come."

THE FROG: THE CONSEQUENCES OF PREMARITAL SEX

Another abstinence lesson of the fairy-tale narrative is that someday your prince will come, but if you choose not to wait, you may end up with a frog. The frog metaphor reverses the fairy tale about a woman's kiss turning a frog into a prince, symbolically emphasizing the negative consequences of sexual activity outside marriage.

Frog imagery is popular in abstinence resources such as bookmarks and stuffed animals. One bookmark reads, "Kiss a toad and he's still a toad, not a prince."[22] Another line of bookmarks with the tag line "No toads: Accept no substitutes" features photos of toads. One reads, "Okay, let me spell it out for you . . . Toads marry toads. The princess gets the prince. Got it? Good. Now live it."[23] Another reads, "Do I look like a prince to you? So . . . why waste your kisses?"[24] The back of both bookmarks makes explicit the correction of the traditional frog-to-prince fairy tale and presents a negative consequence–avoidance approach to encouraging abstinence: "Remember the fairy tale of the princess who kissed the toad and *poof* he became a prince? Hello? No matter how many times you kiss a toad, it's still a toad. Forget the promises they make to be more, do more, give more. Toads are users. And while real toads can't give you warts—some people can. So save your kisses. Accept no substitutes. Wait for the real thing and the wedding ring."[25] Here the toad is someone who has not waited to have sex until marriage and thus has contracted a sexually transmitted disease. The toad is the inferior substitute for the "real thing" of marriage.

In Jana Spicka's *The Locket and the Mask,* a picture book "appropriate for fifth grade through high school," the narrative about a princess waiting to give away her virginity (symbolized by a locket in this retelling) to her prince is complicated with the inclusion of a frog and masks of deception.

Following the opening trajectory of *The Princess and the Kiss, The Locket and the Mask* begins with a young girl named Selah who is given a locket at birth as a gift from the Great High King. Her father explains that only one man holds the key to the locket, and it must not be opened until her wedding day. Now a young woman, Selah dons the locket and a princess mask to attend a masquerade ball at the castle. Her father warns her, "Don't be fooled by the masks that others wear. Our true identity lives in the heart."[26]

Selah dances with many masked strangers. She is enthralled by one man masked as a prince, but when he demands to have her locket, she asks him to take off his mask. He is actually a toad. He begs Selah: "I so want what lies within that locket—it will change me into all I am not. Please, trust me with your treasure, and I will become your prince." She removes her mask and responds: "If you would lie and trick me to have a locket that is not rightfully yours, you have revealed what lies within your heart. And you truly are a toad. I will not give my treasure to one whose heart is so selfish and deceitful." The prince Ilori, in whose honor the ball has been given, witnesses the scene and reveals to Selah that he was given a key when he was born that would unlock only one locket. "I have waited all my life for you," the prince says. On their wedding day, they pledge the vow inscribed on the locket and key—"forsaking all others"—which the story points out is a pledge that both Selah and Ilori had lived long before they met each other. "I have waited all my life to give you this treasure," Selah says, and "so the prince and princess began the journey of happily ever after."[27]

In this story the female protagonist has the power to choose a husband, but her choice of the prince turns out to be merely a frog in a prince mask. His frog identity is revealed in his attempt to wrongfully claim Selah's locket. The true prince recognizes the value of Selah's locket and has waited for Selah, just as she has waited for him. Again, the moral of the story is that true love waits, but there is a more equal distribution of agency between the prince and the princess in their ability to choose to wait or not.

THE PRINCESS, REVISITED: MODESTY AS GIRL POWER

Of the three U.S.-focused evangelical abstinence organizations—True Love Waits, Pure Freedom, and Silver Ring Thing—included in this study, one organization uses the imagery of the princess more than the others. It may not be surprising that Pure Freedom, considering its focus on teenage girls, uses princess imagery more frequently in its events and written materials, but it does so in a way that increases the agency of young women. In a subtle shift the definition of being a princess moves from waiting for or choosing a prince to choosing to act and behave as a princess. The power of personal choice moves to the center of the imagery, replacing the centrality of the prince. The argument is based on the premise that God intends all young women to be princesses, so one must choose to act like a princess. However, the role of the prince is not altogether suppressed, because proper princess behavior (as defined by Pure Freedom) is portrayed as more effective at attracting a prince for marriage. In addition, young men are portrayed as having little control of their hormones, so the appropriate behavior of the princess is intended to help the young man act like a prince.

On a brisk Saturday morning in October 2004, 250 mothers and their teenage daughters sat at round tables with white paper tablecloths and autumn floral centerpieces. They were sipping tea from pink and white floral china demitasses in the gymnasium of a Baptist church, a stately red brick church and Christian school complex nestled in a wealthy suburb of Chicago. Soft piano music played in the background as the women and their daughters nibbled Rocher chocolates and Pepperidge Farm cookies. As instructed in a previous mothers-only breakout session, the adult women gave hand massages to the teenage girls using the small bottles of scented lotion with the Pure Freedom logo that were available at each table. The hand massages were intended to establish a loving connection between mother and daughter and to facilitate open conversation. Whether it was the massages or the caffeine and sugar after hours of Bible verses and teaching on purity, the mix of animated conversation, chatter, and laughter suggested that the daughters were enjoying themselves.

Dannah Gresh, the founder of Pure Freedom, was dressed in black pants, heeled boots, and a long black tweed coat. She asked the teens how the tea party made them feel. "Elegant," one said. Gresh asked the teens to consider how they would have felt if they had entered the gym to find tea bags and Styrofoam cups or maybe old ceramic mugs. Presentation matters, she said. How are you presenting yourself? Like a Styrofoam cup, ceramic mug, or priceless china? Are you setting yourself up to be treasured? "You are God's princess!" Gresh exclaimed. The teenaged girls gasped in delight as Gresh told them that the china cups and saucers were theirs to keep as a reminder of their value as princesses. Some have brought their cups to their weddings to remind them that they are princesses that day, she told the group. Describing her own wedding day, Gresh later read to the young women from one of her books: "He was the man of my dreams, and this day was a fairy tale come true. . . . We were the prince and princess of the ball."[28]

Self-esteem and girl power are central to the Pure Freedom message on abstinence. Young women should value themselves because God values them. Mixing metaphors, the teens are princesses because they are as valuable as china. In Dannah Gresh's book *And the Bride Wore White: Seven Secrets to Sexual Purity,* which is the core curriculum for the events, the secret of girls' value is the only secret to which she devotes two chapters. The first chapter uses the Styrofoam-ceramic-china metaphor and presents girls' inherent worth as stemming from God's view of them as valuable: "God says you are a princess. . . . Your behavior and the choices you make must be governed by that value if you are aiming for the sunset ending in your love story. You must present yourself as you would priceless china." The second chapter addresses making choices in dress, locations for dates, and personal conduct ("the royal wardrobe," "the princess's kingdom," and "the conduct of a princess") that demonstrate the young women's value.[29]

The "royal wardrobe," or the issues of fashion and modesty, receive far more attention at the Pure Freedom events than do the other two areas of young women's value discussed in the book. Dannah Gresh introduced the topic to the mothers and daughters at the tea party in Chicago by saying that too many young women "want to live a life of purity, but they are dressing like Styrofoam cups." The problem with this, according to Gresh, is twofold: Their dress demonstrates that they do not value themselves, nor do they value guys, since guys are sexually aroused by Styrofoam fashion and it unfairly causes them to sin. Young men "cannot control these reactions by choice." Using a white board, Gresh described the autonomic nervous system to the mothers and daughters at the tea party and explained that the young men's system is more sensitive than young women's. As she writes in her book *Secret Keeper: The Delicate Power of Modesty,* "If a guy sees a girl walking around in tight clothes or a miniskirt or tiny shorts . . . well, she might as well hang a noose around the neck of his spiritual life. It's not 'just' fashion but a constant source of spiritual failure for men." Quoting Proverbs 5:18 and 19 to the tea party guests, Gresh explained that only one man—a woman's husband—is meant to be intoxicated by her body, so if a woman dresses immodestly and arouses many men, she is committing a sin.[30]

Then the fashion show began. After a false start with a slow ballad, a church volunteer quickly changed the CD to an upbeat Christian pop song as six teenage girls entered the Baptist church's gymnasium, strutting rather awkwardly and self-consciously among the tables to show off their modest fashions, as the audience clapped in time to the music. The "Truth or Bare" fashion show is a staple of the Pure Freedom events for girls, featuring teens picked from among the attendees and the affordable teen fashions they are given to wear (discounter T. J. Maxx is the only retailer mentioned by name). Outfits included a black warm-up suit, a sparkly T-shirt with large vivid pictures, pink camouflage pants, and a miniskirt layered over jeans, with fashion advice from Gresh that "legwarmers are even coming back" and "ponchos are *the* fashion accessory for the fall."

The emphasis of the fashion show is on the Truth or Bare Fashion Tests—Gresh leads the models and the audience through a series of tests such as "Raise and Praise," "Spring Valley," and "Grandpa's Mirror" to determine whether their clothes are modest enough. In Raise and Praise the teens are instructed to lift their arms over their heads in a simulated expression of religious fervor to see if their shirts lift up to reveal their midriffs. The "secret weapon," according to Gresh, is to layer T-shirts over men's undershirts (or "beaters," as one Pure Freedom leader referred to them). Spring Valley tests to see if shirts are too tight (solution: buy a larger size), and Grandpa's Mirror checks to see what others see when the teen is seated while wearing shorts or a short skirt.

Based on my informal conversations with mothers at three separate Pure Freedom events in Wisconsin and Illinois, the fashion show and modesty tests are the highlight of the event for women who are concerned about their daughters' modesty and feel that they are in a losing battle with the influence of a Britney Spears teen culture. Daughters may be less convinced. At one Pure Freedom event, three teenage girls huddled in the church foyer and discussed the upcoming modesty fashion show. "Yeah, long sleeves and baggy pants. We can't have any skin showing," one girl said, as all three laughed.

The emphasis on modest dress could be understood as a fearful retreat by Christians from popular culture or as an oppressive decree designed to restrict female self-expression. In a savvy rhetorical move, however, Gresh persuades her Lindsay Lohan–influenced audience to consider modest dress not so much because immodesty is sin but because modesty is powerful. *Power* is a word that Gresh uses often in her book *Secret Keeper: The Delicate Power of Modesty,* which describes modesty's power as power over men:

> I'm convinced that the practice of modesty in your life is an intriguing and untapped power source. . . . If you stick with me for these few short chapters, you'll be in the driver's seat of this power.

> You have been given all of the power of a masterpiece that is worthy of every glance you receive. And ever since Eve, guys have been glancing. Oh, have they been glancing!

> Your beauty is powerful.[31]

Gresh quotes a male author who writes that, during a critical moment in a baseball game, if a woman removed her top, "the guys would forget the game! (Now that's power!)"[32]

A woman's allure is the power she holds over men: "The thrill *not* of what is seen, but what is yet to be seen is what actually tempts him."[33] Immodesty relinquishes a woman's power and gives it to men:

> Immodesty removes the obstacles and invites any passing guy to desire you in his mind. It's a cheap thrill requiring no investment on his part. It offers him the power of your body at *his* control. He is motivated by lust.

> Modesty becomes a positive "obstacle" that makes a man "work to earn your heart."

> Modesty protects the true secrets of your body for one man, requiring him to invest into your life in order to one day enjoy your allure.

> How does he [work to earn your heart]? Through romance! I don't know about you, but I'll take the candlelight dinners, soft love songs, and carefully crafted love notes of yesterday over today's "liberated" casual sex scene.

> These obstacles issue a challenge for men to earn your heart. Flowers, Valentine's Day gifts, and romantic dinners are some of the ways a man might try to prove himself worthy of your virtue.[34]

Here, modesty is framed as a mode of power and control over men. Conversely, immodesty is framed as a relinquishment of that power to men. A traditional tool of patriarchal oppression—fashion as an accomplice in female objectification—is used to undermine the oppression.[35]

This emphasis on female power and agency borrows a key feminist argument of women's control of their bodies and the right to choose. However, the desired choice here is to attract one man who will demonstrate his worth as a potential husband through the traditional romantic tropes of flowers, candlelight dinners, and love songs, much like the knight who braves the dark woods and dragons as proof of his worth to the princess.

Interestingly, modesty-as-power is portrayed as the moral choice. In an apparent contradiction, if "what is yet to be seen is what actually tempts him," according to Gresh, then modesty could be understood as inherently immoral because it causes young men to be tempted. This power over men—controlling through concealment and subsequent temptation—is promoted as preferable for abstinent girls than exercising a different sort of power through disclosure and overt sexuality. In the process, young men are rendered virtually powerless. The only weapon in their arsenal is to flee temptation, which may mean fleeing girls in general.

THE PRINCE, REVISITED: BOYS WILL BE BOYS

I could hear them before I could see them. At 9:00 A.M. on a warm sunny Saturday in rural Pennsylvania in 2008, I entered the gymnasium of the Evangelical Free Church and found balls and boys bouncing off the walls. Some groups were shooting hoops, and others appeared to be involved in a makeshift game of dodgeball, as boys ran around the gym chasing each other. Christian pop music playing over the loudspeakers mixed with the echoing shouts of the boys and the thwacks of the balls. The opening event of this coed Pure Freedom retreat went until nearly 11:00 the previous evening. Today, the teens were to receive separate instruction by gender. I stifled a yawn, impressed with how much energy was in the room so early in the morning.

After the balls were put away, David, a Pure Freedom leader, took the microphone. "This morning we're going to unleash you to be guys," he told the teenage boys and their adult male group leaders. "This will get sticky." He explained the rules for the popular Pure Freedom "duct tape derby." The objective is to duct-tape a person to the wall. To win, the boy had to remain suspended for eight seconds. As rolls of tape were distributed, the groups sprang into action. One boy hung from a basketball hoop as his teammates worked to attach his limbs to the gym wall. Another boy was held in a horizontal position on the shoulders of his teammates while he was taped. Someone cried "Ow!" as a group peeled tape from his face and arms and started over. One boy fell from the wall before the judging began; he was wrapped like a mummy, with bound legs and feet. A teammate began dragging him around the gym floor by a loose end of tape, to the apparent delight of the wrapped boy. Few remained taped to the wall for the full eight seconds.

Once the balls of duct tape were thrown away, the two hundred or so boys gathered in a classroom down the hall from the gym. In a loose application of the duct tape activity, David told them to avoid "sticky situations" and to "flee from sexual immorality." He gave the young men specific ideas, such as "stay public, stay vertical" and "avoid AOL [America Online] alone." The boys broke into small groups to discuss the various temptations that they face.

While the girls were upstairs in the church sanctuary "doing completely frou-frou things," as Bob Gresh described it to the group, the boys were busy being boys with a full-body version of Rock, Paper, Scissors called Gorilla, Man, Gun; gross-out jokes about women with hairy armpits; and urinal etiquette games. Each period of biblical teaching or sexual morality instruction was broken up with games and activities to keep the mood light and the short attention spans engaged.

After asking God to "teach us what godly men look like," Bob Gresh led the group in a discussion about lust. He began with a vocabulary test. He called out each word as he wrote it on a large white board. "Say *sex*," he called out to the audience. "*Breasts. Masturbation.*" The boys seemed eager to play along. "There's a lot of stuff we can't talk about in mixed company," Bob said. "Nothing is out of bounds [here]." He asked the audience to shout out common objects of lust. Replies of sports, food, and video games came from across the room. "Jeremy," shouted one boy, eliciting laughter from the group. "Glad you guys have a special relationship," Bob responded good-naturedly. Consistent with the heterosexuality of the fairy-tale narrative, homosexuality appeared to be out of bounds in this discussion.

After lunch David talked about triggers for lust. His list included television, surfing the Web, going to the beach or pool, "JCPenney lingerie ads," and the "smell of your girlfriend's sock." To apply the lesson the boys played the "egg protection device game," which sounds as if it might address contraception but instead involves creating crash-proof containers for eggs out of straws as a symbol of protecting one's purity. Gresh challenged the teams of boys to identify as many as twenty different ways to avoid triggers; for each suggestion the team would get a plastic straw for its device. When the teams were ready, Bob stood on a mechanical lift in the gym, surrounded by newspapers and tarps spread out below. He read some of the suggestions: "no Hooters," "no European beaches," "no bedrooms or basements," "kiss like you're kissing your grandparents," or, if that doesn't work, "get an ugly girl-friend." He dropped each egg contraption from the lift to see which ones would survive the fall with the egg intact. The egg seemed to represent both the boys' purity as well as the purity of their future girlfriends. Bob told them, "This egg is your purity or, if you're a dad, your daughter's purity." In this case it is the father's duty to protect his daughter's purity, not the boyfriend's duty. The triangle- and starburst-shaped contraptions had more success at protecting the eggs than the torpedo and ball shapes. A few boys lost interest and began playing basketball in the background.

Themes of controlling sexual desire and managing temptation are central to the boys-only part of the Pure Freedom coed retreat. Boys are taught to identify what triggers sexual lust and how to avoid it. Lust is portrayed as a basic element in what it means to be a male. Bob Gresh described his humorous lust test to the audience of teenage boys: "[We] strip you down naked, and if you have a penis, you struggle with lust. It's 99 percent effective."

In addition to high-energy object lessons involving duct tape and raw eggs, the boys were presented with models of what it means to live lives of purity.[36] A key session of the morning was dedicated to hearing the testimonies of the adult male leaders who had accompanied the boys to the event from their home churches.[37] Their stories focused on the dangers of pornography, masturbation, and going too far physically with your girlfriend. None of the five men (four of whom identified themselves as married) had sex before marriage, although several admit-ted to sexual behaviors that later brought emotional stress into their marriages. As Caleb, twenty-four and married for four years, put it, he and his wife were virgins before they were married, but they were not pure. "We did a lot," he told the boys. The result was the absence of lovemaking for the first year of his marriage. "It felt shameful and wrong," he explained. Jack, twenty-nine and married for six years, said that because he and his wife "fooled around time and time again" when they were dating, now they were dealing with issues of past relation-ships. He explained that the emotional burden of past sexual activity is like carrying to each new relationship a suitcase filled with past experiences. He warned the boys that the contents of their suitcases will be laid bare "while you and your wife are having glorious sex." He ended his testimony by challenging the boys: "Don't make the same mistakes I made. Be a bigger man than I was." This was met with strong applause.

Consistent with the overall message of the evangelical abstinence campaigns, the testimonies emphasized that sex is great in the context of marriage. Dan, a thirty-eight-year-old youth leader, told the group that he waited to have sex until marriage because he was promised when he was younger that it would be great. He affirmed to the boys that it was worth the wait. "Sex is awesome, and I'm looking forward to it tonight, because I've been gone for four days. Don't call my phone tonight!" The guys hooted their approval. As David, the Pure Freedom leader, later told the group, "Sex is like a field goal." He raised his arms and yelled, "It's good! Sex is really, really good."

At the end of the afternoon the lights were dimmed, and the boys were invited to come forward in a type of purity altar call and take a ping-pong ball, write their lust on it, and throw it away. A contemporary Christian ballad was playing over the sound system—"I want more of you and less of me"—as the boys came forward. The leaders hugged the boys, and a few were crying. A hip-looking leader with a goatee and sideburns who was wearing a Mountain Dew T-shirt kept his arm around one boy who was crying. He and the boy stood off to the side for most of the service. A microphone was passed around the audience as boys shared what they would take away from the retreat. It was unclear whether all the games and discussions about temptation and lust made a difference, but a few boys spoke more generally of spiritual recommitment. One boy said, "I'm not alone." Another said that the retreat brought him out of spiritual complacency. Another boy haltingly gave his brief testimony: "I just let the Lord . . . accepted into my life." Someone else said, "The Lord has shown me a different way I can be in."

The church's youth leader told the boys that they were about to rejoin the girls upstairs in the sanctuary, and this news was met with groans from the audience. He told the guys, "The girls have been taught that they are precious and like fine jewelry. Our call as men is to esteem them." He went on to say that feminism exists because men have treated women badly. If they were to treat women with humility and respect, he said, "feminism would die a quick death." As the boys headed out the door, he said, "We have the right and ability to raise women up and make them feel esteemed."

This eleventh-hour call to esteem women seemed oddly disconnected from the rest of the day's activities on lust and temptation. The discussion had been more about staging a retreat from nonmarital sexual desire (and, presumably, from women as the objects of sexual desire) than about mounting an offensive to rescue women from the clutches of feminism. In keeping with the fairy-tale narrative, girls were taught to wait for their prince but that what holds power over boys is an active waiting involving choices, like modest dress. Boys were taught to be the traditional masculine hero who battles evil forces, but the battle is first and foremost for his own body and soul, not for a princess. The prince has arrived at the castle with the princess trapped inside, guarded by a fire-breathing dragon, but this time the prince realizes that he is the dragon, unwittingly holding the princess captive by his own untamed lusts and selfish desires.

WORTHY OF BEING WAITED FOR: SUPPORTING AND SUBVERTING TRADITIONAL GENDER ROLES

The fairy-tale narrative is a fitting rhetorical device for communicating the aims of the evangelical abstinence movement, particularly for its role in supporting the goal of traditional marriage. The refrain of "someday my prince will come" locates the argument in support of waiting for true love in a context of romance and dreams of happily ever after. The fairy-tale narrative reinforces traditional definitions of female and male through the stock characters of the princess and prince. As most of the fairy tales examined in this chapter demonstrate, the princess is defined in relation to the prince; she is waiting for him to rescue her, either from the dark woods or from a life of spinsterhood in her parents' castle. The actions ascribed to the princess and prince define their identities and their level of agency: the princess passively waits, and the prince actively rescues. This disjunction would seem to have a negative impact on the abstinence message, but in each fairy tale the princess is rewarded for waiting by finding her true love and living happily ever after. "True love" is defined in the fairy tales as a prince who has also waited for the princess, remaining sexually abstinent until their wedding day. In the fairy tales the personal character of a prince is equated with abstinence; a true prince cannot be sexually active outside marriage. In one story the prince who demanded sex before marriage turned out not to be a prince at all but a toad.

The fairy-tale narrative implies an audience whose members expect a reward for their sacrifice of sexual abstinence. A consistent element of the fairy-tale genre is the happy ending. In the context of abstinence the promise of a fairy-tale happy ending functions as a promise to teenagers, a reward for abstinence. This suggests that the sacrifice of waiting is not a particularly compelling argument on its own. The fairy tale uses the narrative form instead of logical reasoning to assert that waiting will bring positive benefits to the individual. Although the fairy-tale narrative is not intended for an exclusively evangelical youth audience, it functions as an appropriate rhetorical device for the evangelical teen audience because its narrative structure is consistent with evangelical theological metaphors of Jesus Christ as the bridegroom and the church as the bride, for whom Christ will one day return. As P. L. Travers, author of *Mary Poppins,* writes about the fairy-tale hero, "It is the hero who repairs the past . . . and thus, by repairing the past, he prepares the future."[38] Similarly, Jesus Christ fits the archetypal romantic hero as one who is motivated by love, who possesses the power to save, and whose return ensures a happy ending. The use of the fairy-tale narrative in the evangelical sexual abstinence campaigns is fitting for reasons beyond popular romantic forms of Cinderella and Sleeping Beauty: an audience of evangelical teenagers understands that the ultimate happy ending occurs through a relationship with Jesus Christ.

The fairy-tale narrative also implies that its audience consists of heterosexuals who, for the most part, define their identities as consistent with traditional gender roles. Campaign leaders assume that their audience of teenage girls wants to be rescued by their prince and that teenage boys want to do the rescuing. Use of the fairy-tale narrative supports abstinence critics' claims that the movement reinforces imagery of romantic love, which promotes traditional gender roles.[39] However, a close reading of the fairy-tale narrative across the movement reveals how its articulation of rhetorical agency both supports and subverts traditional gender roles.[40]

The rhetoric of Pure Freedom makes an interesting move in its use of the standard princess imagery. Drawing on feminist arguments about the power of women to choose, a princess is portrayed not as passively waiting for a prince but as actively choosing appropriate princess-defining behavior.[41] The identity of a princess is not defined in relation to a prince; it is defined in relation to the identity of value given to her by God (the "High King" in one story) and her decision to act in accordance with that identity. In a notable example a true princess is one who chooses modesty instead of surrendering her sexual power to men through immodesty.

This appeal to female power in sexual abstinence campaigns reveals a subtle but significant shift from some of the earliest modern-day sexual purity movements. In the mid-1800s books and pamphlets on sexual purity were written exclusively by men for a young male audience. Masturbation was a central concern; the male orgasm represented an uncontrollable threat to the individual and society. Young women were portrayed in these texts as either whores or madonnas. The pure woman, assuming the traditional role in the home, exerted an "absolute sexual power over men." As the historian Carroll Smith-Rosenberg writes, "Men were to assume a dependent sexual position, to obey women, the procreative force." In return for such sexual power, women were to remain subservient to their husbands and children, limiting their sexual desires and functioning as a stabilizing force in the home and society.[42] Thus women's submission stemmed in part from their power.

In the present case, modest fashion for evangelical Christians functions much like the veil or *hijab* for Islamic women. In their comparative study of evangelical Christian and Muslim women in the United States, the sociologists John Bartkowski and Jen'nan Ghazal Read explore gender debates surrounding the issues of evangelical wifely submission and the Islamic veil to show how women affirm their conservative faith traditions while crafting new rhetorics that reflect a more feminist outlook. Just as modest dress hides a young woman's "secret allure," so too the *hijab* hides the female form, creating a subcultural identifier that joins a woman with other veil wearers while separating her from secular culture and allowing her to move freely within it. Veiling the body is portrayed as "a corrective for masculine foibles, including men's apparent lack of sexual restraint."[43] This view of the Islamic veil rejects patriarchal oppression and instead reinforces the power of women's bodies and thus women's power over men.

Similarly, evangelical women who subscribe to a conservative view of male headship and wifely submission subvert the implied notion of gender hierarchy by saying that they choose to submit to their husbands, asserting their personal agency. Also, they argue that it is "men's deficiencies, rather than women's inferiority, that make wifely submission central to a harmonious marriage." The power for wifely submission comes from the wife, who chooses to submit to her husband because he needs to "feel like a man." As one of Bartkowski and Read's interview respondents said about her husband, "Philip feels like such a man when I say, 'How do you want to do this?' . . . He feels big. It definitely helps [men] when they know that they have someone to protect. It puts a lot of responsibility on them, but it makes them act better."[44]

In this way, women portray wifely submission as in their best interests, as R. Marie Griffith points out in her study of Women's Aglow Fellowship, the largest women's evangelical organization in the world. In a section entitled "The Power of Submission," Griffith describes submission as a "strategy of containment": "It is what men need to bolster their fragile egos, and women should comply in order to maintain domestic harmony as well as their own security." Although she acknowledges that this could be interpreted as the internalization of patriarchal values, Griffith asserts that the evangelical women themselves describe submission as leading to freedom and transformation, demonstrating a "broad repertoire of choices" available to women in their understanding of submission.[45]

This subversion of evangelical wifely submission is also found in the abstinence rhetoric directed to the next generation of wives. The princess may be waiting for her prince to come, but in the meantime she is actively pursuing princess-defining behavior and exhibiting control of her would-be suitors by modestly covering her body. In contrast, the valiant prince is charged with the heroic tasks of rescuing and protecting the princess; however, the evangelical rhetoric undermines this authority and power by portraying the next generation of husbands as trapped by their own sexual lusts and desires.

At the closing session of the Pure Freedom coed retreat, guys and girls crowded the front of the sanctuary, mosh-pit–style, as the worship band played. Dannah Gresh took the stage and asked the boys to return to their seats on the right side of the sanctuary, with girls on the other side. She spoke to the girls first. "When did it become okay for Christian girls to embrace the feminist movement?" she asked. She said that one of the lies of feminism is that having a job outside the home is more fulfilling than being a wife and mother. "You guys are on a battlefront," she told the girls.

Then she turned to the boys. "Why is it okay to have a humorous view of wimpy men?" She told them that God designed men to be godly protectors and valiant representatives of the godhead, and women should be obedient and submissive counterparts as a picture of the church. If you dismantle true manhood and true womanhood, she told the young people, then you dismantle our picture of Christ. She challenged each boy to be a man who is a "rescuer, savior, provider, and protector," and she encouraged each girl to be "a woman that's strong enough to be submissive."

Dannah defined true womanhood for the girls as being a wife and mother. She told them that they have "power and authority" and have "the right to be used as a picture of the church." She acknowledged that submission has been difficult for her in her marriage. "It's hard, because when you are a strong woman, it takes incredible strength to stand beside a strong man." She told the young men, "Guys, protect them. . . . Set your desires aside, so she can be a pure and spotless bride."[46]

Instead of asking the young people to commit to abstinence or purity, Dannah Gresh led them in a series of gender-defining questions, to which they were to respond by standing on their chairs and calling out, "Yes, Lord!" Will you be a man who will rise up and protect women? Will you choose to help your brothers by choosing to dress modestly? The audience shouted back the response.

Before the retreat concluded, the church's youth pastor asked all husbands at the event to take their wives by the hand and come up on the stage. Nine couples lined up at the edge of the stage. Bob Gresh kissed his wife on the cheek. Dannah responded by kissing him on the lips, then Bob dipped her for a big, movie-style kiss, to the obvious delight of the audience. In this curtain-call moment, marriage clearly was the goal of the retreat's message. The couples extended their hands over the audience and prayed for the young people, "that God would protect them as they search for that mate."

Feminism is the bogeyman here, as professional and domestic callings are set up as archenemies. And yet one wonders whether Dannah Gresh's actions speak louder than her words: she is a model of the best type of Christian feminism, publicly blending her vocational callings as a sincere follower of Christ, loving wife, devoted mother, and successful author and speaker. Despite calls for young women to submit humbly to their husbands, it is Bob Gresh who displays humility in taking a backseat to his wife's leadership of Pure Freedom. This clearly is her show, not his. Although the retreat's traditional gender-construction conclusion is not particularly surprising, given the abstinence campaigns' gendered rhetoric, I could not help but wish for a more nuanced conclusion to the weekend, one in which Dannah talked openly about balancing her professional and domestic roles and Bob shared how he is able to strengthen his masculinity by submitting to his wife's professional gifts and goals.[47]

And yet it is also important to consider the gendered rhetoric of the Pure Freedom retreat and the fairy-tale narrative in general within the standards and expectations of the evangelical community without imposing a feminist progressive norm. Within this evangelical community, feminism, not patriarchy, is represented as the true oppressor; thus what may appear to be a reinscription of traditional gender roles is understood as a powerful act of agential liberation from a repressive regime of liberalism.[48] As the feminist scholar Saba Mahmood writes in her study of the women's piety movement in Egypt, "What may appear to be a case of deplorable passivity and docility from a progressivist point of view, may actually be a form of agency—but one that can be understood only from within the discourses and structures of subordination that create the conditions of its enactment. In this sense, agentival capacity is entailed not only in those acts that resist norms but also in the multiple ways in which one *inhabits* norms."[49] Within this context, young men's protecting young women and young women's choosing to be wives and mothers constitute acts of agential power; they are inhabiting the norms of evangelical culture. Simply put, both the support and the subversion of traditional gender roles within evangelical abstinence campaigns constitute acts of agency.

Except for the married couples standing side by side, the retreat provided no model or explanation of how controlling men through modesty and protecting women by guarding against misplaced sexual urges would prepare the young people for the prayed-for future marriage. The closing prayer gave it away, when God was asked to protect the young people, instead of to prepare them for marriage. Contrary to the fairy-tale narrative, as it turns out, it is the prince who needs protection, not the princess. In a subversion of the narrative, the campaign portrays young women as powerful, protecting the egos of young men through wifely submission or protecting (and controlling) the purity of young men by dressing modestly. Young men are left in the potentially emasculating position of protecting themselves from their own bodies and desires. The call may be for young women to submit, but the campaign rhetoric also portrays young women as holding the power.[50] The female power argument is an audience-centered argument that is persuasive to a generation of teens who live in a culture that assumes sexual freedom and the power to choose what is right for their own bodies; at the same time the female power argument reasserts conservative religious values like the goal of traditional marriage.

This argument has persuaded at least one teenager to remain abstinent until marriage. Abby Jenkins exhibited the characteristics of a princess, even echoing the language of the fairy-tale narrative as it is used in the evangelical sexual abstinence movement. She chose to behave as a princess and to remain sexually pure while waiting for a prince who was worthy of her love. Abby's waiting paid off. As she explained, her real-life romance followed the fairy-tale script. She was alone in the woods, when her prince arrived on horseback and proposed marriage. Throughout the retelling of the relationship to the thousands of teenage girls gathered in the Dallas sports arena in 2004, Abby referred to her husband as "the prince that I had waited my entire life for." As the organization's name admonishes, true love waits, but waiting is also rewarded with true love. If her prince had not arrived that day in the woods, it is assumed that Abby probably would have kept on waiting for a reward that might never have come.

"Someday my prince will come"—but what if he doesn't? This is one of the challenges of the fairy-tale narrative for the evangelical abstinence campaigns. For all the young woman's power she may still be powerless to find her future husband. However, the fairy-tale narrative also dissuades impatient would-be princesses and princes from not waiting. The risk of catching a frog is portrayed as worse than never catching a prince.

The fairy-tale narrative effectively portrays the ideals of the abstinence message, but does this message resonate with the intended audience of teenagers? I now turn to the receivers of the evangelical abstinence message in the United States to explore how they accept, reject, and/or modify the message. Some abstinent teenage girls may be waiting for their princes to arrive, but the teenagers with whom I spoke offer a more realistic approach to negotiating sexual behavior while they are waiting.

CHAPTER 4

Disciplining Sexuality

How American Evangelical Youth Are Committing
to Abstinence—and Sticking with It

In MGM's 2003 sharp-witted feature movie release *Saved!* about teenage angst at the fictitious American Eagle Christian High School, the evangelical abstinence movement takes a beating. Pastor Skip, the desperate-to-be-hip school principal, instructs a sex education class, "It's all about populating the planet, and good Christians don't get jiggy with it until they're married."[1]

Attending the class is Mary, a senior, who slept with her boyfriend because she had a vision of Jesus as she was nearly drowning in a swimming pool. In the vision Jesus instructed her to have sex with her boyfriend to save him from homosexuality. As Mary contemplates her new mission, she and her friend Hilary Faye (played by the pop star and self-described Christian Mandy Moore), the ringleader of the popular "Christian Jewels" clique, discuss abstinence. The scene takes place at a local firing range:

> *Hilary Faye:* Christian girls have got to know how to protect themselves. I mean, sure, Jesus could restore my physical and spiritual virginity, especially if I lost it to some rapist, but who wants that? I'm saving myself until marriage, and I'll use force if necessary.[2]

Hilary Faye's resolution is underscored by the resounding shots of her firearm as she obliterates the genital region of the human-shaped paper target.

As this movie demonstrates, Hollywood's take on evangelical teens who have pledged to remain abstinent portrays them as weirdly aggressive in their narrowly religious beliefs and laughably naive about the way the world—and their bodies—work.[3] Evangelicals may be using sex to sell abstinence, but what makes some teens embrace abstinence, not sex? In their own words, what does abstinence mean to them? As I learned in my interviews with young people, abstinent teens may be waiting for sex, but they are certainly not waiting to express their sexuality.

WAITING IN THE GRAY AREA: DARCY SUTTON AND MATT ROWE

Darcy Sutton is on time for our meeting, but she begins by telling me that she tends to overcommit herself. She has a lot to say, and she talks fast. "Everything I do, it seems to be, like, 110 percent, like I can't do a half-baked effort." She recently graduated from college and now teaches art for elementary and middle school students. Her college years were busy, balancing work as a nanny, leadership in various campus ministries, and her academic studies in the university's honors college. Despite her challenging schedule, she maintained a 4.0 grade-point average.

When our conversation turns to sexuality and abstinence, I'm not surprised when Darcy tells me that she created a long list of do's and don'ts for appropriate sexual behavior before she ever started dating. "I'm one of those people, maybe it's the driven or organized part of me, that has a set of rules for everything, things like [those] I didn't want to have happen before my wedding day." When she was in middle school, Darcy wrote in her journal that she dreamed that her white wedding dress would represent her purity on her wedding day and that her body would be her gift to her husband. She pushes back her short bobbed hair and crosses her legs. Darcy, twenty-two, clearly knows what she wants and will work to achieve it.

Darcy is driven, but true to the fairy-tale narrative, she is also a romantic. Matt Rowe's family had moved to the area just before his junior year of high school. Darcy, a high school senior at the time, had heard about him from a mutual friend. Aware of how difficult it would be to be uprooted so soon before graduation, Darcy began praying for Matt and his family. The teens met at church one summer Sunday morning. She knew it was "a God thing." "Dang, that girl's beautiful" was Matt's initial reaction, as he told me in a separate conversation. He also sensed that Darcy was out of his league. They liked each other immediately but took a year to develop their friendship, deciding to date just before Darcy left for college.

Darcy was convinced that she would marry the first boy she kissed. She asked Matt to wait a year before he kissed her, so she could make sure that he was the one. But the waiting wasn't easy. "It was hard; it got really hard," Darcy says. She sensed that the kiss was coming during a hiking trip in Washington State. She had prayed that morning that God would not let Matt kiss her unless it was "the real deal." They kissed on top of the mountain. Later, around the campfire, Darcy told Matt about her prayer. He asked her how God had responded, and before she could answer, they both saw a shooting star. "I guess that was my answer," Darcy tells me, as tears fill her eyes at the beauty of the memory.

Darcy didn't realize that her self-discipline was in for a shake-up when she started dating Matt. Although they had a long-distance dating relationship while they were away at different colleges, they saw each other during summer breaks. That's when Darcy's long list of do's and don'ts became shorter and shorter. They both had committed to abstinence and had attended Pure Freedom events together, but, as Darcy puts it, she didn't realize that "the whole sex drive kicks in, and things aren't so black-and-white anymore." She was afraid of being out of control. "It scared me. I was like, Oh, my gosh, like, I desire these things I can't have. . . . I feel powerful as a woman, and it was scary, because I felt like I could see how things could get out of control." Both are still virgins, but she says that they've crossed lines physically that she wishes they had not crossed. "It's not just do's and don'ts," she says, with a hint of amazement in her voice. "There's gray area. It was shocking."

The couple got engaged a few months earlier in a romantic outdoor proposal with roses, hot chocolate, and a hot air balloon ride. The wedding date is a year away, but both Darcy and Matt insist separately that their abstinence pledge is now easier to maintain, not harder. "Wow, there's a finish line," Darcy tells me. "I can see the prize at the end!" True to her task orientation, Darcy is willing to wait and work toward the goal. "We know it's going to happen," Matt tells me matter-of-factly. "We've waited this long, why not wait until then?" Just in case, he has been praying that God will keep them from temptation.

IT TAKES A COMMUNITY

The evangelical sexual abstinence campaigns may be using sex to sell abstinence, but it is true that not all evangelical young people are buying it. Comprehensive sex education advocates are quick to point out that abstinence pledges don't work, considering that they may only delay sexual debut by eighteen months.[4] But abstinence supporters counter by emphasizing that commitments to abstinence have *some* impact. Not all pledgers may make it to their wedding day as virgins, but this is more likely for pledgers than for young people who did not make a commitment to abstinence.[5] Even for those who make it to the finish line of the wedding day, maintaining an abstinence pledge is certainly not easy, as Darcy and Matt's story demonstrates. So how have they beaten the odds?

When I asked this of Darcy and Matt in separate conversations, both replied that they felt they were not alone in their struggles. When their physical relationship started going further than they were comfortable with, they sought the help of their youth pastor and his wife. Darcy and Matt talked with them and laid bare the private details of their relationship. They asked for prayer. And they asked for more than just prayer: Darcy and Matt would tell the married couple when they were coming home from college for the weekend and would be together, and they would ask the youth pastor and his wife to "call us to make sure we're being good." As Darcy puts it, she believes that God has designed their bodies to desire each other, so he knows how difficult it is to wait to have sex; therefore, he wants them to pray and to ask trusted accountability partners to support them.

Studies show that abstinence commitments are strongest when made in the context of a supportive religious community of family and friends. The sociologist Mark Regnerus writes, "If you really want to know what distinguishes youth who delay sex, who are less sexually active, and who have fewer lifetime sexual partners, you must look . . . to how immersed they are in religious plausibility structures and how connected they feel to family and friends who are—for lots of reasons—committed to helping them effectively navigate adolescence and its sexual pressures."[6]

Of the abstinent young people I spoke with who are actively dating, all referred to influential people in their lives who kept them accountable to their pledge, whether concerned parents, close friends, or church members. To their credit, each abstinence organization encourages pledgers to find "accountability partners." Pure Freedom and Silver Ring Thing use e-mail to stay connected with pledgers, encouraging them to maintain their commitment. More than an e-mail, it is the personal relationships that make a difference. Many young people I spoke with mentioned pastors or youth pastors by name. Casual church attendance does not appear to be enough, nor does one-time attendance at an abstinence event. What seems to make a difference in the success of an individual's pledge is whether the individual is surrounded by a community of caring individuals (often older, more mature individuals) who are not afraid to get involved in the intimate details of their lives. Waiting for sex is too tough to manage alone.

THE POWER OF PERSONAL TESTIMONY

Whereas a committed community may be required to ensure the success of an individual's pledge, the appearance of community can begin at the abstinence event, making the pledge itself more appealing. Although the choice for abstinence is portrayed as an individual choice, young people reveal a complex understanding of the role of individual choice in the context of community. The most compelling argument for abstinence is not a logical argument (logos) but the character of a person (ethos). The interview respondents repeatedly mentioned that the most persuasive part of an abstinence event is the personal testimony of a peer who publicly shares that he or she is waiting to have sex until marriage. The testimony becomes an argument embodied in form, suggesting, *If I can wait, so can you*.[7] The testimonies of peers who succumbed to sexual temptation are equally, if not more, compelling, because they offer an embodied argument in support of second virginity.

Katie Peterson, nineteen, attended her first Silver Ring Thing event three years ago as part of a "girls' night out" with her church youth group. She was expecting another "boring seminar" about sex: "Because I grew up in a church, and I was always, Yeah, I'm going to save myself, you know, until I'm married, I'm not going to have sex until then, blah, blah, blah." Katie tells me that, to her surprise, she was "totally blown away" by the lights and music of the Silver Ring Thing presentation. But the reason Katie made a pledge of abstinence that night was not because of the flashy hype; she says it was because of the personal testimonies: "The people who were doing it, I could tell that they weren't just up on stage, like, 'Okay, this is how it goes.' They were really speaking, like, they really believed what they were saying. That was what really drew me to it, especially when I started to get to know the people more, and I realized they were hard core about their decision, and they weren't just getting on stage and doing it—they were living it out, and they were really about it, pretty much." Katie distinguishes between the public and private personas of the testifiers. The consistency between message and behavior added credibility to the embodied argument that she found compelling.

Jake Weber, eighteen, thinks that the Starting Over testimony at the Silver Ring Thing event, given by someone who has had sex but has since made a pledge of abstinence as a second virgin, is the most compelling argument for abstinence. "They've had sex, and they've said, you know, 'Hey, I'm going to start over. I know this isn't right,'" Jake says. "That can tell, you know, to see someone who's done that, it gives you encouragement and says, 'Hey, I know that, I've been where you're at, and I went through that. You can do it, too.'"

Rachel Hollister, twenty-six, recalls that personal testimonies were a regular feature of her church's abstinence message. Once every couple of years beginning in junior high, someone would give testimony to the youth group about how having sex had negatively affected his or her life. The members of the youth group would have the opportunity to fill out a "commitment card" to pledge abstinence and avoid the same fate as the testifier.

When Rachel was a sophomore in high school, she won a competition sponsored by the conservative evangelical organization Focus on the Family and was asked to give her testimony at a True Love Waits event. She recalls standing before thousands of other teenagers gathered in a massive sports arena and telling them about why she was committed to remaining sexually abstinent until marriage: "So myself and a boy had to walk up on the stage and then just kind of share," she recalls. "I just said some kind of like short thing, like, 'Having sex before marriage is like opening a gift too early' or something like that, where if you want the gift to be special, you need to wait."

Although Hollister was one of those who shared her testimony with her peers, she says that she was motivated to maintain her abstinence commitment because of the testimonies of the Christian celebrities at the event and the feeling that she was part of something larger than she. "Of course, when you're in high school and you have these artists and speakers that you just think are so cool, and then they're saying also how they're going to wait, how they waited and everything. That kind of thing obviously is part of that whole pep rally feel of everyone else is on board, too," Rachel says.

POSITIVE PEER PRESSURE

In addition to the role of testimonies, Rachel cites the importance of the sheer numbers of like-minded teenagers in the audience and the feeling that one is not alone in one's decision to be abstinent. Personal testimonies provide embodied arguments as to why an individual should choose abstinence, but a large crowd of teenagers who are publicly choosing abstinence provides positive peer pressure that suggests that a decision for abstinence is a decision to be part of the teenage mainstream. Although the choice for abstinence itself may be countercultural, it appears to be mainstream when an individual is surrounded by a sports stadium full of abstinence-pledging teens. Rachel describes the impact of positive peer pressure at the True Love Waits event:

> You have an entire arena full of junior high and high school students. So, all of a sudden, being the only kid at your high school that you felt, like, was waiting and then you're in this huge dome full of students. . . . And then, I remember, as the event went on, we were to sign pledge cards, and, then, as the pledge cards were signed, they stacked them all one on top of each other. And then they had a string all the way up to the roof, so that you could see that all the way up to the roof there had been colored pledge cards all the way up. So it was just kind of a neat visual representation of that there were that many people who were saying they would do that. . . . I think it's so compelling to be with other people. It's like positive peer pressure.

Katie Peterson says that she already knew she should wait to have sex until marriage, but attending the Silver Ring Thing event made her feel part of a larger group of teens who also were waiting to have sex. "And this kind of made it, like, solid, this is how I'm really going to do this, I'm really committed to it now," she says. "And not that I wasn't before, but it's kind of like, okay, you know, I know that there are other people out there doing this now, that I'm not the weird girl, like, who's not going to have sex until she's married, you know? So that was cool." Katie's response suggests an element of implied accountability that comes with the positive peer pressure. Now her commitment to abstinence is more solid because she knows that she is not alone in her commitment. There is also safety in numbers: for Katie Peterson, making a pledge of abstinence with a room full of other teenagers made the exceptional decision seem normative and less weird.

An implied corollary to the significance of positive peer pressure is that if making an abstinence commitment establishes membership in a particular peer group, then not making or breaking the abstinence commitment could result in the ostracizing of an individual. Rebecca Blithefield, twenty-one, had already signed an abstinence pledge card at a large denominational church rally during junior high, but she felt pressured to sign another card when her church's high school youth group conducted a Bible study series on why teens should wait to have sex. "I guess it was because maybe I lost my other card or something," she says. "I don't know. It was because everybody was doing it. I just did it again. I had already made that commitment. . . . Everyone around me [signed a pledge card]. . . . It would have been odd if I hadn't signed it."

The power of teenage peer pressure can erode the power of the individual commitment. Although Rebecca had already chosen to remain abstinent, she felt pressured to sign another pledge card so that it would not appear as if she had rejected abstinence and wanted to have sex. It is also possible that teens who had not made an abstinence pledge would also feel the same pressure of conformity, creating the public sign of membership in the group while continuing private sexual behavior that would go against the standards of the abstinence community.

MAKING MY OWN CHOICE

Testimonies of abstinence commitments and peer pressure to choose abstinence can provide compelling embodied arguments, but they also can mask false commitments and appear too didactic, resulting in a backlash of adolescent agency.

Abstinence was not the reason that Jodi Simmons attended a Pure Freedom retreat in 1998. She wanted to go because she heard it would be about sex and because "it was a way to get away from the house." A self-described "bad kid" in middle school, Jodi hung with the wrong crowd, smoking and shoplifting and generally disobeying her parents. "I wasn't really into church or God or anything at that point in my life. I was pretty against it. I went because my friends went," she says.

Jodi, who was twenty when she spoke with me, committed to abstinence at the Pure Freedom retreat, but it was not her first abstinence pledge. Because she had grown up attending church, she was sure that she had taken a pledge before. This time, however, was different.

"They'd do those, like, you know, True Love Waits things at youth group, and I really was just very much a follower, like, you know, if my friends would go up to the altar, I would go up to the altar, that type of thing, you know? And just up until that retreat, it had never been a decision [I] made for myself," she acknowledges. The significance for Jodi was that this time she did not just go along with the crowd; she made the decision on her own, even going against her peer group. "Actually, at the end of the retreat, the main thing about that decision that I made was that it was completely on my own, like my friends really persecuted me for doing that," she recalls. "Rather than joining, or me joining them, it was really something that I stepped out on my own, you know."

The choice for abstinence was significant in Jodi's mind because she did not succumb to peer pressure. She says that friends from her church youth group teased her after she made her abstinence pledge, calling her a hypocrite and "little Miss Christian." "I think they saw my changes as like a threat to their lifestyle," she says, acknowledging that her friends were even more rebellious than she was.

Jodi thinks that a lot of her friends took abstinence pledges but have since broken them because they merely went along with the crowd and did not make the commitment for themselves. "Yeah, I know that there's been a lot [of broken pledges], just because it's just such a, like, you know, if you are at a True Love Waits thing, it's, like, 'Now everyone come up and sign this pledge form,' you know, like, people don't make their own decisions, really, a lot of the time and just, like, fill out a form and not really, like, mean what it says, you know? I think that happens a lot," Jodi says. The difference for her was that she ignored peer pressure and made her own choice for abstinence: "Well, like I said, it was because it was a personal decision, that I stepped out on my own, you know, that, like, God called me, like, singled me out and said you have to make this decision on your own rather than me just, like, following some of my friends."

Making a choice for abstinence can mean parting ways with friends. Katie Peterson's story is similar to Jodi Simmons's: "So I definitely wasn't supported all around for my decision," Katie says. "And a lot of my friends didn't go [to the Silver Ring Thing event]. A lot of my friends weren't Christians, so that was kind of hard for me, too. It kind of came to the agreement point where I was, like, 'This is how I'm going to live my life, this is how I believe you should.' And they didn't feel the same way." Instead of weakening her commitment to abstinence, the rejection of Katie by her friends solidified her commitment and forced her to find new friends who shared her views about abstinence.

Positive peer pressure may contribute to the abstinence message by providing a feeling of community and a sense that one is not alone in making the commitment, but as Jodi Simmons's story illustrates, this is not always the case. Peer pressure can have the negative effect of encouraging false commitments. In Jodi's case, the strength of her abstinence commitment came from her decision to step away from her peer group and make a solitary decision. Here was weakness, not strength, in numbers. Her strength of commitment lay in making an individual decision.

Just as peer pressure may result in forced or false abstinence commitments, so too testimonies may be perceived as too didactic, prompting a backlash that suggests that teens do not want to be told what to do; they want to experience life and decide for themselves.

Jonathan Ebersol, nineteen, doesn't like to be pushed. Growing up as a preacher's kid in a small farming town in the central plains, Jonathan decided when he was three and a half that he wanted to accept Jesus as his savior, but his parents wanted him to wait because they thought he was too young to make such a big decision. He had made up his mind and was able to convince his parents that he knew what he was doing. When he was a teen, Jonathan's mom tried to talk him out of dating. She wanted him to read *I Kissed Dating Goodbye*, the courtship book by Joshua Harris. "She'd always push the books on me," he says.

Jonathan says that he "never got into the whole True Love Waits" thing, although a lot of his friends did. He says he viewed it more as a marketing scheme to sell rings. He knew about the importance of abstinence from school sex education classes and from church youth group discussions, as well as the Christian dating books his mom made him read. He knew that as a Christian he was supposed to save sex for marriage, but he was feeling pushed into it:

It's things like your parents will push it at you, and all these older people push it at you, especially when you're sixteen or seventeen, you're, like, it's something I want to try to find out for myself. Or how-do-you-guys-really-know kind of a thing—Just the whole . . . your parents talk about abstinence and things. You'd always be, like, "Well, they're being overprotective. They're trying to push this. Never date a girl." My mom was almost [saying,] "Never have a relationship"—[that was] almost [her] mind-set. I know she was just trying to protect me and things like that, but whenever I was in a relationship she would just always bring me questions about it. She was in the mind-set [of] you only date to marry. Which I would agree with now, but at sixteen or so was not that way.

In typical teenage fashion, Jonathan chafes at being told what to do by his parents. Even though parents were teenagers once too, the age gap could make a difference in the perceived credibility of the message. "So I definitely think with students today, and just the way that parents and older people push things on them, that's kind of where I think some problems are caused where, when you're fifteen, sixteen, seventeen, you're curious and you want to find things out," Jonathan says. "You're getting to the age where you think you know what you want to do and you understand life. And when things are pushed at you, you kind of reject that and don't always want to listen." Like Jodi Simmons, who broke away from her peer group to make a decision for abstinence, Jonathan Ebersol suggests that breaking away from his parents and making his own choices based on his "own free will" could make for lasting decisions.

WORTHY OF BEING WAITED FOR

Another reason that young people—particularly young women—are committing to abstinence is because it increases their self-esteem. When I asked my female interview respondents to describe what they viewed as the most compelling part of the abstinence message, most said that the message to wait to have sex taught them that they were worth waiting for. The subversive girl-power rhetoric of groups like Pure Freedom is gaining resonance. For young women, abstinence places a hedge of protection around their bodies and sexuality so that they can learn to value themselves for who they are, not how they are dressed or what they are willing to do with a guy on a Friday night.[8]

Nora Williams says that the abstinence message she heard at a Silver Ring Thing event in 2000 made her feel good about herself. "I think it was that they challenged us to find self-worth and to realize that you are worth waiting for; that you don't need to fill your life with things, you don't need to do drugs, and you don't need to have sex to make your life better and to make you feel better about yourself," she says. "You can wait, and people are still going to respect you, and ultimately that you are worth waiting for. I really liked that, how they made me feel good about myself. I really liked it a lot."

Her newfound self-esteem gave Nora the courage to break up with the guy she was casually dating at the time (a "cheesy high school relationship," as Nora, twenty, now calls it). Upon hearing that she had made an abstinence pledge, the guy told her, "'That is the strangest and most stupidest thing I have ever heard in my life,'" Nora recalls. Since he had that attitude, she knew that the guy was not worth her time:

> So I was just kind of like, "Alright, well, then, I don't need you." But it was great, because I actually learned that attitude from Silver Ring Thing, that if people don't respect your morals and the boundaries that you lay on in your dating life, they are not for you and not worth it. So, it saved me a lot of pain fighting for this relationship where he didn't respect me. He could have pressured me, I mean, we could have had sex, but, you know, because I went to Silver Ring Thing, it kind of stopped me from making those mistakes in high school.

Rebecca Blithefield did not have a boyfriend to break up with after she took her two abstinence pledges because she does not believe in dating. She views dating as a "big waste of time," particularly when she could be spending time with her girlfriends and developing her own potential:

> If you spend a lot of time with the opposite sex on dates, you aren't developing friendships with girls and your girlfriends, speaking from the perspective of a girl. You aren't developing just having good times with your own best friends doing innocent, fun things. And you're off with a guy who really doesn't love you and just wants to take advantage of you, or vice versa, a girl could take advantage of a guy. And it just seems like a big waste of time and a big waste of emotional energy when you can develop skills, developing your education to go on and do things with your life.

The girl-power attitude in Rebecca's comments is especially interesting because she holds conservative evangelical views on wifely submission, courtship instead of dating, and saving the first kiss until the wedding ceremony. Just as Pure Freedom's focus on modesty and a young woman's "secret allure" increases her power over men, so too, Rebecca's response suggests, does a separatist feminist-type power over men that takes the abstinence pledge a step further and opts out of the dating game altogether.

The abstinence message gives young women a sense of self-worth by connecting a message of God's view of their worth with God's demand that they save sex until marriage. Young women are taught to have self-worth because they are worthy of God's love. At a Pure Freedom retreat, Jodi Simmons gave up her rebellious ways, rededicated her life to God, and discovered a new affirmation in being a woman. "I think the main things that really got me were, like, [the retreat leader] talked a lot about self-esteem and how that's really good to, like, dating relationships and then physical stuff and just really encouraged the girls that we are worthy, that in God's eyes that we have great worth and stuff like that and that meant a lot to me," Jodi says.

The most important part of the retreat for Jodi was the message "that girls have great worth in God's eyes. Self-esteem issues and stuff. . . . All the reasons why to say no to sex and all that stuff relates back to the fact that we have worth in God's eyes." She recognized that she had worth because God thought that she had worth. She says this message freed her from her rebellious past and feelings of condemnation:

> Like, that's like the main thing that I got because, like, I've been, I've felt, like, condemned my whole life. Like, I felt, especially those past couple of years, just because my parents were really strict and obviously I was being really rebellious, so it was like a constant, like, "me getting in trouble because of God" type of deal, you know? And so, it just really meant a lot to me to know that God didn't just, you know, like, he wasn't just up there to condemn me, you know, but like he really cared for me, and that because of that he wanted me, he wants us, to wait to share our bodies with someone else. Does that make sense?

Jodi goes on to explain that she thinks that most teenage girls connect self-esteem with sexual activity:

> I think a lot of girls get their self-worth out of boys and out of relationships. And I think the reason why so many people are so loose sexually is because they feel like that is the only way they can feel good about themselves, you know? Or feel like they are loved, or feel intimate, you know? So, I think that our culture and just the way things are have really degraded women and made us feel like we don't have any worth, like we don't have any worth to the community other than as sexual, like, creatures, you know?

The evangelical abstinence message addresses young women not just as sexual beings but as spiritual and emotional ones as well. Jodi Simmons's perspective on the connection between the sexual behavior of teenage girls and their self-esteem suggests that the most compelling evangelical abstinence message for teenage girls is that they can find their self-worth from another source (God), not from sex-hungry boys.

CONSEQUENCES FOR YOUNG WOMEN

One explanation for the focus on young women in the message of self-worth and the benefits of abstinence may be that many of the consequences of not choosing abstinence change the lives of young women. Few respondents mention any consequences of nonmarital sexual activity for teen boys. Both male and female interview respondents cite consequences of nonmarital sexual activity as consequences for young women: namely, pregnancy. Of the eight interview respondents who referred to friends who had not been abstinent, five spoke of a young woman who became pregnant. Three of the five pregnancy stories came from male respondents. In one case the male respondent mentioned a young woman from his high school who had become pregnant. In another case the male respondent mentioned his best friend from his church who had gotten a young woman pregnant. They married and had to quit school to go to work and support their child. Here the consequence of the pregnancy is shared between the male and female in the story. The moral of the story, according to the respondent, is that "it's not worth it."

Jonathan Ebersol recounts the female-centered testimonies of past abstinence events:

> We'd always have people come from the Crisis Pregnancy outreach center. They'd always bring a girl who was, like, seventeen or eighteen who already had a child or an abortion or something. Just talking about things they go through. And I think that caters towards the females. I don't know if they really had the whole male side of the issue figured out as well in schools. It's weird. It's always these consequences seem like for the girls—you'll get pregnant or the guy will leave you; he's just after sex; he doesn't care about you. And [for] guys, it's kind of like, "Yeah, don't do it."

As a male, Jonathan felt left out of the abstinence message, which was directed primarily at young women. Here, the objective for young women is to avoid teenage boys, who are portrayed as the harbingers of the negative consequences of sexual activity. Boys are told "don't do it" but are not given a reason why. The agency for saying no is placed on the young women. "It always seemed like they were always catering towards the female audience and leaving it up to them to say no," Jonathan recalls. "I've never really [been] told, 'You guys should say no, too.' It's always more teaching girls how to say no to their pushy boyfriends or things like that." By possessing the power to say no, young women are given the responsibility for the consequences as well as the privileges of female power and self-worth.[9]

Although pregnancy is a highly visible consequence of nonmarital sexual activity, sexually transmitted diseases are not as visible, and therefore they seem not to be as compelling a negative consequence of choosing to be sexually active. "I think that the whole idea of the disease part of it is so true but overplayed. I think the people know that," says Rachel Hollister. When asked about the fear of disease, Jonathan Ebersol replies that teenage boys are not motivated by diseases or negative consequences in general. "It's the whole mind-set. A teenage guy does not think it will happen to them," he says. "Even now a lot of things guys do in college, crazy little pranks we'll pull or stunts we'll try to do, these things can get us hurt or in trouble. But you just don't think about it at the time. It's really kind of funny how I think a lot of guys don't understand hindsight when they do something. Consequences aren't contemplated very well."

In contrast, the fear of consequences appears to be a strong motivator for young women. "I think I was so scared," recalls Rachel. "I think I had heard so many talks about the consequences of screwing up from youth pastors . . . and we had a girl live with us who was twentysomething who had pretty much wrecked her life by having sex with so many guys and everything. So I think that at that stage I don't even know that I consciously was thinking, 'I'm going to set boundaries.' It was almost like I had this fear of *what if*."

SETTING LIMITS TO PHYSICAL INTIMACY

The story of Darcy Sutton and Matt Rowe's relationship is the prototypical evangelical abstinence story. They are both attractive and winsome; they are serious about their faith and church participation; their relationship follows a romantic narrative, including shooting stars and a hot-air balloon; and they are on track to remain virgins until their wedding day. What at first glance may not seem as common for abstinent youth—their ongoing struggle with sexual temptation—is, in fact, a key part of what makes Darcy and Matt's story so typical. Quantitative studies of sexual abstinence unfortunately give the impression that young people are either abstinent or sexually active, which does not account for the range of sexual activity that may be acceptable even to abstinent teens. Although abstinent teens may focus on the delayed gratification of sex within marriage, most young people I spoke with acknowledge struggling with sexual temptation in their current relationships. The commitment to delaying sex until marriage does not mean that abstinent teens are not engaged in various forms of sexual activity. This is a key break in message reception from the producers of the campaigns to the teenage receivers: the abstinence campaigns tend to focus on not having sex but generally avoid the gray area of defining how far is too far, aside from sexual intercourse itself. Abstinent young people are still sexual beings, and they are left to negotiate their sexuality on their own.

Although all my interview respondents stated a commitment to delaying sex until marriage, most acknowledged engaging in various forms of intimate physical activity, apart from sexual intercourse.[10] The young people discussed boundaries in their dating relationships, but the responses displayed a variety of acceptable limits to their physical expression, including the concept of courtship as an alternative to dating, with courtship defined in part by its lack of physical intimacy. The interview respondents revealed a nuanced working concept of purity that allows for a diversity of views on the question of limits to physical intimacy by focusing on the concern for respect for others, not gratification of self.[11]

Jake Weber dated two girls in high school, both of whom, like Jake, had made a pledge of abstinence. At a Christian camp one summer, a kitchen worker to whom Jake was attracted asked him to come home with her and spend the night, "and I was, like, 'No, I can't do that,' and she couldn't wrap her mind around that," Jake remembers. He defines abstinence as the "polar opposite of sexual immorality": "If you go to the Grand Canyon, are you going to run right up to the edge and try to stop, or are you, you know, going to, like, keep your distance? I definitely think that abstinence shouldn't be, like, let's see how close we can get to having sex without having sex, because a lot of times, you know, those hormones are going to kick in, and it's going to just push you over the edge and that's, that's not good." For Jake, pushing the boundaries of acceptable sexual behavior is not part of committing to abstinence, as his Grand Canyon analogy illustrates. Hormones, as he points out, can defeat self-control, so limits need to be set before the ultimate limit of sexual intercourse. Hormones may be powerful, but individuals possess the power to control their hormones and thus their bodies.

Jodi Simmons says she had been physically intimate with guys in the past but has not had many opportunities to date: "I'd like, you know, made out with boys before and stuff and never really felt bad about it." But Jodi also says that she has struggled with sexual temptation since making her abstinence pledge. A junior at a Bible college that has strict guidelines for dating relationships, Jodi says that she has broken some rules. "Like, I've had a couple of boyfriends where it's been a struggle, you know. But I think I've always, it's always been, like, it's never been a losing battle."

For Katie Peterson, sexual temptation was easier to handle because her boyfriend of a year and a half had also made a commitment to sexual abstinence. "Because we both knew that we were going to wait until we were married, then it was so much easier as a couple to wait, because we knew, like, what our tempting situations would be, and, you know, we're not going to push our limits, we're not going to see how close we can get." Although it was easier to wait, Katie acknowledges that she was tempted. But she points out that sexual desire is healthy, since God created it: "I think in any relationship, there is going to be temptation, because God created us to, you know, desire, but it's so much easier to overcome that temptation when you know that the other person is waiting."

For Jennifer Bartell, focusing on the hopes of future marriage helped to curb sexual temptation with her boyfriend during her freshman and sophomore years of high school. "We had a point where we came that close and it was just, like, no, no, it's not happening. We both agreed that it would . . . ruin anything that we would have in marriage," Jennifer says. After breaking up in high school, the two recently got together again and now are planning an August wedding.

Reflecting on her upcoming nuptials, Jennifer wonders what it will be like to finally be able to have sex. "It seems to be almost like a free-for-all," she says. "I mean, it's, like, wow, that's a huge step. It seems so odd to me." When asked to elaborate, she replies, "I don't know how to describe it. Up until you are married, you are not allowed to do things, I mean, not allowed is in a good way, and afterwards you are allowed, and it just seems like a huge gap." Jennifer's gap is similar to Jake Weber's Grand Canyon, describing a boundary between when sexual behavior is considered bad and when it is considered good.

Like Darcy and Matt, Colin Smith, twenty-two, acknowledges that he and his girlfriend have struggled with sexual temptation, especially after they became engaged. For Colin the key is balance. He thinks the physical, emotional, and spiritual aspects of a relationship need to be in balance, without one aspect dominating the others. Yet he reaffirms the role of nonintercourse physical intimacy in the dating relationship. To describe the appropriate role of physical intimacy, Colin offers what he calls a kind of cheesy analogy of a cake, where the relationship is the cake and the physical aspect of the relationship is the frosting: "And so if you look at a cake, a really good cake has a lot of cake to it, and then the frosting is within limits. But if you have a cake that has a ton of frosting, it's just way too sweet, and you're like, hey. It's good for a minute, but then you get sick. Whereas a dry cake, well, that's boring." Most young people with whom I spoke agree that it's okay to be physically intimate with your girlfriend or boyfriend, but you should make sure that it is within limits. For abstinence pledgers the only clear limit is not to have sex.

Jonathan Ebersol agrees that the Christian definition of abstinence involves saving sex for marriage, but he points out that within the black-and-white rule of not having sexual intercourse is a large gray area of acceptable physical intimacy. "As a Christian you're supposed to save sex for marriage. . . . Everybody says it kind of a little bit different. But it's really kind of hard to figure out," Jonathan says. "I don't think there's maybe a consistent message besides 'Do not have sex.' I think they'd all agree on that. But how they get there, levels leading up to that are different in a lot of the [abstinence] talks." Jonathan acknowledges that in his previous relationship with his one serious girlfriend of four months, it was difficult to determine where to set the boundary of acceptable physical intimacy:

> We never set up a line to begin with. It was one day after I think we had kind of a crazy night or something, the night before was really "All right, we need to have some rules. . . ." We didn't really come up with anything spectacular. Just like, okay, we definitely won't have sex. Just try to make sure that clothing stays on and things like that was really what we decided. . . . You find that when a line was pushed it's hard to go back. You can't . . . you can say things start being expected in a relationship physically after it happened the first time.

COURTSHIP AS A DATING ALTERNATIVE

Darcy asked Matt to wait a year before their first kiss, but two other respondents place their limits of acceptable physical intimacy much further away from sexual intercourse than that. Two young people with whom I spoke, both college students, are in what they describe as a courtship relationship with another person. Courtship is a sort of backlash to traditional dating, and it is increasingly popular among a small minority of evangelical Christian young people, distinguished by the relationship's serious focus on marriage and lack of physical intimacy.[12]

Rebecca Blithefield has been in a courtship relationship with another student at her college for more than a year. They developed their friendship over two years within a group of friends. She says that she made clear her commitment to courtship in various conversations with guys in her group of friends. "And it was not that I was afraid of a relationship; at that point I was just not ready for one," Rebecca says. After two years of being friends, the young man asked Rebecca's parents for their permission to pursue a more "marriage-direction relationship" with their daughter. "And then he asked for my permission, if I would agree," she says. "And I did."

Rebecca was raised as an only child in a Christian home in the South, where she was homeschooled and her family attended a large Southern Baptist church. A self-described homebody and bookworm growing up, Rebecca preferred classical music to Christian contemporary music because it "seemed shallow and just kind of repetitive." Her parents talked to her early on about the "heart-wrenching nature of recreational dating" and encouraged her to consider a courtship relationship as she got older so that she could be "spared the grief of on-and-off relationships with guys." Rebecca says she wasn't excited about the idea at first, but as her friends began to get boy crazy, she thought that her parents' advice was wise.

Guidelines and boundaries are important parts of a courtship relationship. Distinguishing factors of a courtship relationship are the clear boundaries for physical intimacy. But the commitment to purity begins with the individual before it expands to the couple. Rebecca is clear that she made her own decision to pursue a courtship relationship; it was not forced on her by her parents or her church. The reason she maintained the commitment to herself was that she recognized its benefits: "I've always been very firm in my decisions, and I think through very carefully why I decide what I've decided," she says. "And I can see the benefits so clearly of keeping that covenant that I made [with] myself, that decision to stay pure and to stay within those boundaries that I set for myself, that it was not a temptation to overstep those boundaries." Her courtship relationship is also based on clear boundaries. "We made very clear guidelines from the very beginning based on our commitment to ourselves in the past, and we made the commitment to each other once we started our relationship that there are certain lines that we would not cross, certain things that we would not do together," she says.

Those guidelines include not kissing and not praying when they are alone together. Initially, the couple did not hold hands, but Rebecca says that it is part of a process of intimacy with much more to come: "So right now it's very sweet just to have good conversations with him and learn his heart and what he loves about life and what he's interested in. And I'm more enthusiastic about having a good conversation than physical indulgence. So it's a process. And we're definitely more physical than we were when we started, but it's still very minimal. It's done with an understanding that there's a lot more to come and that just needs to wait." Rebecca says that their conversations steer toward the practical, like housecleaning and other standards for marriage, instead of the emotional in order to find out if they are compatible.

Perhaps the central distinguishing factor of Rebecca's courtship relationship is that she is waiting for her first kiss until her wedding day. Although the evangelical abstinence message stresses saving sex until the wedding day, Rebecca sets a more conservative boundary for what many young people would consider an acceptable early stage of physical intimacy. She says that she wants to wait for her first kiss so that it can be a covenant of their marriage and so that premature kissing will not cheapen it. "I want to be so head over heels in love with this man that I'm ready to do that with my whole heart. I don't want to do it too early and think it's yucky, I guess," she says. Rebecca also acknowledges that kissing can lead to more physical temptations, and she does not want to be forced to deal with that, since they both have a few more years of school before they can get married. Rebecca's description of her desire to wait for her first kiss sounds both conservative and countercultural, even for evangelicals. She describes her conservative view on acceptable physical intimacy not as an imposed limit on her own freedom and enjoyment but as her personal decision to strengthen her future marriage and to protect her freedom now, as a single college student.

Not all abstinence pledgers would agree with Rebecca Blithefield's decision. "I think it's absurd," says Jonathan Ebersol, referring to the decision that some make to wait to kiss until their wedding day, "because it's a natural expression, I think, very much of caring for a person. Just kissing in and of itself isn't this huge thing that's going to lead to more things. It's levels of kissing or making out or whatever that can get you into more trouble. . . . I think it's a very natural part of dating relationships. But definitely it should be discussed beforehand, when or how it will happen. Just boundaries need to be set before you get there." Jonathan explains that he feels that the physical side of a relationship is just as important as the emotional and spiritual sides; all must be developed together within the protection of specific boundaries as a couple progresses toward marriage, he says, echoing Colin Smith's cake analogy in which physical intimacy is the frosting.

Recalling Jake Weber's Grand Canyon analogy, Jonathan Ebersol's description of the boundary of appropriate sexual behavior is perhaps more like a hill than a canyon, with a progression of physical intimacy as the relationship matures. Rebecca Blithefield also describes her courtship relationship as a process of growing physical intimacy, although she sets the boundary at a significantly different level than both Jonathan and Colin. All, however, define themselves as evangelicals and say they are committed to abstinence. Their responses illustrate the diversity of abstinent adolescents' views on acceptable sexual behavior.

REDEFINING PURITY AS RESPECTING OTHERS

Abstinent young people offer a variety of acceptable boundaries for physical intimacy while maintaining their commitment to abstinence, but they generally adhere to a definition of abstinence as purity that is similar to the definition used by evangelical abstinence campaigns. However, the young people with whom I talked reveal a nuanced position on purity that includes a theological view of the body as God's temple and a practical view of respecting others, emphasizing individual self-worth in dating relationships.

Broadly, the interview respondents define abstinence in terms of purity. Krista Willette's response provides an example: "Personally, I tend to use the word *purity* because abstinence raises the question[s] of how far is too far? and what makes a virgin? and all this stuff and what is intercourse? And a lot of people just don't have the education. So I use the word *purity* because it's not about having a line in the sand. It's following a direction, and it's towards Jesus Christ. If it doesn't honor him, it's not being pure." Krista uses the word *purity* instead of *abstinence* because purity does not focus on specific boundaries of physical intimacy or "having a line in the sand." Instead of a negative commitment not to have sex, a commitment to purity, as it is constructed in the evangelical sexual abstinence campaigns, is a positive call to actively pursue a lifestyle that honors Jesus Christ.[13] Krista uses this focus of honoring Jesus to define purity.

Jennifer Bartell struggles to define abstinence, but she knows that it has something to do with a kind of purity that goes beyond actions. "I would say it is purity in actions but also in your thoughts, where you . . . I'm trying to think of the right words . . . It's purity of . . . I guess I don't know how to describe purity . . . because you are abstaining from certain situations that would compromise, perhaps, emotions, like your heart feelings, and the emotions of that other person, too. I'm not sure if that's a complete enough answer."

Nora Williams begins her definition of abstinence by saying that it means "withdrawing yourself from something," but she goes on to describe sexual abstinence as "a lot more than just saying you're not going to have sex. It's kind of an entire lifestyle and making sure that you remain pure—even though you're not going to have sex, you need to remove yourself from the other junk that comes along with it and making sure that your dating relationships are pure and healthy." Similarly, Amanda Carter defines abstinence as a "pure lifestyle" that includes "pure thoughts and actions and not looking at impure things, pornography, that kind of thing."

Rebecca Blithefield defines abstinence as all that she is saving for her future husband, including her emotional as well as her physical self. She defines purity as freedom from sin. "Purity is unashamed in my actions and thoughts. I'm free," she says. "I have nothing to hide. Nothing to be ashamed of. I am righteous in my actions, apart from sin that we all struggle with in our human nature. But as far as what I have done, I'm above reproach."

The positive and expansive message of purity over abstinence is being successfully communicated to evangelical young people. Abstinence is defined as purity, which is portrayed as more than just not having sex. Purity involves more than appropriate physical intimacy, including purity of thoughts and freedom from sin. As the response from Krista Willette points out, sexual purity for evangelical teens who are abstinent has more to do with following God than with following specific rules and guidelines for not having sex. The young people with whom I spoke are not without boundaries in their sexual behavior, but they display far more diversity of viewpoints than simply "don't have sex." The simultaneous focus on both purity and boundaries is resolved by understanding that the guideline for establishing boundaries is defining purity as following God. Part of following God is an understanding that one's body is created by God. Quoting scripture, respondents refer to their bodies as "God's temple." If all bodies are God's temples, then the body of a boy's girlfriend is God's temple too and worthy of respect. The interview respondents resolve the tension between godly purity and the gray area of appropriate physical intimacy before sexual intercourse by articulating a practical view of respecting others. Placing others' needs before their own, the interview respondents offer a nuanced view of purity.

Krista Willette cites Romans 12:1–2, which, she says, talks about "your body as a temple and to worship God with your body." Rebecca Blithefield articulates a "WWJD" (What would Jesus do?) view of the body as God's temple. "And he has ordained our bodies are his temple; that he dwells in me and is present in everything I do," she says. "And kind of the mind-set if Jesus were to walk in a room and see what I'm doing, would he be pleased with what he sees? Am I indulging in sin and what the world would have me do? Or am I keeping myself focused on his word and on his holiness and trying to implement that as best I can through his strength?" As Rebecca points out, if the body is God's, then the person is responsible for appropriate stewardship of the body. Stewardship of the body as God's temple is pleasing to God. Personal self-worth and respect come from this view of belonging to God.

According to this view, then, respecting one's boyfriend or girlfriend as well as oneself qualifies as stewardship of God's temple, which is pleasing to God. So where do the abstinent teens draw the line for appropriate physical intimacy while staying true to their commitment to purity? They draw the line where they feel they are still respecting the other person. Rebecca Blithefield uses the word *respect* to describe how she treats others. She views others with respect because she feels they are created by God: "Being aware of the value of my life because of my life with Christ and also respecting the other people around me as wonderfully made by God and special to him." According to Rebecca, a physically intimate relationship does not demonstrate respect for the other person because it is disrespectful to God. She believes that one can become distracted from serving God if one is "indulging in a sensual relationship." She explains: "You're not seeking the best for the other person and just taking what you can get for pleasure."

Jonathan Ebersol also uses the word *respect* to describe how his faith and commitment to abstinence dictate how he treats the young women he is dating. "For me it would really be the honor and respect thing and making sure that, especially if I'm dating someone, that I'm treating my sister in Christ with a love and respect that you're called to," he says. "Just making sure you consider others more important than yourselves."

Although Jonathan says that he never made a public pledge of abstinence, he always knew that he wanted to save sex for marriage. He established boundaries for his sexual behavior by asking himself if his behavior was treating his girlfriend with respect: "It would always be, in the back of my mind, 'Am I treating my girlfriend with honor and respect or how is selfishness playing into this?'" Jonathan acknowledges that in a past relationship, he and his girlfriend did not set clear boundaries. As a result, their physical intimacy accelerated rapidly. The focus of the physical pleasure was on self-gratification. Now a sophomore in college, Jonathan says that he will date again only if he can place the young woman's best interests before his own. Although Jonathan is not talking about pursuing a courtship relationship, he says the next time he dates, it should be with the goal of marriage: "Truly, for me, it's if I'm going to date again, it's going to be definitely with a purpose and definitely knowing that it has to be a conscious choice, like, every day that you have to consider the person more important than yourself, and you can't go about it in a selfish way. Just knowing that dating should be something that should lead towards marriage. I think it shouldn't be something you just do for fun or just for the conquest of it or things like that, that a lot of guys can seem to get caught up in." Respect for the other person helps set the boundaries for physical behavior, since the end goal is marriage.

For some, like Rebecca Blithefield, who is saving her first kiss until her wedding day, the line of appropriate sexual behavior is met much earlier in a relationship than for someone like Jonathan Ebersol, who describes a much more physically intimate dating history. Despite their differing views on specific boundaries, both articulate a view of respect for the other person in their dating or courting relationships that guides them as to where to create appropriate boundaries for their behavior. In the evangelical abstinence context, respect for the other always means no sexual intercourse outside marriage, but as the abstinent teens show, it also can mean everything from no kissing or holding hands to much greater physical intimacy.

For Darcy Sutton and Matt Rowe, accelerated physical intimacy became a problem in their relationship. Physical intimacy in general was not the problem; Darcy was fine with kissing. But things went further than she wanted, when she realized that her body wanted more. She felt out of control in the relationship.

What Darcy didn't tell me, and I learned later in a private conversation with Matt, is that their sexual behavior had threatened to end their relationship. The previous semester they broke off the relationship. Matt tells me that it was largely because their relationship had become "more centered around the physical stuff." Matt starts spinning his cell phone on the table between us as he talks. He acknowledges that he "went off the deep end for awhile" after the breakup. He drank a lot and "did a lot of stupid stuff. . . . I know I had opportunities; I could have run with other girls." I believe him. At twenty-two Matt is tall and athletically built, with sandy blond hair. He spent a night at a friend's house at college and woke up to find a girl kissing him. Although he and Darcy were technically not dating at the time, he was afraid of how Darcy would react. He waited a week to tell her. Matt looks down at the table. He tells me he tries to forget what happened. Darcy and Matt eventually got back together, and they are on track for their white wedding this summer. Matt tells me that, when he was younger, he thought that sexual immorality was the worst sin you could commit. With the wedding only a few months away, the goal is in sight, but the temptation to have sex still lingers. "It's always a struggle," Matt says. "It will not happen until we get married," he says definitively. "That's all I have to say about that."

CHAPTER 5

The Fractured Fairy Tale

When True Love Doesn't Wait

Monica Bonneville, twenty-two, captures attention when she walks into a room. With her Bettie Page bangs and vintage emerald green tulle party dress, Monica doesn't look as much like the homecoming queen as the homecoming queen's bad-girl rival. She is short and curvy, with a sparkling smile and a quick laugh. Her dark red hair, black liquid eyeliner, vintage black patent kitten heels, and candy apple red lips and nails complete the retro-glam look. She looks more like a modern-day pin-up model than a sales clerk at a children's clothing store.

Monica looks hot, and she knows it. Her fashion choices are intentional, but she knows her boundaries. "I'm not going to lie. I love the attention with the way that you dress and the way that you act and the flirtiness. But I never let myself get too involved in it where it was like I couldn't control [myself], where I made poor choices." In this Monica falls right in line with evangelical views on modesty. She is covered up—no cleavage or bare midriff here—and recognizes that her fashion and her body are powerful tools to control the attention of men. She likes to draw guys in, but she doesn't let them get too close. Some might even call her a tease. She prides herself on her reputation as the woman who doesn't let guys touch her, not even a casual hug.

The hour is late, but Monica is full of energy. She speaks quickly, almost nervously, and in full paragraphs. She tells me the story of her life in the manner of one who is still trying to make sense out of the contours of the plot. What is apparent early on is that Monica is a true romantic. She talks about abstinence, sexuality, and her sexual past in fairy-tale terms. She refers to her history with men as her "love story," one that God is writing. She frequently refers to Eric and Leslie Ludy's book *When God Writes Your Love Story,* as influencing her perceptions of her own love story.[1] As she talks, it becomes clear that Monica desperately wanted God to write her love story, but she thought that she would help him out by filling in the blanks. The result was a fractured fairy tale, one without a happy ending.

This study focuses on what makes the evangelical abstinence campaigns so persuasive. In the course of my research I talked with dozens of young people across the country who have pledged abstinence through their participation in events sponsored by groups such as Pure Freedom, Silver Ring Thing, and True Love Waits. But this doesn't mean that all the young people with whom I spoke are still virgins.[2] Broken abstinence commitments can result in broken hearts, as the abstinence campaigns insist and my interview subjects attest. But the reasons for the broken commitments go deeper than just wanting to have fun on a Friday night. I heard stories of personal loss, self-doubt, eating disorders, unwanted pregnancies, severe depression, divorced parents, and sexual abuse. Sex becomes a substitute for self-worth or an escape during times of tragedy. For some the pain of past relationships casts a long shadow over current relationships and complicates forgiveness: What happens to the dream of happily ever after if the prince or princess did not wait? For others the success of their abstinence commitment is causing them pain: What if they never get married and never get to experience the reward of great sex for their years of waiting? Although many evangelical young people subscribe to the fairy-tale story of romance and are happily waiting for their prince or searching for their princess, in real life the tale of true love has many twists and turns.

WRITING THE PERFECT ROMANCE: MONICA BONNEVILLE

Monica Bonneville's story begins like a typical story of a young evangelical. She was raised in a Christian home, and when she was five, she asked Jesus into her heart—twice, just to make sure it stuck. Her whole family would gather in a circle and hold hands for prayer each evening. Monica attended a private Christian school for a few years, and then she was homeschooled through high school. Although she liked going to school in her pajamas, she felt that she was missing out on the social life she saw her friends enjoying. She missed being around boys and being the center of attention. Her older sister, who was not home-schooled until high school, was popular with the boys at school. Monica describes her sister as the cute one, and although Monica idolized her, dressing like her and following her around, Monica acknowledges she sometimes felt overshadowed by her more popular sister. "I always wanted to be pretty, but I knew she'd always be prettier," Monica says, quickly adding, "It was never anything she did. She always did every-thing to build me up and do my makeup or do my hair and, like, tell me the boys liked me."

A turning point came for Monica at a church youth camp when she began to see her sister in a different light. Her sister, while still a virgin, did not know how many guys she had kissed. Soon Monica's friends, all in their early teens, began sleeping with their boyfriends. Monica decided to take a different path and "just really go after God." She decided that she was not going to date or have sex. Her parents had always encouraged her to wait until she was married to have sex. She recalls her parents' talking to her about waiting when she was twelve years old. They gave her a ring with a pearl and diamonds and told her "just to wait and how sacred it could be, not just to my husband [but] also to God." Her new commitment may have been to God, but it also moved her out from under the shadow of her older sister.

She attended an evangelical youth conference and vividly recalls a young woman her age who was standing on the stage with a bouquet of roses. The teen described how dating and sexual activity with dif-ferent guys is like giving away your roses of purity. "By the time you get [to your wedding day], you used to have this beautiful bouquet of flowers the way that God intended it to be, but when you get there, you have one single rose and it looks matted and almost destroyed," Monica says. "But that's all you had left because everything else you handed off to other people. So I never wanted that. I decided that wasn't for me. . . . I wanted to be treasured just the way like God intended me to be treasured."

Being treasured became an important personal theme for Monica, so much so that some might say that she locked herself up and threw away the key. "I was kind of the untouchable little girl. That's what I turned into, because people knew that I wouldn't do [something] even as simple as a kiss or I wouldn't hold your hand." Just as Monica liked the attention from boys because of her appearance, so she liked the new attention that she received from her physically conservative ways.

She decided that the first guy she kissed would be her husband. "I knew that God made who I was supposed to be with. So when that guy came along it was the guy I wanted to kiss." Prompted by the Ludys' book, Monica was on the lookout for the man God had prepared for her. She was convinced that God was writing her love story and was eager to uncover the main plot line.

When she was eighteen, Monica knew that she had found the man she was going to marry. "[He] just fit into everything from the worldly perspective—nice car, looked good, muscles. He was going to go into the same profession as my brother and brother-in-law. So why wouldn't this be it?" She had found her future husband, and so she let him kiss her before she left for camp the summer before she started college. But she ignored his preference for alcohol over God. While she was away, she became more certain that the relationship was not right, that they did not share the same morals and values. She broke it off the day she returned from camp. They had been together one month.

By the end of that summer, still puzzling over the red herring in God's love story for her life, Monica had met Tim. He seemed perfect, especially in comparison with her first boyfriend. They met at a college ministry event, and Monica was immediately attracted by his handsome appearance. As they began talking, she discovered that he loved God and was raised with the same standards as she. She was convinced that Tim was the one she had been waiting for. On their first date, Tim told Monica that he respected her standards and that she could take as long as she needed before she was ready to kiss him. Before the night was over, however, Monica says that he gave her a hug and tried to kiss her. She successfully deflected his advances, at least until the next night. It's okay, she thought. Tim is meant to be my husband. Within a month of starting to date Tim, Monica was taking off her clothes and giving and receiving oral sex.

"I wanted to give my heart away. [And] I did, way too soon." Monica nervously picks at her chipped red nail polish as she tries to make sense of her actions. "I just threw everything into it. I just pretty much, like, 'This is what I saved, so please take it.' I [couldn't] wait to give it away almost, instead of holding on to it and really praying about it and really making sure," she says, her voice trailing off.

Monica knew that what she was doing was wrong, but she desired the physical intimacy. She was reluctant at first to perform oral sex, but she says that she felt as if she owed it to him and this was the only way she could get him to hold her. Adding to her confusion, she acknowledges, was that the sexual desire in the relationship was not one-sided: "Once [your sexual desire] is awakened, once you know what it feels like, then you want to do it. I just wish I would have never done that because it was so hard to lay there with him at night and not feel like I wanted to do everything. I'd wake up almost every day [and] I'd cry or almost every day I'd talk to him. 'I can't do this. This is not what I want to do.'" Monica rationalized her conflicted feelings: on one of their first dates Monica explained that she was waiting for the right person, and Tim said that he was, too. This must be it. Their sexual activity was justified because both were experiencing it for the first time. Or so she thought.

A year later the relationship reached its breaking point when Tim revealed that he had been sexually active—including having sexual intercourse—with five girlfriends in the past. Monica was crushed. She felt betrayed. Instead of leaving him, she prayed for God to give her the strength to forgive him. "I went back out with him because my heart was attached and I thought I loved him. I wanted to marry him. I was connected to him because of the physical aspect. I promised myself whoever I did anything with, that was who God [had planned for me to marry]. . . . I only wanted to give my heart away one time. I never wanted to be the girl with the [damaged] bouquet of roses."

Tim accepted a job offer across the country but promised to marry Monica within the year. The physical separation gave Monica the courage to tell Tim that she knew God had called her to serve in Christian ministry to young girls and that she couldn't stay in a relationship with him and serve God at the same time. But the physical separation did not end their physical relationship. She would periodically travel to visit him, and "if I was with him, I was messing up again," she says. Privately, Monica wondered how God was going to be able to use her anymore. When she was younger, she felt that God was calling her to share her story with other girls about waiting for God's best, because God was writing her love story. Now she wondered if it was too late.

Then God gave her an epiphany. "It was the dumbest epiphany ever," she acknowledges, "and I should have figured it out way before I was in a relationship." She used to pray, asking God why she was unable to resist temptation when she was with Tim. "Am I not stronger than my hormones?" she would ask. God answered by telling her that she is not meant to be strong in those times. "You're supposed to have that desire to be intimate in those ways. And so you're never going to be strong when you put yourself alone with a guy you care about. . . . You're never going to be strong because you're not made to be strong, because when you're married, you don't have to [be strong]." Monica says she now understands why God made sex for marriage.

Things did not change overnight. She liked that her relationship with Tim—the travel, the gifts—made her stand out, just like her emerald green dress. She was convinced that God had placed her in Tim's life to help him be the man God wanted him to be. She found it difficult to acknowledge that her story was not turning out the way she had thought. Soon after their two-year anniversary, Tim broke up with her. Even so, she prayed desperately that God would repair the relationship.

Although the breakup happened more than ten months ago, it's clear that the wound is still fresh. Monica tries to process what went wrong. "I planned out my life, and that was my first mistake," she says. "I planned out my story, and that was the worst thing I could have ever done for myself. Instead of giving myself completely to God, I gave myself to God but told him I was going to write my life story." She now sees her pride in being the "untouchable girl" as contributing to her downfall. Despite the tears, she says that the heartache was worth it, because she traded her false intimacy with Tim for true intimacy with God. "[It's] like the relationship I always wanted but I never knew what it meant when people said find the intimacy with God. . . . I'm like, you can't be intimate. Intimacy is sex. Intimacy is physical. And I can't have that with God, so that's weird. But intimacy is so much deeper than that. It was just the fellowship of knowing he loved me for me, and he loved me just because he created me. And I've never felt more of a peace in my life."

GOD IS MY BOYFRIEND

Through the breakup in her relationship with Tim, Monica found a new relationship: burned by an earthly romance, she found a divine romance with God. Here she presents God as a boyfriend discovered on the rebound. Only after realizing that Tim could not give her the intimacy she longed for, she discovered that intimacy in God. Lynn S. Neal, in her study of readers and writers of evangelical romance novels, found that the ideal love stories portrayed in the novels teach their female readers about God's divine, unfailing love for them. She writes that the romance novels portray God as "the ultimate lover who pursues them and will always be there for them." Romance novels are a prime example of the pervasiveness of the fairy-tale narrative in evangelical culture: the dashing hero who saves the heroine—regardless of what she has done—is symbolic of the creator God's unconditional love for his people. Readers' spiritual lives are strengthened by stories of God's romantic pursuit, and readers' increased faith romances God in return.[3]

For some young people, focusing on a divine romance with God can function as a substitute for (or avoidance of) earthly romances. As one of my evangelical male college students told me, girls have turned him down for dates because, as they put it, they are too busy dating Jesus. It can also set up an unachievable model for heterosexual relationships: How can your boyfriend's attempts at romance compare with God's unconditional love? The difference between the role of the romancing God in evangelical book clubs and that in evangelical sexual abstinence campaigns is subtle but significant. Romance readers use the idealistic stories to deepen their understanding of biblical descriptions of a God who is love. Abstinent teens tend to use the biblical descriptions of God's divine love as a model for their earthly relationships, which will inevitably fail in comparison.

Monica insists that God has now given her a new story. "And I kind of am liking this story better because more people can relate to it," she says. "It's not the 'I did it the perfect way so you can do it the perfect way,' because life's not perfect. Life's hard, and the choices you make are hard. And life's decisions are sometimes you have regrets and you can't go back. You really can't go back. But you can move forward."

Monica has moved forward into a new relationship. She met Scott Schultze at church as he was ending a relationship, three months after her own relationship ended with Tim. Monica likes that Scott listens to her and sends her text messages saying that he is thinking about her. She likes that they pray together and receive counseling from their church's young adult pastor and his wife. She likes that he was willing to give her high fives instead of hugs. She insists that she is taking things slow this time. They waited a month before their first kiss, and even then she was reluctant to stretch her newly restored boundaries. She insists that she has not given him her heart. "God has my heart, not him. . . . Am I falling for him? Absolutely. Is it scaring me? Absolutely. But it's the kind of falling in love I always dreamed of and never knew existed."

THE CHALLENGES OF BEING PRINCE CHARMING: SCOTT SCHULTZE

While Monica was helping God write her love story, Scott was searching for comfort after a string of personal tragedies. He found it in sex and alcohol.

I first met Monica and Scott at their church before a Silver Ring Thing event. Scott, twenty-five, is a marketing consultant with an easy smile and movie-star stubble. We arranged times for me to talk with them separately. I talked with Monica at the church later that night, and I met Scott the following morning at a family friend's condo that he had offered to paint. I sat in the middle of the empty living room floor as he rolled light beige paint on the walls and told me his story.

Scott has all the makings of a Prince Charming. From his physical build it's easy to tell that Scott was a jock in high school. He participated in four sports and edited the school newspaper. Scott, who remembers praying in the backseat of the family car and asking Jesus to be his savior when he was four, regularly volunteered with a Christian after-school sports program for at-risk youth. Weekends usually brought outdoor activities like riding his motorcycle and hiking with buddies or just hanging out at someone's house and watching movies. Scott's faith and his friends were important to him.

Scott dated in high school, but it was never anything serious. Although his church youth group never talked about sexuality, Scott was committed to abstinence because his parents taught him that you are not supposed to have sex until marriage. Some students at his high school were into the party scene, but none of his friends was having sex. "It was kind of just understood you don't do that," he says. Scott first heard about Silver Ring Thing from a friend in college, but he wasn't impressed. "I just thought, 'Well, I don't need to wear a stupid ring. I know I'm going to save myself. Like, what's the point of going to one of these things and putting that ring on? That's just stupid,'" Scott recalls. "[The] Lord has opened my eyes on some stuff since then," he adds.

During his senior year, a string of tragedies—including two fatal car crashes—shook Scott's small town. After the most recent tragedy Scott was scheduled to share his testimony during the worship service at his church. He sensed that a lot of people were questioning God, wondering why he would let these deaths occur. In front of a packed house Scott shared his faith and challenged the crowd to ask God what he was trying to show them through this, not just why he was doing this to them. "He doesn't have to justify himself. He is God," Scott told the few hundred people gathered in the church. "And it's not that he is the one that caused these deaths to happen. So we needed to trust in that." Scott was also upset by the recent deaths, but he still had his faith in God, and it felt good to share it with others. "God really used me," he recalls. "I was really able to help a lot of people."

Two months later one of Scott's close friends died in a motorcycle accident. For Scott this was the final straw. "Everything I just spoke on . . . was just out the window," he says. "Like I couldn't believe anything anymore that I said. My heart just got, like, instantly numbed and hardened to God." As he tells me his story, Scott continues to roll the paint on the wall of the condo. He doesn't pause to turn around. His friend's mother asked him to help carry the casket at the funeral. "That is the worst thing in the world, to have to be a pallbearer at your best friend's funeral. That's an indescribable thing," he says, to the even pace of the paint roller.

Scott, who had wanted to be a youth pastor when he was in high school, received more opportunities to share his testimony. Before Scott headed off to college, a youth pastor offered him a position as an assistant. Scott turned him down. "I know my heart's not right. I'm going to go to college. I'm going to want to party. I'm going to want to drink. And I wouldn't feel right doing that and trying to pour into kids' lives and stuff. I'd just feel like a hypocrite so I turned him down," he says. But he did accept some opportunities to speak at youth retreats. "It's just embarrassing to say that I went there and spoke, and I wasn't really able to buy into anything I was speaking on," Scott now says.

Scott went away to college, and his life was soon filled with alcohol and girls. He lost his virginity in a one-night stand. "There was nothing remotely special about it," Scott recalls. "It was just a searching for something . . . other than God." His college friends all knew that he had been a virgin, and no one was surprised when he caved. Scott felt ashamed that he had violated his standards, but now that he had messed up, it was easier the next time. He's had four sexual relationships since then.

With one girlfriend Scott tried to reset his standards, and he told her that he was not going to have sex with her. The girl, who was a virgin, knew that Scott had slept with other girls and didn't understand why he would refuse to sleep with her. She insisted that Scott was the one for her and that she was ready to give her heart to him. It became a wedge in their relationship. Scott eventually gave in and they had sex. The relationship didn't last.

At about this time a campus minister helped guide Scott back to his faith in God. Scott was raised in the church and realized that he knew all the right answers as a Christian, but his heart was not in the right place. "I call it Christianese. Like you just knew what to say. You knew how you were supposed to fool people. And I was ending up fooling myself in the process," he says. Even though he was starting back on the right track, Scott did not change overnight. He met an attractive Christian girl and vowed not to have sex again until he was married. He explained to her what he valued in a relationship, and she respected him for it. Because they both trusted their Christian commitment, Scott now sees that they put themselves in situations where they thought they could push the limits physically and nothing would happen. Regular sexual intercourse soon followed.

Scott began attending a new church, and the youth minister helped him to see that he had to end the relationship. "It's incredible how many fresh starts God can give you," he says. When I ask him what abstinence means to him now, he replies, "[It's the] opportunity to do right again—to correct what I screwed up before." Soon after Scott started attending the new church, Monica caught his eye. Part of the attraction is Monica's desire to serve other people. He says that he is surprised she even was willing to talk with him. He says that he feels like a T-ball player swinging for the fences in the major leagues. But he explained to her that he was not ready to rush into a relationship. They began talking on the phone each evening for hours at a time and reading the Psalms together. They run together and have even bungee-jumped together. "We're not the typical dinner-and-a-movie kind of couple," Scott says with a laugh. They mostly see each other at church, where they both are actively involved in the young adult ministry.

Although the couple is seeking after God, their sexual pasts cast long shadows. Scott knows that Monica has done everything but have sex. She acknowledges that his sexual past is difficult for her to overcome, because she technically waited and he didn't. He can tell that she is concerned about being compared with his former girlfriends. He insists that there is no comparison, but it's clear she doesn't quite believe him. Scott says he knows that God has forgiven him his sexual past, that he has a "clean slate, and it's out of God's memory," but Scott finds it difficult not to condemn himself when he sees how his past is hurting Monica. He has to remind himself and Monica that this time is different, that this time their relationship is centered on God. Last year they attended a Silver Ring Thing event and purchased abstinence rings. They've written down a list of their sexual boundaries. Sex is not an option for either of them. "We're making sure it's not going to happen," Scott says.

Whether they have sex or not, both Scott and Monica bring complicated sexual pasts to the relationship that may make things difficult going forward. But both are sincere in their Christian faith and are surrounding themselves with accountability partners and a caring community of support. The time I spent with Monica and Scott illustrates for me why so many of the statistical studies on abstinence pledges feel inadequate: the binary categories are too black-and-white, assuming that one is either abstinent or sexually active. For the young people with whom I spoke, like Scott and Monica, abstinence and sexual intercourse are two ends of a gray spectrum. The abstinence pledge is more akin to the evangelical's born-again commitment to Jesus Christ. A Christian does not cease being a Christian because she struggles with sinful behavior, just as a young person may pledge abstinence while still struggling with sexual behavior. For a sexually active teen an abstinence pledge may represent a desire for a change in lifestyle, but the change may not happen overnight.

WHEN THE CHINA TEACUP GETS CHIPPED: HANNAH BATTEN

Hannah Batten does not look like a rebel. Petite and attractive, with blond hair and bright blue eyes, she responds politely and thoughtfully to all my questions. Her story begins like so many others: She was raised in a Christian home with three younger siblings. She accepted Christ as her personal savior when she was five. Church was a regular part of her life, although she remembers it as kind of boring when she was a child. She says that she hated high school and wasn't really into academics, but she enjoyed playing on the soccer team.

Hannah never dated much and was generally known as a "good girl." She took an abstinence pledge as a member of her church's high school youth group. Her boundaries were set. Hannah's few dating relationships lasted a couple of months each and mostly amounted to going to movies and holding hands. Her spiritual faith and church involvement continued to be an important part of her life. During this time Hannah says that she was "very much for God."

She went on a mission trip to Haiti the summer before her senior year of high school. What was intended to be a spiritually uplifting experience ended up contributing to a crisis of faith for Hannah. She returned from the mission trip to find that her best friend had started dating her ex-boyfriend. She says that they "pushed her around," and even friends from her church youth group turned against her. Now, ten years later, as Hannah and I sit in Starbucks sipping hot tea, she stumbles over her words and struggles to describe the pain fully. She acknowledges that it seems petty now, "but it drove me away from the whole church thing." Looking back, she says that she was "sick of being the good girl all the time."

Once during her senior year she and a male friend had sex. She doesn't remember how or why it happened, but she knew that she was tired of trying to live up to the expectations of being a good Christian girl. The relationship lasted for a couple of months. I ask her what her abstinence commitment meant to her then. "What am I going to do about it now?" she wondered at the time. "I can't get [my virginity] back." She felt she had "screwed up too bad."

After high school Hannah got involved with the wrong crowd and smoked pot and drank too much. She moved out of her parents' house when she was nineteen and began attending community college. She started dating another guy. How would she characterize the relationship? She grimaces, then laughs. "Where do I start?" He was "white trash," never had a car, always needed a job. "I was his mother," she says. The sexual relationship connected them, and they dated for three and a half years. He turned out to be a drug addict. Hannah ended the relationship with her boyfriend when she dropped him off at a rehabilitation center. She says that she felt as though she had strayed so far from her abstinence commitment that she didn't know how—if ever—she would get back.

Hannah continued with a string of damaging relationships. After college she thought that she had hit rock bottom. She still partied a lot, but she felt drawn back to church at the invitation of a friend. Slowly, things began looking up for Hannah. She felt that her life was getting back on track.

Within a few months she met a good Christian guy. They attended the same church and worked at the same shopping mall. But, Hannah now ruefully adds, "Boys will be boys." She later discovered that he was addicted to pornography. "I thought he was this nice Christian boy," she says. Since she had been in sexual relationships in the past, she didn't know how else to be loved. "I thought he loved me, but he was a very selfish person." She recognizes that they brought out the worst in each other. A year and a half later, she was happy to end it. Reflecting on the relationship, Hannah says that she wanted a relationship with a godly man. What she found was a boyfriend who went to church with her but became a different person when he wanted sex. She couldn't put it into words. It was lust, pure and simple, she says.

While she was still dating the not-so-perfect Christian guy, she volunteered at a Silver Ring Thing event hosted by her church. Her boyfriend did not go, but she bought a ring for herself and one for him, too. She thinks he never wore it. She enjoyed the program but felt uncomfortable because of her past sexual experiences. Although she made a commitment to abstinence that night, she continued in her sexual relationship with her boyfriend. She says that she didn't actually think it was possible to be in an abstinent relationship. "Now I don't know how you could not," she says. "It was always about us—our own ability—trying not to have sex. We need the help of God."

It has been nine months since her last relationship ended, and she has not dated anyone since. Does she think that God is preparing someone for her or is she content in her singleness? "I'm ready to find the man I'm going to marry. I think that's what I wanted all along." This time she would create strict boundaries for the physical relationship. She has moved back in with her parents, which she acknowledges will make it more difficult to be alone with a guy. Hannah, who is now twenty-six, recently started work as an administrative assistant at a Christian school. It's important to surround yourself with good people, she says.

Throughout our conversation it's clear that Hannah still carries the burden of her sexual past. I ask her if she feels that God has forgiven her. She pauses and looks down at her tea. "Yeah," she answers tentatively, "but sometimes I can't believe the things I did." She brushes her hair out of her eyes. "He forgets your past. We still remember it, of course."

Those who look askance at abstinence campaigns may blame Hannah's lingering guilt and pain on the campaigns themselves. The problem is not sex, they may say, but the unrealistic standard of waiting for sex that is thrust on teens by the church. If Hannah were to reframe sex as something positive and not something that a "bad girl" would do, she could spare herself the pain she now feels regarding her past choices. The sociologist Laura M. Carpenter, in her book *Virginity Lost,* advocates such a reframing. She declares that her study "represents an empirically based challenge to the claim that virginity loss before marriage, or during adolescence, inevitably causes physical and psychological harm."[4] True, sex before marriage may not inevitably cause harm; in fact, one of the implicit fallacies perpetuated by the evangelical sexual abstinence movement is that sex before marriage will inevitably feel both emotionally and physically awful.[5] If sex is so great, wouldn't it be great all the time, both in and out of marriage? As Hannah's story shows, as do the stories of other young people with whom I spoke, sex before marriage may cause physical and/or psychological harm to some. One solution apparently would be to change one's view of virginity loss to eliminate the accompanying shame. Carpenter identifies three main metaphors that her interview subjects use to describe their virginity—as a gift, a stigma, and a rite of passage—along with a fourth metaphor—virginity as an act of worship—which appears in only two of her sixty-one interviews.[6] Carpenter concludes her study by pointing out that "men and women who view virginity loss as the most significant event of their sexual careers may be more likely to experience adverse outcomes than people who do not see virginity loss as uniquely important."[7]

The solution, it seems, is to devalue virginity, in essence, to change the rules if the rules do not accommodate one's desires. Carpenter advocates a process orientation to virginity loss, and she suggests that those who view virginity as a gift or stigma reframe their interpretation so that virginity loss is a natural step in becoming an adult, no shame required. Arguably, abstinent evangelicals also view virginity loss as a rite of passage, except that the rite is celebrated by the wedding ceremony. Yet Carpenter's approach of self-interested metaphor switching is problematic for religious young people who seek to shape their identities by living in accordance with a set of biblical standards outside their control. For evangelical young people, the solution is not to value virginity less but to value God more. Evangelical theology provides for the inevitable feelings of shame and guilt by emphasizing God's redemption and forgiveness when one fails to live up to the biblical standard. Indeed, a central tenet of evangelical theology focuses on the life, sacrificial death, and bodily resurrection of Jesus Christ, the son of God, on behalf of the sins of the world. On the other hand, if evangelicals placed less value on abstinence and the avoidance of nonmarital virginity loss, perhaps the wedding ceremony could indeed mark the beginning of the marriage and not merely the long-awaited moment of sexual debut. As it stands, the high value placed on abstinence threatens to devalue marriage, making it just about sex. Carpenter concludes her book with this final charge: "We would do well to give teenagers the tools to help make their virginity-loss experiences as healthy, safe, and happy as possible."[8] Evangelical abstinence campaigns have heeded the charge, insisting that the only healthy, safe, and happy way to enjoy sex is in marriage. The problem with this persuasive message, as discussed in previous chapters, is that although the timing of sexual debut is different for evangelicals, it's still about sex as a tool for the individual's personal happiness. In practice, according to the young people I spoke with, the commitment to abstinence is a sacrifice and may bring pain and loneliness.

To borrow a metaphor from Pure Freedom, it's difficult to repair a broken china teacup. Like Hannah, many of the young people with whom I spoke who had broken their abstinence pledges felt that they themselves were broken or damaged goods; they might as well keep having sex. While the evangelical abstinence rhetoric insists that God forgives and that virginity can be found again, a number of young people like Hannah still find it difficult to forgive themselves.

FORGIVING THE FROG

If Hannah Batten started out as a member of the Good Christian Girls' Club, Samantha Adams would be its club president. She was raised in a Christian home and made a pledge for abstinence at a Silver Ring Thing event in the ninth grade. To Samantha, abstinence means not just waiting to have sex but remaining "pure before the Lord," which includes avoiding the murky areas of permissible sexual activity, such as fondling, French kissing, and oral sex. "If holding hands feels sexual, then that's not pure," she says. Samantha decided in high school not to date, since she understood that the purpose of dating was to find a husband, and "I don't think it will ever stick with these boys," she thought at the time.

When I ask Samantha, who is now twenty and a junior in college, if she has ever had a boyfriend, she tells me with an embarrassed giggle that she and her "best guy friend," Thomas, had just decided two days earlier that they would begin dating. They met their freshman year of college in their art and biology classes. He had just broken up with a girlfriend, and their personalities clicked immediately. She soon discovered, however, that her prince was actually a frog. The former girlfriend came back into the picture and announced that she was pregnant. Thomas and his former lover tried to repair the relationship for the sake of the child but were unsuccessful. Now Thomas has a fourteen-month-old son.

Second or renewed virginity is a key theme in the evangelical sexual abstinence campaigns.[9] The message of second virginity centers on the power of God's forgiveness, which gives individuals the power to forgive themselves. None of the campaigns, however, addresses how to forgive someone else for lost-and-found virginity.

Samantha sounds matter-of-fact as she recounts her story, but she acknowledges that she was upset when she found out. "It was a hard thing to deal with, but love covers a multitude of sins," she says. After attending a recent Silver Ring Thing event at her church, she says she came home and "God and I had a good cry. I thought it wasn't fair that I had made a choice that [Thomas] didn't." Although Samantha is still a virgin, she realized that Thomas was not the only one who had sinned. "His sin happened to be sexual and mine are other things. God brought some peace about it." She says that at least she doesn't have to worry if he will be a good father someday.

Before their decision to date, Samantha and Thomas consulted their young adult pastor and spent one month in individual prayer about it. At the end of the month Thomas, accompanied by his son, drove Samantha back to her campus dorm room, where they prayed together. When they were finished, Thomas asked her if the decision to date was official, and Samantha replied that it was. She tells me that "God showed me that I was emotionally ready, and he helped me overcome all my hesitations." Samantha and her mother babysat Thomas's son recently, after which she felt more secure about being able to raise a stepson.

Samantha says that she and Thomas have set boundaries for their physical relationship. They have agreed that holding hands and hugging are fine but not a lot of cuddling. A goodnight kiss is okay if it's just a goodnight kiss. And no sex before marriage. She says that Thomas renewed a commitment to abstinence after his son was born. He doesn't wear an abstinence ring, but she insists that he wants to. He wanted them to get rings together at the recent Silver Ring Thing event at their church, but she didn't feel comfortable since they were not officially dating yet. They will probably order rings together now, she says.

Samantha is convinced that "the purpose of dating is to find your potential spouse, and it is not a subject to be taken lightly." They have been dating for only two days but have already talked about how many children they want to have and where they want to live. She acknowledges with a laugh that they are taking things a bit too fast and that she doesn't want to have that conversation again for awhile.

Forgiving but Not Forgetting

Jodi Simmons's current boyfriend had sex with a previous girlfriend in high school. She insists that it does not make her feel second best because she knows that God has forgiven him. "See, I really don't, I don't feel inferior or I don't think about it, like, it doesn't bother me, because I know his life is different and that God has changed his life and changed his heart and forgiven him for that. But he has a hard time, still sometimes, accepting the forgiveness," Jodi says.

God may have forgiven her boyfriend, but the young man's inability to forgive himself is causing problems in their relationship. "It's really hard," Jodi says. "We've gone through a lot of rocky times, just because he, it holds him back in a lot of areas, and it really condemns him still a lot, and it causes him to be, get, really scared in relationships and stuff like that, so, it's really, really been, it's been, it's really been hard." Despite the difficulties, Jodi says that she could marry someone like her boyfriend who is not a virgin. "I don't see that when I look at him or when I think about him, like, I see a forgiven person," she insists. "One thing Dannah [Gresh, the founder of Pure Freedom] talks about at her retreat is quote unquote second virginity and which is, if you've already messed up like that, you can be pure again, like, in God's eyes and stuff. That's kind of how I feel."

About six months into her relationship with her boyfriend, Amanda Carter, twenty-six, learned during a phone conversation with him that he had had sex. He had been talking about previous girlfriends, and when Amanda asked him if he had had sex, she recalls that it got "real quiet" on the phone. Amanda, who signed a True Love Waits pledge card in 1996, says that she felt sick to her stomach. Not that she was head over heels in love with him at that point, but "it broke my heart because I had had this vision, or I had had this expectation, that whoever I would marry would be a virgin and would have that same commitment that I had." He said that he had asked God to forgive him, and he asked Amanda to do the same. She says it took her awhile to work through it, but she decided that if God could forgive her boyfriend, she should, too. The couple stayed together for a year, then broke up. He wasn't very mature in his faith, she says, and his previous sexual experience was hard for her to deal with.

But "God worked on both of our hearts," Amanda says. The two continued attending the same church, and she noticed that he was growing spiritually. Although he had already said that he was done with sex until marriage, he signed a True Love Waits pledge card online. He could do it because "it doesn't say anything about past. It says it's from this day forward." Soon after, the couple married.

Amanda Carter says that the commitment she and her husband made to purity during their dating relationship has helped them in their marriage, because their marriage is not based solely on physical attraction and desire. Yet Amanda acknowledges that every so often she thinks about her husband's having had sex with somebody else. She doesn't worry that he is comparing her with other women, since he had sex with only one and it happened so long ago, but "I can't say that I've never thought about it again and thought about him being with somebody else, because that's—," she pauses. "I've thought about it. It's popped in my mind, but I just kind of have gotten over it or just accepted God's forgiveness for that. But it has come to mind, I guess."

The evangelical abstinence campaigns promote the ability of anyone to choose abstinence, whether he or she has been abstinent in the past or not; but as the stories of Jodi Simmons and Amanda Carter illustrate, second virginity is not the "get out of jail free" card that it can appear to be. Sometimes forgiveness does not erase doubts and emotional baggage that can be carried into marriage.

Memories of Sexual Abuse

Jessica Ralston, twenty-one, found freedom from emotional baggage through second virginity, not because she had had nonmarital sex but because she had experienced sexual abuse as a child. Jessica was among the first to make a commitment to abstinence through True Love Waits in 1993. Six months later a close family friend began sexually abusing her. Jessica says that she experienced a great deal of hurt and wondered if she was "damaged goods." She wondered if her period of sexual abuse rendered her abstinence commitment invalid. She says that she was tempted to become sexually active because she did not want her last memory of a sexual experience to be an abusive one. She figured that she was already messed up, so she might as well try to fill the empty hole in her heart.

Thankfully, Jessica says, she began to experience God's healing in her life as she realized that she did not choose to break her abstinence commitment. "You know what, even though if somebody else might have taken things that belonged to you, I didn't give that to them," she says. "So there is a difference in giving . . . I can say, I can still tell him, I didn't give away what belonged to you, and there can be forgiveness in that." Jessica's commitment to abstinence helped her realize that her virginity was a gift, and she had not lost it or given it away. Her virginity was taken away. She realized that actively engaging in sexual relationships would only add to her pain.

Jessica Ralston says she has a newfound compassion for those who haven't been able to live up to their abstinence commitment, because "Christ's righteousness . . . covers you." She says that she has friends who are struggling with past sexual abuse and wishes that the church would talk about it more. She likes the True Love Waits emphasis on second virginity. She respects her friends who have committed to second virginity, "because I think that once you've had sex, my friend told me one time, she was, like, 'It's like pushing a button that you can never turn off again,' and she was, like, 'It's just really hard.'" Although she is not currently dating anyone, Jessica acknowledges that she may not end up marrying a virgin, but she is okay with that. On the other hand, she says, "nobody likes to be compared."

Sadly, Jessica's story is not unusual. I spoke with other young people—both men and women—who had been sexually abused. Although all have moved on in their lives, the memory of the pain still lingers. The message of second virginity is a central and important part of the abstinence campaigns, just as the gospel message itself is one of hope for the broken and repentant. No one is left out, even if that person has willingly lost her or his virginity or had it taken. Abstinence is a daily, renewable choice. The campaigns present second virginity as a message of hope, but the reality is not quite as rosy. Second virgins are struggling with the challenges of forgiveness, painful memories, and deep regrets.

WHEN THE PRINCE NEVER SHOWS UP: THE SILENCE ON SINGLENESS

Sex as the reward for abstinence may be a slam dunk for the chastity campaigns, but virtually none of the organizations in this study deals head-on with the challenge of singleness. It's one thing to pledge abstinence as a teenager when one's Friday nights are typically spent home alone with popcorn and a DVD instead of in the backseat of a car with a member of the opposite sex. It's another thing altogether to maintain that pledge into adulthood, through college and career, with no Mr. or Ms. Right in sight. It's the ultimate dilemma of the forty-year-old virgin.

"It's like singleness has a stigma about it," says Heather Hunter, who is twenty-six and single. "If you're not married by twenty-seven, then you're an old maid."

I met Heather in one of those awkward moments when both of us were alone in a crowd, and the flow of humanity pushed us together. It was a Sunday evening gathering of the young adult group at a large evangelical church. More than a hundred young adults were packed into a self-styled club in one wing of the church building. Contemporary Christian music videos played on television screens suspended from the ceiling. Café tables and booths with vinyl-covered benches filled one side of the room, as small groups of young men and women munched on chips and sipped sodas. Menus behind the bar featured candy and fast food, but tonight someone had donated the food, and large trays of make-it-yourself nachos lined the countertop. People looking for more substance than popcorn could purchase a Christian book at the other end of the bar, on topics ranging from discovering the power of the Holy Spirit to finding a soul mate. The other side of the room featured arcade video games and pool tables. The atmosphere was more like a Saturday night party than a Sunday night church group.

Heather is tall and willowy and seemed relatively shy. She spoke quietly in the noisy room, acknowledging that "large crowds of unfamiliar people scare me." She appeared to be alone. We chatted about the evening, and I asked Heather about the Silver Ring Thing event her church had hosted the night before. She told me that she had gone, "just to check it out. I was smug about going . . . I think it was designed for high school students." But she bought an abstinence ring at the event, which she wears on her left hand. "I thought it would be a good tool—an outward symbol of my abstinence. I tell my friends it's my waiting ring."

Soon we all were ushered into the sanctuary for the service. The senior pastor of the church was the evening's guest speaker, continuing with a theme of biblical sexuality. Heather and I sat together and agreed to talk by phone again later.

Heather is educated and has a full-time job, but she has never dated much. Her only dating relationship lasted a month during her freshman year of high school. Usually, she and a group of friends would go to the school dances together. Besides, between extracurricular activities and a part time job, she was too busy to date, she tells me. Following graduation from a Christian college, she began working on a master's degree in physical therapy. Still no dates. She now works in a private clinic and lives at home with her two older siblings; her dad, who is retired from General Mills after more than thirty years of service; and her mom, a homemaker. Her parents "kind of coexist," Heather says.

As she tells me her impressions of the abstinence event the night before, she says that she was particularly moved by the testimony of the young woman who talked about singleness. Heather could relate to the loneliness. She says that all her friends are either married or in relationships, and she has felt left out. "I hadn't quite come to terms with my singleness," she told me. But then she read a book talking about how singleness is a gift, and she realized that "I can use this time to grow my relationship with Christ." What does she think about all her friends' getting married? "Now that doesn't bother me. Eventually it will happen."

She acknowledges that she hasn't heard many church sermons about singleness. "They try not to focus on it," she says wryly. She feels as though her family is embarrassed that she is still single. Neither of her adult siblings is married, either, but at least they are in relationships.

Heather assures me that "I am content in my singleness," but she has filled out a profile with eHarmony, the Christian online dating service, anyway. "It doesn't really work," she says, giving an example of a match with someone who is old enough to be her father. What if Mr. Right never comes along? Heather hesitates. "Maybe God is calling me to singleness." Then she adds, "I kind of think that this is temporary. That there is someone out there for me." She is waiting and trusting God. "Because he wrote the book; I didn't."

Heather's friend Laurel, who is eighteen, also does not date and wonders if this is a sign of things to come. She equivocates about whether she wishes she were dating right now, as if she is trying to convince herself as much as she is trying to convince me: "As much as I really, really desire that, because I feel like I'm old enough now where I'm of age, I don't think it would be good for me right now, as in, like, this school year, I think I have some growing to do, and I think, yeah, that's what I think, as much as I desire it, [and] I truly desire that a lot."

Laurel has led a fairly sheltered life. She and her two younger sisters were homeschooled in the suburbs. Now she lives at home and attends community college between regular babysitting jobs. She doesn't know yet what she wants to study. She had thought at one time of getting a psychology degree and going into Christian counseling, but now she is thinking that maybe she should go into education. She accepted Christ as her savior when she was four years old, but she says that she made a real commitment when she was eleven years old at a church summer camp. She made a commitment to "give him her whole life." Two years later, when she was thirteen, Laurel and a friend attended a Silver Ring Thing event at a nearby church. She says that her family had talked a lot about purity in the home, but she had never been to an event where they talked so openly about sex. She was also surprised by the "hilariousness" of it. One of the testimonies had a particular impact on her: she remembers a young woman saying that she pictured herself on her wedding day in a white dress with nothing cluttering her mind. Laurel made a commitment to abstinence that night and bought a ring. She still wears it. "It sounds weird, but I never take it off. I have quite a tan line," she laughs. Some kids she babysits ask what the ring means. She tells them, "I'm saving myself for my future husband."

Last winter she and her mother and sister went on a mother-daughter cruise sponsored by *Brio* magazine, a periodical for young women that was formerly published by the conservative Christian organization Focus on the Family. Dannah Gresh, the founder of Pure Freedom, was the keynote speaker. Laurel recalls that Dannah talked about modesty. "Whenever we dress immodestly, we are intoxicating men," she says. Laurel, wearing jeans and a scoop-necked T-shirt, describes her own look as classic, saying that she shops at Ann Taylor and J. Crew.

Laurel enjoys spending time with her family. She plays tennis with her sister and enjoys running and swimming. Right now, she and her family are watching the BBC series *Pride and Prejudice*, rented through Netflix. She loves going out to eat, particularly Chinese food. Most of her friends are away at college, but when they get together, they often go out for dinner and a movie. Laurel has never been in a dating relationship. She's not sure whether this is because of her parents' influence or her personality. She wonders if it is because her dad has been a significant part of her life. Her dad is the parent who takes Laurel and her sister shopping for clothes. They always head straight for the clearance rack, because they know that's where he wants them to look. "He tells us what he thinks is appropriate. He really does have a good sense of fashion," she quickly adds. A couple of times a year, each daughter will have a special night out with Dad, like dinner and a movie. Laurel's friends aren't dating either, and she says that she hasn't been exposed to coed groups. She began attending the young adult group at her church a few months ago, which she acknowledges is a different atmosphere than she's used to. "It's not a dating ministry. There's no pressure, . . . but definitely it's a good place to find somebody, if you know what I mean."

Like her friend Heather, Laurel is convinced that this season of singleness is allowing her to focus on her relationship with God and to discover his purposes for her life. "I think I need to become more grounded in what he has for me and trusting him with my life and my future," she says. "As opposed, like, if I was with somebody, if I had a boyfriend, I think a lot of my time and energy would go to that relationship as opposed to just affirming my relationship in Christ and knowing that I'm going to trust him with my life and where I'm going to be going in the future."

Laurel hesitates when I ask her about the possibility of a lifetime of singleness. "As bad as I think that sounds right now, I know that whatever God has for me is going to be his best. I don't think I would like that at first if I realized that, you know, maybe I was called to a life of singleness. I think that that would be a huge place where I would need to grow in being content with that, but I'm just going to have whatever God wants for me, basically." She pauses. "But it would be very difficult."

Young people like Heather and Laurel, who claim that their singleness is a calling from God, are just fooling themselves, according to a new and provocative crop of Christian books for young women aimed at promoting marriage. They argue that single women are just trying to make themselves feel better despite their bad situation. Debbie Maken, author of *Getting Serious about Getting Married,* uses scriptural references to argue that singleness is unnatural because "*it is God's will for people to marry.*"[10] She takes issue with the idea of singleness as a gift when "it's the kind of gift that makes us cringe and smile politely while we desperately search for a gift receipt so we can return it." Virginity may be a gift, but some single Christian women in their late twenties are angry about their abstinence commitments, wondering why they should give their diligently saved virginity as a reward to a man who waited so long to marry, which has made the woman lose precious years of companionship, sex, and perhaps fertility.[11]

Although Maken, a self-described homemaker and conservative Christian, supports abstinence, she states matter-of-factly why it doesn't work: "First, the vow of abstinence is on a collision course with teens' very nature, and, second, they have no hope [of ever being married]." Her first point sounds similar to abstinence opponents' claims that teens are bound to have sex sooner or later because that is the way their bodies are hardwired. Although evangelical abstinence supporters use this argument to fuel their counterclaim that teens can choose to control their bodies and wait for sex, the overall message of the abstinence campaigns supports their opponents' view: God made individuals as sexual beings; therefore, sex is good. The main difference is that evangelicals assert that sex will be better within the covenantal confines of marriage. Maken's second point cuts to the heart of the abstinence campaigns' implicit promise of marriage. Maken feels that our culture of "protracted adolescence" lets men off the hook, not requiring them to commit to the responsibilities of a wife and children. She says that the church is also to blame for condoning singleness. Marriage is a social institution, not a private one, and a failed or unrealized marriage can hurt society: "Singleness is not purely a private choice, but one that has a public cost because it fails to form a family. It costs someone a spouse, it costs us our own children, it costs grandparents grandchildren, and it fails to replenish the church nursery."[12]

Although Maken's arguments sound hyperconservative and outdated at best, she frames her solution to the problem of singleness as supporting women's rights, in an echo of the modesty-as-power argument of the abstinence campaigns (see chapter 3). She advocates arranged marriages, whether through parents or dating services, in an attempt to restore to women the power of pursuing marriage.[13] Although Maken is to be applauded for taking on the issue of singleness, she gives short shrift to the possibility that singleness could be an active choice or a religious calling, as fulfilling and sacred as marriage. The main problem here is that marriage is offered as a solution to the problem of singleness, just as marriage is offered as a reward for the commitment to abstinence.

The abstinence campaigns may be persuasive with their culturally savvy sex-is-great argument, but the emphasis on marriage—with no talk about extended singleness—may be setting abstinent teens up for heartbreak. Perhaps the most telling testimony of singleness I heard came from Nora Williams. I first spoke with Nora four years earlier, at a Silver Ring Thing event in 2004. After attending an event and making an abstinence pledge, she had been so moved by the work of Silver Ring Thing that she decided to volunteer as an intern. With her college degree behind her, Nora, now twenty-four, is working part time teaching piano lessons and volunteering with her church's youth group. She also works part time at a bookstore and babysits to help pay the bills.

When I caught up with Nora for tea at a bakery near her home, I asked her what was different in her life since the last time we had talked. "I still haven't dated anybody, haven't been asked out on a date," she replied. Taking a sip of her chai tea latte, she reflected on her original abstinence commitment, made more than eight years earlier. "To be honest, and why not, I think I made the decision as almost a defense mechanism. In high school I never dated anybody. I was almost abstinent by default. I was awkward and really insecure, and so that way I could at least use it as an excuse. 'Oh, why aren't you dating anybody?' 'Oh, because I'm waiting.'" Nora acknowledged that she used her abstinence pledge as a cover for her lack of dating relationships, but she now insists that her lack of opportunities to test her abstinence commitment means she has more time to focus on herself. "If I have to wait forever, then that's okay. I got to work on me and become the kind of woman that I want to be, traveling and pursuing my art and my vision and learning. And if a guy happens to come in, then that's great."

The topic came up again later in our conversation, and Nora acknowledged that she has moments of being tired of waiting. "I just turned twenty-four, and [I'm] looking at my life and going, 'I don't have a house, I don't have a boyfriend, I don't have a full-time job.' And thinking, like, 'Oh, man, when I turn thirty I'm just going to go to a bar and pick up a guy.' You know, like you have thoughts like that. Like, what am I waiting for? If he's not out there, what am I waiting for? Why does it matter?"

The stigma of singleness can come from the church, not just peers and family members. Nora expressed her frustration that the Christian church is not encouraging of young adults in their singleness. "I just get aggravated that even in the church community no one asks us how our ministry is going. No one asks me how my relationship with God is. They just want to know who I'm dating. You know? It would be nice to see that make a turnabout where we care about people's integrity and their adventures in life rather than, 'Oh, you're single? What's wrong with you?'"

Despite her outward bravado, Nora still seems to be struggling with the stigma of singleness, just as she did in high school. The only difference is that back then she used her abstinence commitment as a cover. Now she focuses on the opportunity for self-improvement:

> People think relationships are the end-all, be-all. After I graduated from college I should have found my husband in college, so that we could be married right out of college and have kids by the time I'm twenty-five, so that we can have our family and send them to college and they can find their future husbands. It's like, what is that? If I was dating somebody I would be even more poor than I am right now. I would be frustrated. I would never have time to focus on myself. I would be constantly worried about pleasing someone. We're trying to grow up so fast and no one enjoys life. No one travels anymore. People are getting married at nineteen. And, yeah, I don't doubt that they love each other, but you don't even know who you are. I don't even know who I am. I don't even think a thirty-five-year-old woman knows who she is. How are you going to try and tie yourself to someone for the next fifty years?

Membership in the abstinence community helps to dispel the stigma of virginity, but the campaigns inadvertently create a new stigma of singleness. Initially, an abstinence pledge made in middle school or high school can provide a convenient cover for a lack of dating relationships. But as the pledger grows older—and still has no dates or serious relationships—the pledge becomes stale with no reward in sight. The goal of abstinence may be a future good marriage, but what if the future does not hold marriage for the faithfully abstinent teen? Implicit in the abstinence message is that abstinent teens do not have to give up sex, just postpone it until marriage with the promise of making marriage—and sex—even better. Marriage involves double agency—two individuals must choose each other; it is not enough for one individual to choose to be married someday without another individual making a choice in return. Does the argument for abstinence crumble if the goal of abstinence—marriage—is unattainable? It certainly makes it less persuasive.

Heather and Laurel talk about this period of singleness as a time to pursue their relationship with the Lord: sort of Jesus-as-my-boyfriend-by-default. Nora, on the other hand, uses a more secular argument to claim this as a time to focus on improving herself. Her front-row seat for her own parents' marital struggles undoubtedly contributes to her mixed feelings about marriage. Her self-improvement argument in support of singleness echoes the sex-is-great argument in support of abstinence: both focus on personal gratification. If marriage is the reward for abstinence, then bright young single women like Heather, Laurel, and Nora could be made to believe that their abstinence commitment is rendered empty and meaningless.

WHEN THE PRINCE IS WAITING FOR HIS PRINCE: THE SILENCE ON HOMOSEXUALITY

Promising marriage as a reward for abstinence is problematic not just for heterosexual singles but also for singles with a same-sex orientation.[14] A pledge of abstinence until marriage does not make sense for a gay teen, when gay marriage is not widely legalized. None of the abstinence events that I attended addressed the challenges of homosexuality and purity.[15] This is not a surprise, in light of evangelical Christian beliefs that hold homosexual activity to be sinful.[16]

Denny Pattyn, founder of Silver Ring Thing, affirms that gay teens are welcome at all Silver Ring Thing events and that the campaign encourages gay teens to commit to sexual abstinence, although the campaign does not publicly address homosexuality at its events. Pattyn states in an e-mail that "the number of gay/lesbian/bisexual/transgendered persons is estimated by some to be as small as 1–2% of the population and therefore not a significant enough issue to deal with in front of the whole audience. The media makes the issue 'bigger than life' but in reality, we have more important issues to deal with in the short time we have with the teens." He says he has responded to as many as fifty inquiries on the issue, mostly from reporters, and has received another fifteen e-mails from students after they attended an event. "The homosexual debate needs to be somebody else's issue," Pattyn writes. "Ours is abstinence and evangelism of teenagers. We generally discuss this topic privately when questions are asked."[17]

Addressing homosexual activity as sexual sin would fit with the abstinence campaigns' focus on second virginity and God's forgiveness. However, the reason Denny Pattyn gives for why gay teens should be abstinent has little to do with biblical injunctions. Instead, Pattyn focuses his attention on sexual health. He writes that the age at which a teenager initiates sexual activity and the number of sexual partners an individual has during a lifetime is directly related to the transmission of sexually transmitted diseases: "If we can help gay teens to put on a ring, delay sexual activity and limit the number of partners they have in a lifetime, then we have helped them very much."[18] In the case of Silver Ring Thing, its leaders may privately believe that homosexual activity is sinful, but the campaign's public response emphasizes healthy choices, not spiritual condemnation.

The campaigns may not specifically focus on homosexual young people, but this does not mean that nonheterosexual teens may not attend the events. One of my interview respondents mentioned in an e-mail that two of her gay friends from high school had attended an abstinence event. They both made pledges of abstinence out of their love for God. According to the respondent, both young men struggled with their faith and their sexuality. She has kept in contact with one of them, and she knows that he has had boyfriends but kept his commitment to sexual purity. The respondent, who used to volunteer with one of the abstinence campaigns, said the organization has "a warm and welcoming staff, full of people who care deeply for others, do their best to love as Jesus loved. If a gay student came to any of them and wanted to pledge abstinence, I'm sure they would have received . . . prayers and encouragement." She acknowledges that marriage as the reward for abstinence is not an option for her friend. So what does abstinence mean to him? "I think it's waiting until it is right," she writes. "Waiting for when he's in love inside a monogamous, long-term relationship [in which] he feels safe and cared for genuinely. Even if it can't be legally sanctioned as marriage. I have no idea if this would be a disappointment to the standards of [the abstinence campaigns], but I know it's not a disappointment to me. I would prefer my friend to give his love carefully and when he's ready."

What my respondent describes would indeed be a disappointment to the abstinence campaigns: evangelicals generally believe that it is not a sin to be homosexual, but they consider it sinful when one engages in homosexual practices. The evangelical theologian Stanley Grenz writes that evangelicals tend to "treat homosexual feelings, attractions, urges, desires, and longings as temptations to be mastered, rather than as sins to be confessed. Sin . . . emerges only when a person acts . . . on these urges."[19] In a similar fashion, evangelicals believe that it is not a sin to be heterosexual; it is only a sin when one engages in sexual activity outside marriage. The difference between the homosexual and heterosexual cases, of course, is the location of the sexual activity: For the gay teen, sexual activity always is sin. For the heterosexual teen, sexual activity is sin when it occurs apart from the marriage relationship.

Some evangelicals do not separate homosexual identity and behavior, considering both to be sinful. In an appendix to *Who Moved the Goalpost?*, the book used in conjunction with the boys-only Pure Freedom events, Bob Gresh includes a letter from a pastor and board member of Exodus International, an organization that promotes conversion to heterosexuality. The testimonial describes homosexuality as a choice: "In spite of God's calling and revelation, I chose to pursue homosexuality." The writer, Alan Chambers, describes how one day God spoke to him in a gay bar: "That night I made a choice. I never returned to a gay life." The letter goes on to encourage boys who may be struggling with homosexuality that "[God] loves you, gay or straight" and that "God will do amazing things in you if you trust Him and give Him time." The letter is infused with a tone of acceptance, not condemnation, emphasizing that "God loves you no matter what." The letter is vague, however, regarding whether an individual is supposed to choose to abstain from homosexual activity or choose to become heterosexual. The final paragraph offers some clarity: Chambers writes that now he is a "husband to my wife" and "I am not a homosexual in action, thought, or identity."[20] Like the testimonies in the abstinence campaigns, this testimony offers marriage as a kind of goal or reward for a pure life. In this case, however, one must first become heterosexual to receive the reward.

The distinction between sexual identity and sexual activity is an important one for evangelicals, and should be important for the abstinence campaigns: a heterosexual teen and homosexual teen may claim different sexual identities, but both may commit to abstain from sexual activity.[21] Indeed, evangelicals would say that both the heterosexual and homosexual teen must practice sexual abstinence. It may seem as if the gay teen is at a disadvantage since evangelical theology does not recognize gay marriage (nor do the laws of most states). But the homosexual teen and heterosexual teen face a similar predicament. For a homosexual teen who espouses evangelical Christian beliefs, a pledge for abstinence is tantamount to a pledge to lead a life without sex.[22] So too for the heterosexual teen: although marriage is a possibility, it is not a promise; thus the commitment to abstinence also may mean a life without sex. This may seem too big a burden for a teenager, whether homosexual or heterosexual. And yet evangelical theology affirms that personal fulfillment and individual identity are not grounded in one's ability to have sex; instead, Christian identity is to be found in Christ.[23]

By neglecting a language of sacrifice and suffering in the promotion of abstinence, the campaigns miss an opportunity to talk about lifelong abstinent singleness (not to mention the day-to-day rigors and banality of marriage) as sacrifice. This would also provide space for the campaigns to address chastity within homosexuality. Whether one is single and heterosexual, single and homosexual, or in a heterosexual marriage, one can actively choose to manage one's sexuality, acknowledging that God-given sexuality reminds us of our longing for full communion with God. The sociologist Lisa Graham McMinn writes that this "holy longing" motivates us to live in relationship with others, but it will not completely fulfill us. In this sense, marriage is not the ultimate goal; it simply "provides a temporal home, a place to put down roots to stay the unease of being alone in a universe, separated, for a time, from the Creator from whom we came."[24] This larger dimension of the sacrifice of sexuality as worship of God is largely missing from the campaigns.

The self-fulfillment argument for singleness and marriage makes sense in a culture of individualism and consumerism. Perhaps expressions of abstinence in a culture that does not readily offer the stuff of self-improvement such as fulfilling careers, money, home ownership, cars, and travel would present a different side to the sex-is-great argument. I decided to travel to sub-Saharan Africa to find out.

CHAPTER 6

Fearing God, Not AIDS

Abstinence in Africa

For the American evangelical Bruce Wilkinson, addressing the AIDS pandemic in Africa came as a call from God: "God ripped open our chest, took out our heart, dug a hole in Africa, put it in, covered it with soil and said, 'Now, follow your heart and move down to Africa.'"[1] His sudden interest in Africa came as a surprise to many. Wilkinson, founder of Walk Thru the Bible Ministries, achieved national attention in 2001 as the author of *The Prayer of Jabez,* which topped both secular and religious book charts to become the fastest-selling book of all time. In 2002, after resigning from his organization in order to move to Hollywood to make movies, Wilkinson searched without success for a new home in California. During that time he felt God calling him and his family to Africa.[2] Wilkinson moved to South Africa, where he began outreach efforts to care for AIDS orphans and to train pastors and church leaders in HIV/AIDS prevention and care.

Kay Warren, wife of Rick Warren, pastor of Saddleback Church, first learned about AIDS in Africa from a magazine article in 2002. She was shocked to read that twelve million African children had been orphaned because of the pandemic. "In that moment, God shattered my heart," she says. She decided to do something about it. Warren read the article just as her husband's book *The Purpose Driven Life* was becoming a national best-seller. In 2003 Wilkinson invited the couple to Johannesburg, South Africa, to help lead an HIV/AIDS conference for pastors. Rick Warren was moved by the overwhelming needs of the local people, and he asked God to show him how he could help. "When David takes on Goliath, God gets glory. What are the problems so big that no one can solve them?" By 2005 the Warrens found themselves in Rwanda at the invitation of Rwandan president Paul Kagame, who had read Rick Warren's book. The Warrens resolved to make Rwanda the first "purpose-driven nation," investing significant financial and human resources in the local church to help combat AIDS and poverty and to promote reconciliation of Hutus and Tutsis.[3]

On May 27, 2003, President George W. Bush outlined a "great mission of rescue" comparable to the historic Marshall Plan, Berlin Airlift, and Peace Corps. He called the HIV/AIDS epidemic "one of the greatest medical challenges of our time." That day he signed into law H.R. 1298, the United States Leadership Against HIV/AIDS, Tuberculosis and Malaria Act of 2003, an emergency effort to provide $15 billion over five years to fight AIDS in twelve sub-Saharan African countries and two Caribbean nations where AIDS is concentrated. The commitment was hailed as "the largest international public health commitment in history aimed at a specific disease." Funding was reauthorized in July 2008, providing an additional $39 billion for AIDS efforts over the next five years.[4]

Clearly the need is great. Roughly 10 percent of the world's population lives in sub-Saharan Africa, but the region is home to more than 65 percent of all people living with HIV/AIDS. Ninety percent of all children younger than fifteen with HIV are living in this region. Young people continue to be at risk: 45 percent of new HIV infections occur among fifteen to twenty-four year olds. Half of all people living with HIV are women. In sub-Saharan Africa the percentage is higher: more than 3 in 4 women (77 percent) older than fifteen are living with HIV.[5] Women are at greater risk of sexual abuse, rape, sexual exploitation, and coerced first sex, all of which can be associated with an increased risk of HIV transmission.[6]

American evangelicals have found a new venue for their abstinence message: sub-Saharan Africa, as a response to the rapid spread of AIDS.[7] In Africa the context shifts from teen pregnancy to AIDS. True Love Waits began abstinence education efforts in Uganda soon after its founding in the United States in the early 1990s, and it expanded its efforts to five other sub-Saharan African countries in 2007. In 2005 Silver Ring Thing expanded to South Africa, where the club-style events reached 67,032 young people with 102 shows, at which an average of 70 percent of attendees committed to abstinence. In 2004 Pure Freedom's founder, Dannah Gresh, traveled to Zambia at the invitation of the Zambian government. Her abstinence curriculum is now administered by a Zambian health agency. Some of the evangelicals' efforts in Africa are financially supported by the U.S. government, including Bruce Wilkinson's AIDS prevention training sessions for African pastors.[8]

Although the presence of the evangelical abstinence campaigns in Africa may be recent, evangelical involvement in Africa has a long history, in terms of both missionary activity and humanitarian efforts. However, the spread of AIDS in Africa presents a new challenge: a humanitarian crisis precipitated by a disease that evangelicals believe to be caused, in most cases, by immoral behavior. The first documented cases of AIDS in the United States in 1981 were among gay communities in New York and Los Angeles.[9] Dubbed the "gay plague," the illness was seen by some evangelicals as the consequence of sinful homosexual behavior.

When the spread of AIDS in sub-Saharan Africa first hit the headlines in the United States, American donors to evangelical organizations were not particularly eager to aid those engaging in sinful practices. World Vision, a Christian relief and development partnership with a history of close ties to evangelical leaders, surveyed its donor base in 2000 before launching its Hope Initiative to alleviate the AIDS crisis in Africa. The marketing department told World Vision CEO Richard Stearns that work with HIV/AIDS would not resonate with the organization's donors: "Our top people in brand building told us that we have a very wholesome child-focused image. People equate us [with] helping children and families in need. If we start talking about AIDS, prostitutes, drug users, long-haul truckers, and sexuality, it will hurt our image." Ken Casey, head of the Hope Initiative, called the results of the donor survey "devastating news": "We asked [respondents] if they would be willing to give to a respectable Christian organization to help children who lost both parents to AIDS. Only 7% said that they would definitely help while over 50% said probably not. Surveys in Canada and Australia found the same thing. It was stark and clear that our donors felt that AIDS sufferers somehow deserved their fate."[10]

The challenge for evangelical relief and development organizations was to change donor perceptions about the causes of AIDS and the role of human behavior in disease transmission. A quick survey of organizational annual reports and Web sites suggests that one way the organizations have attempted to overcome this bias is to focus on the image and narrative of the symbolic "AIDS orphan," the vulnerable and innocent victim of the AIDS epidemic whose parents have both died of AIDS. The emphasis on the child's innocence stresses a lack of culpability, and the emphasis on vulnerability creates space for the potential donor to respond and make a difference.

Now AIDS-in-Africa ministries are springing up across U.S. evangelical congregations, sending money and people to aid in prevention and palliative efforts. The AIDS crisis is seen as a "great opportunity" for the church, as one individual from the evangelical Wooddale Church in Minnesota portrays it: "The Early Church grew rapidly as it responded to the most desperate needs of its time, including epidemics and plagues. It became clear to us that AIDS is not only the greatest health tragedy in history—it's also the great opportunity of the Church. With World Relief's help, we identified families affected by AIDS in Mozambique, prepared 5,000 care kits, and began a prayer ministry for the victims and their families."[11]

World Relief is a leader in the U.S. evangelical abstinence movement in Africa. In the first round of USAID funding from the President's Emergency Plan for AIDS Relief (also known as PEPFAR) in 2004, World Relief received the largest single grant, totaling $9.7 million over five years. The grant supported the abstinence component of World Relief's Mobilizing for Life initiative, which was expected to reach 1.8 million young people in Haiti, Kenya, Mozambique, and Rwanda with "church-centered AIDS prevention strategies focused on abstinence." As part of this goal, World Relief was establishing 1,750 youth clubs to train and encourage youth to remain abstinent. The broader AIDS initiative also included establishing groups to provide basic care for people living with AIDS, distributing emergency food supplies, creating community banking programs, and providing care for AIDS orphans.[12]

According to its Web site, World Relief is a wholly owned subsidiary of the National Association of Evangelicals (NAE). The organization began as NAE's War Relief Commission in 1944 and today is involved in emergency relief and community-based development in more than twenty countries. Its motto is "Churches Helping Churches Help the Hurting," emphasizing the organization's focus of working through local churches. The organization reported $51 million in total support and revenue for 2007, with nearly half coming from federal government grants ($24.6 million).[13]

In this chapter I examine the work of World Relief and its partner agencies because of its central role in evangelical abstinence efforts in

Africa. I will explore the differences between abstinence campaigns in the United States and in African countries. I interviewed abstinence educators and organizational leaders in Nairobi, Kenya, and Kigali, Rwanda.[14] I also talked with young people at four church-based abstinence youth clubs supported by World Relief in Kigali.[15] World Relief's abstinence curriculum is largely an American product, but the ways in which it is received in the African context reveal that it is different from the "what's-in-it-for-me" orientation of U.S. evangelicals.

Producers of the abstinence message in Kenya and Rwanda borrow the rhetoric of the U.S. campaigns, focusing on key themes of sexual purity and second virginity, with a stronger emphasis on the fear of AIDS. Avoiding AIDS brings hope for the future, both for oneself and one's country. African evangelicals promote abstinence by focusing on AIDS avoidance, but they acknowledge that African young people are not motivated by a fear of AIDS in a context where other diseases and threats to life seem more urgent. To overcome this problem of message reception, African evangelicals also promote abstinence by focusing on fearing God. This shift from the fear of AIDS and death to the fear of God attempts to provide a transcendent argument for abstinence that focuses on pleasing a transcendent God through moral lifestyle choices.

Rwandan young people frame abstinence both as an act of obedience to God and as a sign of salvation and a sin-free life. Rwandan young people express limited acknowledgment of their physical desires and the need to set boundaries to tame them. Far more often they express a form of circular reasoning, saying that true Christians are not tempted sexually and do not sin and so the best way to pursue abstinence and avoid temptation is to become a Christian. A Christian who gives in to sexual temptation was never a true Christian. Such reasoning emphasizes the power of conversion to Christianity. Additionally, it weakens the role of personal responsibility in sexual temptation and activity, which may account for the persuasiveness of the argument. True agency is placed on God to convert the sinner and bring new life.

In this chapter I offer a cross-cultural comparison of the evangelical abstinence messages in the United States and sub-Saharan Africa. Is it the same message, and how does it resonate with young people in a different cultural context? I argue that while the message may be basically the same, an argument for abstinence based on individual agency makes less sense in a cultural context in which choices are already limited.

THE POWER TO CHOOSE

The loud music sounded more like a raucous party than a church service. Inside a Pentecostal church in the Kabeza district of Kigali, the voices of a dynamic choir of about fifteen young people, distorted by the sound system, reverberated off the corrugated tin roof and partial wall of red brick. An attentive audience of more than one hundred people—some from the church, some from the community—sat on wooden benches and took in the performance. Half a world away from the pop music and laser lights of Silver Ring Thing, an abstinence youth meeting sponsored by World Relief was gearing up for a November afternoon of community outreach. This was a teen club, Rwandan style. While World Relief workers observed from the audience, the event was led by Rwandan teens who had pledged abstinence and were now encouraging others to do the same.

After the thumping music a teenage girl came to the stage and offered a dramatic recitation of a poem she had written: "Mothers are crying and babies are suffering. Oh, AIDS . . . is it a punishment from God? Let us fight . . . where there is a will there is a way. In the future generation, I want to make a strong Rwanda."

After the poem five teenage boys dressed in jeans and matching white Nike T-shirts took the stage and performed two dances—one traditional and one hip-hop (or "MTV-style," as a translator explained)—to prerecorded Rwandan Christian pop music. The audience clapped along. More dancers followed, including a group of young women dressed in traditional sarongs and ankle bracelets made of bells. A humorous skit about a wealthy man whose business was failing elicited laughter from the audience. At the end of the skit a character playing a Christian confronted the wealthy man about his lavish lifestyle: "You have to choose your destiny, choose life or death. Jesus brings life: if you choose women, you choose death."

As in the U.S. campaigns, abstinence in Africa is presented as a choice for young people. John Mwangi of Scripture Union, a partner of World Relief in its abstinence education in Kigali, sees his role as offering information and guidelines so that youth can make wise choices concerning their sexual behavior: "You can't prevent them from making the wrong decision, but you can help them make informed choices. . . . We say it is for you to make the decision." Youth possess the ability to choose abstinence among competing claims about appropriate sexual behavior. "Abstinence is not a one-time decision; it is a choice you make every day. . . . Your culture could be saying to [go] for it, but you can say no." Acknowledging the agency of youth to make choices is to acknowledge that they may make choices contrary to what has been deemed the best or wisest choice; however, World Relief promotes the choice of abstinence as the best choice. The title of its abstinence curriculum emphasizes these themes: "Choose Life: Helping Youth Make Wise Choices."

Most curricula offer activities that allow youth to practice making decisions and anticipating the potential consequences. This type of trial-and-error exercise aims to encourage wise decisions. The *True Love Waits Leaders' Manual* for Kenya presents four situations involving drugs, teen sex, and sexual favors in return for school fees in a section called "Choices, Choices, Choices—What Do I Do?" The stated purpose of the exercise is "to help youth realize that they have many choices in life, that they are responsible for the choices they make, and that choices have consequences."[16]

The agency to choose abstinence is described in terms of control or power over one's body and physical desires. "Can You Tame the Tiger?" an appendix to the True Love Waits leaders' manual for abstinence education in Uganda, describes sexual desire as a wild tiger that needs to be controlled: "As the debate rages: 'Is it possible to control our sexual desires? Can the raging tiger be tamed?' I say we can control our sexual desires. It is this ability to choose what to do with our emotions and desires that separates us from animals which are driven by instinct."[17]

AVOIDING AIDS

A primary way that abstinence educators in Africa communicate the importance of the choice for abstinence is to focus on the consequences of choice in general, and the specific consequences of promiscuity. The primary consequence mentioned by the leaders whom I interviewed is the contraction of HIV/AIDS and subsequent death. "We talk about [how] premarital sex has consequences," says Tabitha Ogango, an abstinence trainer hired by Focus on the Family. The organization's "No Apologies" curriculum teaches youth to make wise decisions by using a "decision tree." The potential consequences of choosing nonmarital sex instead of abstinence are printed in the workbook and include STDs, pregnancy, and abortion.[18] Although abstinence campaign leaders mention a number of potential consequences of not choosing abstinence, such as unwanted pregnancy and abortion, the most frequently cited consequence is contracting HIV/AIDS.

Abstinence education is taught as HIV/AIDS prevention. The covers of the "No Apologies" workbooks display the AIDS ribbon with "HIV/AIDS Prevention" written across it. The introduction to World Relief's "Choose Life" curriculum sets AIDS as the context for its abstinence education: "In some countries in Africa up to half of our youth will not reach age 40. Why? Because they got a disease they did not have to get—AIDS. It brought an end to their life and the life of their sexual partners before they could even begin life as an adult. . . . Obeying God's plan is 100% effective in preventing the spread of AIDS through sex." A potential consequence of nonmarital sex is AIDS: "The decision to become sexually active before marriage can lead to AIDS and prevent you from living to see your children or grandchildren." The introduction to the *Worth the Wait* training manual highlights AIDS as a consequence of sexual promiscuity: "Sex in the context of marriage is beautiful. Otherwise it is painful and destructive. One only needs to look at the AIDS pandemic to know there is something terribly wrong with sexual promiscuity and infidelity."[19] Evangelicals in Africa use the possibility of contracting HIV/AIDS, which results in death, as a negative motivation for African youth to avoid nonmarital sex. The message is that to avoid AIDS, one should choose abstinence.

Rwandan young people are getting the message. Members of the abstinence youth clubs equate having sex outside marriage with illness and death. Sexual abstinence is portrayed as the remedy. "You cannot give away your life as a solution to a small problem. You will try by all means to escape having sex because it is giving your life to death," says a young man at an evangelical church in the Kimihurura district of Kigali. "One has to keep himself away from a bad thing. The first thing is to know how this sickness is very dangerous and how it kills," says another.

Abstinence can help to eliminate the fear of disease. In a survey of 320 Rwandan young people aged thirteen to twenty-three conducted in 2003 by World Relief on knowledge, attitudes, and practices of sexuality and HIV/AIDS, 84 percent responded that they did not believe that they were personally at risk of contracting AIDS, although they acknowledged that AIDS is a serious problem.[20] This may be attributed to the claim by 93 percent of survey respondents that they are practicing sexual abstinence.

The threat of disease motivates abstinence. In a few cases respondents shared that they had been sexually active but then became Christians and adopted abstinence. One young man tells of facing the potential consequences of his behavior and feeling compelled to save others after learning that he had escaped HIV:

> We are to live abstinent so we can escape disease. Before I got saved, I lived a loose life—sex with many people. Now that I am saved, I am convinced I cannot live that way. I wondered if I was sick. After I learned I was not sick, I kept abstinent because I know that one day I will have a wife. I keep myself away from having sex. The way I got this burden in my heart, before I had a test, I saw a movie of the consequences, then I found out I was not sick. This has given me the burden to tell others.

The primary motive for abstinence for this young man is to "escape disease." He suggests a causal link between his spiritual salvation and his conviction that he could no longer live a "loose life." However, he also discusses a fear of discovering that he is sick and an awareness of the consequences of his lifestyle choices as affecting his decision to be abstinent.

HOPE FOR THE FUTURE

Abstinence educators offer, as a corollary to the argument that AIDS is a consequence of nonmarital sex, a positive motivation that choosing abstinence gives youth hope for their future. The logic follows that if one avoids HIV/AIDS, one avoids the death that results from HIV/AIDS and thus has hope for the future. Choosing nonmarital sex is equated with choosing death, just as choosing abstinence is equated with choosing life, as heralded by the title of World Relief's curriculum, "Choose Life." For evangelical Christians the double meaning here is that *life* refers to both physical life—avoiding death from AIDS—and to eternal life, the result of salvation through Jesus Christ. The choice is both for abstinence and for God, as the choice for abstinence is a physical manifestation of one's spiritual choice to follow God.

The circulation of the evangelical slogan "Choose Life" from the U.S. context of abortion to the African context of AIDS radically alters the slogan's meaning. In the United States "choosing life" refers to the choice of a pregnant woman to bear her ostensibly unwanted child. In Africa "choosing life" refers to the young woman's (or young man's) making a choice in support of her (or his) own life—avoiding sex to avoid death. The choice of abstinence functions essentially as an antinatal stance. Although sexual intercourse can bring disease and death, it can also bring pregnancy and new life; hence, the avoidance of sexual intercourse (abstinence) brings the avoidance of new life. In Africa the exhortation to "choose life" becomes a call to reject the possibility of new life in favor of preserving one's own life, which, ironically, sounds similar to arguments in the United States in favor of abortion rights. Although it would be inaccurate to characterize the evangelical abstinence movement on the whole as antinatal, since the call for abstinence lasts only until marriage, some African abstinence educators are aware of the tension inherent in equating choosing abstinence with choosing life in a culture in which pregnancy in general is viewed as a blessing, not as a threat to one's health or plans for self-development.

Just as abstinence educators use the imagining of negative consequences of nonmarital sex as a deterrent, so they use the positive consequences of abstinence as a motivation. But it makes one wonder how persuasive a message of hope can be to a generation of young people who witnessed the atrocities of genocide only a decade earlier. The World Relief staff confirms that most young people I met were directly affected by the massacres, and many were eyewitnesses. How does one choose life after witnessing such death? The message of hope becomes one of hope for the nation, not hope for the individual. "They are the future leaders of this country, and they need to safeguard their health," says World Relief's Rwanda country director. "The biggest threat to that is AIDS through risky behavior. As Christians, they have biblical values to help them. The biggest argument [in support of abstinence] is that they are the future." The motivation for avoiding death and securing a future extends beyond self-fulfillment to an obligation to other citizens. In a country such as Rwanda, where a significant portion of the adult population has been eliminated by civil war and genocide, this argument places the action of the individual in the context of the community and country as a whole. A choice for abstinence, then, means a choice for the future of Africa.

"EVEN A ROAD ACCIDENT, YOU CAN DIE"

The appeal to young people to choose abstinence in order to avoid AIDS and to gain hope for the future is pervasive, but it may not be persuasive: abstinence educators acknowledge that these appeals are not particularly effective with African young people.[21]

A prevailing reason why youth do not fear AIDS is because the specter of death is already part of their daily lives. In the African context AIDS is a less significant threat than malaria and malnutrition. "But people have closer concerns than AIDS," World Relief Rwanda's Emmanuel Ngoga acknowledges. "They are poor. They are not sure they're going to survive because of it. Even food, the basic needs. When you are thinking about these basic needs, it's very hard to think about future plans." Focus on the Family Kenya's Tabitha Ogango agrees: "Our young people don't seem to fear HIV. They don't seem to think it's a big thing. . . . They are going on, and they're having sex with many people as they are. They don't really care." The reason, according to Ogango, is a form of fatalism, not lack of knowledge: "They know everything [about HIV/AIDS], modes of transmission. They know because it's also been incorporated in the curriculum. You tell them [that with] HIV you can die. They say, well, you know, even [with] malaria you can die. Even a road accident, you can die."

Some evangelical leaders in Africa suggest that perhaps African youth have not really seen the effects of AIDS. Although most African families have been affected by AIDS, either directly or indirectly, one respondent suggests that Africans are reluctant to attribute deaths to AIDS, so it is possible that young people may grow up not being fully aware of what the disease looks like.[22] "There still is this feeling that AIDS is for somebody else," according to Colette Cunningham of World Relief. She tells me of an object lesson that some trainers use to illustrate the transmission of AIDS. A group of young people is divided into two groups, with one group given cups of water and the other group given cups of water with a clear chemical in it. The youth are encouraged to mingle and to pour some of their water into the cups of others. Afterward, the trainer adds red dye to the cups to display the presence of the invisible chemical, which by now has traveled throughout the groups, illustrating the number of young people "infected" through the fluid exchange. The youth are often surprised to find that their water has turned red.

Even so, witnessing AIDS and understanding its transmission may not be an effective deterrent. Even if African youths are knowledgeable about HIV/AIDS transmission, they still do not seem to fear it as a consequence of promiscuous behavior. Other threats to their lives—malaria, car accidents—seem more urgent and real.

FEARING GOD

Although abstinence educators state that the most compelling arguments for abstinence are the fear of AIDS and hope for the future, a third argument in African abstinence rhetoric successfully avoids the contradiction that African youth are not motivated by arguments about AIDS and the future: the fear of God. In some cases aspiring to please God is explicitly stated as more important than avoiding disease. The introductions to the True Love Waits curricula for both Kenya and Uganda create a hierarchy through a list of seven beliefs, including the belief that youth are able to commit to sexual purity and that the "safer sex" message is not the solution for Africa. Fearing God is listed as the primary motivation; fear of disease is secondary:

- The primary reason for youth to save sex for marriage is because it is God's plan for them and it results in joy and peace;
- HIV/AIDS, teen pregnancy, STD's, etc., are only secondary reasons for challenging youth to delay sex until marriage[23]

John Mwangi of Scripture Union said that in a test given in schools before abstinence training, students who were already abstinent gave the reasons for their making such a commitment, in order, as "God," "disease," and then "parents." "It has to be more than HIV" for youth to remain committed to abstinence, according to Mwangi. " 'This is what God expects of me.' . . . This is God who created you who expects it that way."

Directing the motivation for abstinence toward God and away from disease sidesteps counterarguments that one could engage in nonmarital sex and not catch HIV, potentially reducing ambivalence about the fear of AIDS and death as a motivating factor. Sheila Muchemi of Crisis Pregnancy Ministries Kenya puts it this way:

And then of course God has been a big factor. I realize that. We keep asking ourselves when we are abstaining, "What if we died today, would we abstain?" You say if you knew you'd die in a week's time, would you rush to go and have sex? . . . If we're doing it unto God, then it makes more sense. Then I don't have to feel like I'm just doing it for myself and just to keep pure for myself. That is when I have a higher goal, for me that has been . . . helping me. Okay, Lord, it's for you. If I never get married, even if I die today, it would still have been worth it for me to have abstained or to have been sexually pure.

This response indirectly addresses the fatalism of youth who feel that AIDS is less of a threat than other, more immediate threats to their lives. Escaping death or enjoying life and the future are no longer the only motivations for abstinence. Fearing God provides a "higher goal." Edgar Makona, a leader of True Love Waits in Kenya, places the motivation for abstinence on a transcendent God in part to separate abstinence from its function as merely a tool for AIDS prevention. "This commitment is not for us, it is for God," he insists. "We tell them not to wait just because they are scared of HIV/AIDS. The disease might go away, but they need to stay abstinent for God." Even if the AIDS pandemic is cured, abstinence would still be necessary to please God. The motivation for abstinence shifts from an inward-directed view of the self (avoid disease) to an outward-directed view of a transcendent other (please God).

Although members of the abstinence youth clubs in Rwanda mention fear of disease as a motivating factor for abstinence, the most frequently mentioned reason is fear of God. Some explicitly counter the assumption that their actions are a response to the fear of AIDS. "It is not by fear of that sickness, but mainly the fear of God," a young woman at an abstinence club in the Kimihurura district of Kigali says. One of the young men in the group agrees: "Sometimes we refuse to have sex, not because of the outcome, but because we know we are to be obedient to our God." As the abstinence educators suspected, the fear of God provides a stronger motivation for Christian youth who are not motivated by the fear of contracting HIV/AIDS.

The fear of God is expressed as a responsibility of obedience to the lifestyle expectations of God: "When we say about fear in God, it's because he loves us and we want to love him. We know that God hates sin. We hate it too, so we can be a friend of God." According to a young man from an abstinence club in the Nyamirambo district, non-marital sex "is the worst sin God doesn't like."

The respondents repeatedly describe their physical bodies as "God's temples" and "new creations," intertwining the spiritual transformation from sinner to saved with a physical transformation from sexual behavior to abstinence. The description of the body as God's temple exemplifies the fear of God as obedience through stewardship: if my body is no longer my own, but God's, then I must engage in a lifestyle that keeps my body pure and disease free, much as a janitor takes care of a building. The lyrics of a song performed at an abstinence club in the Kabeza district express this sense of stewardship: "Stop joking, because AIDS is dangerous and we are God's temples."

The description of the physical body as a new creation similarly suggests an ongoing stewardship, but it also can be used to describe a perfecting transformation that is completed at the moment of conversion. The nuance is significant: the body as God's temple suggests a process of perfection with a high degree of agency in maintaining the temple, whereas the body as a new creation suggests achieved perfection with a low degree of agency in maintaining that which was already attained. The view of the body as a new creation emphasizes the agency of God, which empowers an individual to escape sexual temptation and disease. The distinction between God's agency and personal agency is often blurred. "When we are saved, we become new creations," says a Rwandan teenager. "We are not allowed to do those things. We are to follow the life of Jesus. It is God's grace." A young woman agrees: "We are living abstinent because we are fearing God—new creations. The word of God tells us that we are God's temples. From seventeen years [of age], they are on fire. They want to have sex, but the power of God will keep you."

Becoming a new creation by salvation through Jesus Christ is described as a method of disease protection. Jesus is described as a protector from and healer of AIDS: "If you don't know Jesus, AIDS could get into you really fast." A World Relief abstinence trainer talks about God as helping to promote the abstinence message: "Our position is that although it is difficult, we will continue to promote abstinence. Because God is almighty, whatever the problem is, we will succeed." God can bring healing for AIDS, too. The pastor of an evangelical church in the Nyarutarama district, in describing a video about HIV/AIDS prevention that he produced, says that the video was about "how they can get the right remedy, which is Jesus."

The view of God as healer functions as a source of hope for those who have already contracted HIV. This hope was expressed at one Rwandan church by a young woman living with AIDS. Dressed in a blue and yellow African print dress, she sat silently for much of the abstinence club meeting. The few times she participated in the conversation, she spoke softly and slowly wrung her hands as she talked. Near the end of the session she said that she had been a widow for five years. Her husband had died of AIDS. She was not married long, and she has no children. She told me that she is studying the Bible and hopes to be a pastor in three years. She hopes to marry again. According to the translator, "She is planning for her future like someone without AIDS. God told her she will recover. She waits for the healing."[24]

SALVATION = NO SIN

The fear of God is more than just a motivation for abstinence for the Rwandan respondents. Salvation itself—becoming a new creation—is portrayed as eliminating the possibility of sexual temptation or behavior. In this sense, God does not provide just the ongoing power to resist temptation or the promise of protection and healing from AIDS; God's salvation transforms the physical being into a spiritual being who is no longer capable of sin. "Your spirit says you won't sin, but your body can be tempted, but you can't really sin," according to a teenage boy from an evangelical church in the Nyarutarama district of Kigali. A club member at a church in the Nyamirambo district says, "Abstinence is to give up the thing you liked before. It is not easy in a human being unless you have Jesus. That is why if you don't have Jesus, it is not easy to do it. That is why those who are not saved are easily drawn into fornication."

The opposite is also true: someone who says that he is a Christian and then sins was never an authentic Christian. In response to repeated assertions by youth at various abstinence clubs that their abstinence was the result of their faith in Christ, I pressed them to consider how they handle sexual temptation. In most cases the young people merely reasserted that they do not face temptation now that they are Christians. Evidence of sinful behavior in a Christian does not lead to Christian behavior in the form of repentance and forgiveness; instead, the sinful behavior is evidence of an imitation Christianity: "When you are passing through those ways, you do not have Jesus," one teenage boy told me. "You are only imitating those who have Jesus. So to succeed, you must be a real changed Christian."

This view that authentic Christians do not engage in sinful behavior like sexual activity outside marriage was evident in responses to a story involving a sexually promiscuous young man. I told the story to each abstinence club. Although exact words may have varied slightly with each retelling, the plot remained the same:

> There was a young man about your age. He was handsome and smart and very popular. He had a girlfriend whom he cared about very much. They

frequently would engage in sexual intercourse. One day the young man broke up with his girlfriend and started dating another girl. He cared for her very much and had sex with her. But eventually, they broke up, too. The young man continued to have a number of girlfriends, one after the other. He cared for each of them and engaged in sexual intercourse with all of them. None of the girls became pregnant, and the young man did not spread HIV or catch HIV from any of the girls.

The most frequent response to this story was that the young man was not a Christian, although the protagonist's religious background is not mentioned in the story. Some abstinence club members suggested that the young man's behavior did not match God's standards for behavior. "Even though he was having sex and not giving sickness, the future of that boy is not good, because his way of life is not what God had planned for him, so his future will not be good at the end of the day," according to one male respondent. "What this boy was doing was not good, because one has to keep his life holy," according to another young man.

That the young man's behavior in the story successfully avoided two frequently cited consequences of sexual activity outside marriage—transmitting sexual disease and getting young women pregnant—does not validate his behavior, according to the respondents. The protagonist did not achieve a standard of goodness higher than merely avoiding negative consequences. As one of the World Relief trainers said, "They say use a condom, but you are sinning even if you use a condom or don't get AIDS." This view is consistent with the club members' emphasis on the fear of God over the fear of disease as the primary motivation for abstinence.

Another frequently repeated response to the story of the promiscuous young man was that he will get HIV if he keeps having sex. This view of the inevitability of contracting HIV suggests an understanding of HIV/AIDS transmission and its prevalence in sub-Saharan Africa. However, when considered in the context of the view that the young man was not living up to God's standards and thus not demonstrating an appropriate fear of God, the inevitability of contracting HIV/AIDS could be understood as a punishment for inappropriate behavior. It is unclear whether God actively administers the punishment or whether disease transmission is the natural consequence of behavior that goes against God's standards.

This is consistent with the findings of a World Relief survey of 320 Rwandan youths in 2003.[25] Although most survey respondents (94 percent) said that sexual intercourse is the primary manner of HIV transmission, 14 percent also indicated that HIV can be transmitted through curses or evil spirits. This is twice the number of respondents who cited the impact of evil spirits in a baseline survey conducted by World Relief in 1999. Considering that less than 1 percent of respondents said they had no church involvement (87.7 percent self-identified as Protestant, 9.18 percent as Catholic, and 2.5 percent as Muslim), some of those who believe in the ability of curses or evil spirits to transmit HIV also believe in God. Although the relationship between the spirit world and God in the minds of the survey respondents is unclear, the concern for the agency of evil spirits casts the fear of God in a new light, if God or some transcendent power has both the power to heal and the power to punish through disease.

TAMING PHYSICAL DESIRES

Despite the prevailing emphasis on the fear of God and the view that salvation equals no more sin, comments by some respondents acknowledge the existence of physical desires and the need to tame them.

One frequently used metaphor equates the physical desire for sex with the physical need for food. Although specific elements of the metaphor varied slightly with each retelling, the story was told on five separate occasions during my time in Kenya and Rwanda by both abstinence educators and abstinence club members. At the True Love Waits affiliate in Kenya, the Baptist AIDS Response Agency (BARA) uses the metaphor as an object lesson. The abstinence club leader takes a plate of ten *mandazi,* or donuts, and asks the youth to describe them. The youth typically say things like, "I thirst for it," "It is beautiful," "It is soft," and the like. "They are describing a woman," says BARA's Edgar Makona. Then the leader injects poison into one of the donuts and rearranges the plate of food, hiding the contaminated donut. The leader offers the donuts to the youths. They all decline. "We call it choices," Makona says. "They make choices."

In Rwanda some youths clearly had either participated in a similar exercise or had heard a story about it. Substituting oranges for donuts, one Rwandan youth offered this response to explain why he is abstinent: "If someone gives you some oranges, and in some have poison, which one will you choose? There are bad, and some are good, but I don't know, so I leave them all."

Another Rwandan abstinence club member began by recounting a similar illustration: "I want to take the same example of cakes, and one has poison. This is our problem—which one would you like?" Instead of suggesting that all cakes should be avoided, the respondent goes on to suggest that the hunger for food is more powerful than the threat of poisoning. Turning to the World Relief staff member responsible for abstinence education in Kigali, he said, "Even you, Louise, have said that sex is God's plan for our bodies." Addressing the rest of the club, he said, "You have cakes—some of them are poison—but I am so hungry, so I need to eat. So what do I do?"

Although the purpose of the oranges/donuts/cakes illustration may have been to reveal the tempting disguises of disease carriers and the consequences of poor choices, equating sexual desire with physical hunger may be problematic for the abstinence message. As the last respondent's comments highlight, physical hunger needs to be satisfied for survival. In a poor country that during the time of my visit was experiencing a famine that had tripled the price of food, the average Rwandan is fortunate to eat one meal a day. Eating from a plate of cakes, even knowing that one cake has been poisoned, is a choice that a hungry Rwandan may be willing to make. The young man pointed out that World Relief has emphasized the goodness of sex. Based on the logic of the illustration, it is difficult to refute the club member's wish to fulfill his sexual desire.

A young woman answered the male respondent's question by reaffirming the abstinence call to wait and the corresponding emphasis on traditional marriage: "I will answer your question. Everything at the right moment. When you decide, you get married." Keeping within the metaphor of the illustration, she charged the young man with gluttony—"Please don't eat every cake you find!"—which elicited laughter from the club members.

BOUNDARIES OF SEXUAL BEHAVIOR

If Christians can be tempted as much as non-Christians, personal agency is needed to set boundaries for appropriate sexual behavior. This was one of the responses to a story about two sexually active Christians. I told the story to each of the abstinence clubs:

> Once there was a young woman about your age. She was a Christian and loved Jesus with all her heart. Her whole family loved Jesus. One day at school she noticed a very handsome young man. She found out that he was

a Christian, and his whole family was Christian. She began to get to know the young man. They began dating and spending time together, taking walks together, going to the café for Fantas, and talking. They liked each other very much. They even loved each other. Both families were very happy. The young woman hoped that one day they would be married. Then one day the young man pressured the young woman to have sex with him. She knew it was wrong, but she loved him very much, so she had sex with him. The young woman became pregnant. When the young man found out, he left her, saying he could no longer marry her. Almost more crushing for the young woman, when her church found out, they said she had to leave.

One of the repeated responses to this story was that the young man and young woman did not set boundaries in their physical relationship. "I think what they lacked is to protect themselves. I think the young Christian should be told how to have friendships without going further," one young man says. "What I can share, although we are saved, we are still in the human nature," says another male club member. "We must be wise as people who have known girls. For example, the teenager is the same, saved or not, but we have different ways of behaving in different situations. So we must measure the relationship between the boy and girl—set boundaries."

Despite this articulated understanding of the role of agency in the creation of boundaries, this view was in the minority at the abstinence club meetings. At a Pentecostal church, multiple respondents suggested that the young man and woman in the story were "not really saved." They also said that they were not really Christians because they "lacked self-control." One respondent referred to the Old Testament story of Joseph's fleeing sexual temptation by suggesting that the young woman in the story who had sex with her boyfriend was not a Christian because she did not flee temptation as Joseph did: "There is something they call to fly the scene. In this story, they are both saved. I mean, the man was a temptation put in front of this girl to see if she is really a Christian. Maybe she had not really made a decision for Christ. If this girl was a real Christian when the boy asked her to have sex, she would have thought of the glory of God and said she would not do this."

FEMALE RESPONSIBILITY

Perhaps the most striking theme of all the responses to this story was that most abstinence club members blamed the young woman. It is significant that respondents did not blame the young man, who pressured the young woman to have sex. Respondents were not prompted to place blame for the outcome of the story.

Blaming the young woman for her behavior—as well as the young man's behavior—was a theme of many responses. As the example illustrates, the young woman is charged with not being a "real Christian" and is faulted for not thinking of the "glory of God" when her boyfriend asked her to have sex. The boyfriend does not receive the same charge of being a fake Christian. He is merely a temptation, a plot device in a morality play. One male respondent described a situation in his promiscuous past that was similar to that in the story. He praised past girlfriends who played hard to get, while blaming others for giving in to him too quickly, prompting him to move on to other young women. In effect, he blamed his promiscuous behavior on the behavior of promiscuous young women. One respondent took liberties with the plot to magnify the young woman's culpability: "The girl was to blame for always clinging and saying, 'I love you,' and that she missed him when they were apart for five minutes." Others suggested that the young woman stopped loving her boyfriend after she got pregnant, effectively giving the boyfriend a justification for leaving her.

In contrast to the story of the promiscuous young man who did not get any of his girlfriends pregnant or transmit any diseases, the story of the Christian couple ends with a direct consequence of nonmarital sexual activity: the young woman becomes pregnant. The presence of a visible consequence may have prompted club members to assign blame for the consequence, labeling it a sin. "There are consequences of sin," one male respondent says. "The girl sinned. It is the consequence of the girl's sin." Another male respondent agrees: "It is the sin of both, but most consequences for the girl, unless the boy is infected with AIDS."

Blaming the young woman for mutual nonmarital sexual activity is consistent with Rwandan cultural values that ignore male sexual promiscuity and allow "boys to be boys." Some male respondents expressed the view that if a young man does not have sex before he is married, he is considered abnormal. Even the World Relief abstinence trainer made a distinction between the roles of males and females and their different levels of responsibility regarding sexual behavior. At the end of the abstinence club meeting at an evangelical church in the Nyarutarama district, the trainer stood up and addressed the youths. He began by addressing the young women: "Sometimes I speak and a young lady said that she fought with her husband every day. The girl had had sex [before she married], and he hadn't, so now they fight. He said, 'You will deceive me again.' Girls, if you want to have a good family, practice abstinence now. It will bear fruit later. Otherwise, [your future husband] will always remember it. If you do a small mistake at home, he may blow up. Please practice abstinence and wait for your future." Here the future happiness of the young women's married lives is dependent on their choice to be abstinent now. Sexual promiscuity could turn their future homes into fields of landmines of the young women's own creation.

The trainer had a second point for the young women: "Be careful of people who say they love you. A boy who says he wants to marry you, he is not serious. If you agree to have sex, he will keep it in his mind that you are easy." The first argument offered the husband's response to his wife's previous sexual promiscuity. The second argument offered the boyfriend's response: he will consider her easy, therefore undesirable and not a good prospect for marriage. Although it appears that young men may use promises of love and marriage to get young women to have sex with them, the argument in support of abstinence is a cautionary tale for young women who give in, not for young men who make empty promises.

The final brief point for the young women addressed the fear of God and the fear of disease: "You girls, even if you don't fear sin, fear also AIDS." By placing this argument as the third and final argument directed at the young women, the trainer effectively created a hierarchy, with the threat of contracting AIDS as the least important reason for abstinence. The threat of AIDS is presented as a lesser motivation for abstinence, so that abstinence is considered "even if" one does not fear sin, which is presented as the greater motivation. The threat of the physical harm of disease is presented as a last resort to convince young women to practice abstinence. The organization of the arguments suggests that the threat of an unhappy marriage or failed marriage prospects—along with an assumed fear of God—is a stronger motivation for young women to pursue abstinence than disease and death.

After his message to the young women at the abstinence club, the World Relief trainer turned his attention to the young men: "You boys, what you are doing, if you are deceiving girls, your sisters will be deceived, too. If you desire to have sex, it is not a sin, but try to dominate it." The contrast between the message to the young women and men is significant. Here the young men are portrayed as strong ("dominate") and sex driven ("desire to have sex"). They are absolved of their desire to have sex with the reassurance that "it is not a sin" (which, it can be assumed, refers to sexual desire, not sexual intercourse). The suggested solution to the problem of sexual desire is an act of brute strength: try to dominate it. The message to the young women is filled with consequences: bad marriage, no marriage, and AIDS. In the message to the young men, young women are still the bearers of the consequences of the young men's sinful behavior. Instead of chastising the young men's sinful behavior of "deceiving girls," the World Relief trainer points out that the young men's sisters are the victims of other young men's deception. Presumably, this is an argument in support of abstinence in that the young men will want to stop their sexual activity so that their sisters will not become the objects of other young men's sexual exploits. What is notable here is that the consequences are implicit for the sisters but not for the brothers.

None of the respondents blamed the young man or the church in the story of the young Christian woman who became pregnant. Two female respondents offered somewhat softened critiques of the young man's behavior. "How could this boy have left this girl?" one young woman asked. "As a girl I have to be very careful of who says he is my friend." Another female respondent said, "Girls are more vulnerable. If you are a boy, you . . . If a boy asks you to have sex, then he doesn't love you. If it happens, keep it quiet, don't kill [the baby]." The responses function more as cautionary tales to the other young women than as finger-pointing at the young men. Both responses reveal the deceptive tendency of young men and offer warnings to young women. A young man who says that he is your friend may not be, and a young man who asks for sex does not love you. The last response offers direct advice for young women who have not heeded the other warnings and who have been deceived by a young man and become pregnant. They are told to "keep it quiet," acknowledging cultural views that disapprove of out-of-wed-lock pregnancies, and not to destroy the fetus, acknowledging Christian views against abortion.

Respondents did not fault the church for turning away from a person in need; instead, they interpreted the church as appropriately punishing a sinner. When pressed for responses to the church's behavior, club members explained the actions of the church in the story as consistent with the actions of Rwandan churches. "When they discover if you have had sex, they say they are a sinner and immediately there are punishments," reported one male respondent. "You are not allowed to do anything in the church—sharing, singing—until you repent yourself."

Overall, between the story of the promiscuous young man and the story of the young Christian woman who becomes pregnant, the story of the young Christian woman elicited the most responses. It appeared the fictitious scenario was a familiar situation for some abstinence club members. At an evangelical church in the Nyarutarama district there was a lengthy pause after I told the story and asked the club members to respond. I heard a great deal of murmuring and whispering, but no one wished to respond. The Kinyarwanda translator confirmed that the group understood the question. "They know girls like this," the translator said. "It happens."

CHOOSING GOD

Rwandan young people portray abstinence as a choice, but they portray it as a negative choice or prohibition. In contrast to African evangelical abstinence educators who emphasize abstinence as a positive choice for purity, Rwandan youth discuss abstinence only as ceasing a bad or sinful activity. This discrepancy suggests some degree of lack of message saliency. Although a straightforward explanation is not clear from the data, the discrepancy suggests a difference in cultural scripts: the rhetoric of the African abstinence educators, with its positive focus on purity, is more similar to the rhetoric of U.S. abstinence educators than to that of Rwandan youth. This is not a surprise, considering that the African abstinence educators in this study are all associated with U.S. evangelical organizations that work in Africa. Rwandan youth, in contrast, may be informed by a uniquely Rwandan or African cultural context.

Rwandan abstinence youth club members demonstrate the tension displayed by the abstinence educators' contradiction of focusing on fear of disease as the primary motivation for abstinence but acknowledging that young people are not motivated by disease. Young people acknowledge the context of AIDS that surrounds the abstinence movement in Africa, but they say that the fear of God is a stronger motivation for abstinence than a fear of disease. They go beyond leaders' discussions of the role of religious conversion in transforming behavior to construct a view of evangelical Christianity as determining abstinent behavior: If one is saved, then one will not be tempted sexually.

This shift in focus offers a nuanced view of agency and its role in motivating abstinent behavior among Rwandan youth: the individual possesses personal agency, but the power to choose is to be used to choose God. Once an individual has become a Christian, the other choices, such as bodily self-control, are no longer an issue, as they were before one submitted one's life to God's authority. Personal agency is subsumed under God's agency. If a new believer is a "new creation," then the agency is God's as the originator of the new sinless creation. If a Christian gives in to sexual temptation, the emphasis is not the act of sexual sin as much as it is the earlier sin of false conversion: the individual was never truly a Christian, as demonstrated by his or her lack of bodily self-control.

Despite prevailing themes of the Christian body as a new creation and the emphasis on the agency of God, respondents reveal a complex and seemingly contradictory understanding of agency by saying that individuals need to set boundaries for their sexual behavior. Christians may be new creations, but they also are "God's temples." This phrase emphasizes the agency of the individual to act as caretaker of the body as an act of worship and obedience to God. Using the metaphor of food such as cakes or oranges to represent sex is problematic for abstinence, since it relies on a threat of negative consequences as motivation for abstinence. By presenting a moral equivalency to appetites of the body, whether for food or sex, the choice of abstinence becomes an avoidance of personal harm instead of an act of obedience to God.

The responses from the abstinence club members imply a high degree of agency for females, not in terms of choice but in terms of responsibility. Young women are characterized as bearing the responsibility for sexual promiscuity, acting as temptresses and displaying the proof of their sinfulness in their out-of-wedlock pregnancies. Their choice of abstinence lacks an empowering rhetoric of self-worth. There are no fairy tales here. Instead, young women are blamed for the sexual promiscuity of young men. Societal gender inequalities were painfully apparent during the group interviews: young women were largely reluctant to respond to questions, although they frequently constituted nearly half the group.

As my discussion in this chapter demonstrates, abstinence education is not culturally neutral. The rhetoric of choosing abstinence is much different in the United States than in Rwanda, where choices in general are limited. Table 1 distills five key thematic differences between the U.S. and sub-Saharan African cases. This chapter addresses the first three themes of positive versus negative focus of the abstinence messages, differing conceptions of the relationship between the pledger and

TABLE I COMPARISON OF KEY THEMES FROM THE EVANGELICAL SEXUAL
ABSTINENCE MOVEMENT IN THE UNITED STATES AND KENYA/RWANDA

United States	Kenya and Rwanda
Positive focus on sex/marriage/purity.	Negative focus on fearing God and AIDS.
Pleasing God has tangible benefits for the individual.	Pleasing God is an end in itself.
Females possess power over their bodies.	Females bear responsibility for their bodies.
Sin/behavior is an individual problem.	Sin/behavior is a structural problem.
The condom is a tool of promiscuity.	The condom is a tool for saving lives.

God, and the differing role of young women as possessing power over
or responsibility for their bodies.

In general, the U.S. evangelical abstinence message lacks a degree of
salience in sub-Saharan Africa. Central to this lack of salience is differing conceptions of agency. There is an internal tension in an abstinence
message that offers a solution through individual agency to a problem
that is dictated by social structure and oppression, not by the individual.
To further explore this tension, I turn in chapter 7 to an analysis of the
condom, which addresses the final two comparative themes listed in
table I. Rhetorical constructions of the condom, a subject of consider-
able debate among evangelicals, illustrate who truly has the power to
choose.

CHAPTER 7

The Condom Conflict

Saving Lives or Promoting Promiscuity?

Franklin Graham is no stranger to controversy. Graham, the head of Samaritan's Purse, an evangelical relief and development agency, is the son of the evangelist Billy Graham. In an interview with *Christianity Today* magazine, Franklin Graham recounted an invitation he received from the former ambassador Richard Holbrooke to offer a benediction at an AIDS fund-raiser in New York City. Graham recalled that he asked if he could say a few words to the audience; Holbrooke agreed, so long as Graham did not "attack homosexuals." Graham's pledge to help save the lives of the millions infected with HIV was met with applause. Then Graham said, "I'm pro-life," which was met with silence. "I think it's just as important to save the life of an unborn child as it is to save the life of a man or a woman eaten up with AIDS," he continued. "We can't do this without God's help. That's why I'm here to ask for God's help."[1]

For Graham, the audience's reaction typifies secular approaches to solving the AIDS crisis: "The number one obstacle is the world's concept: Just give me a billion condoms and we can solve this issue. What the world wants to do is to continue in a sinful lifestyle."[2] In his retelling of the story, Graham connects opposition to his prolife stance, ambivalence about asking for God's help, and support of condom distribution as a solution to AIDS. Like many evangelicals, Graham supports efforts to curb AIDS, but he views the use of condoms as part of those efforts— and the lifestyles they support—as tantamount to sin.

Although American evangelicals are generally in agreement about the importance of abstinence education for youth in the United States and in African countries, one important point of disagreement is about the use and promotion of the condom. In the United States, a key criticism by abstinence-until-marriage advocates of comprehensive sex education programs is that providing details about condoms and how to use them dilutes the message of abstinence and implies that teenagers have no choice but to be sexually active. They believe that condom education constructs youth as possessing limited agency in regard to their bodies and reduces the credibility of educators who promote both abstinence and condoms. Abstinence advocates insist that the condom is a tool for promiscuity.

Despite the unfavorable reputation of the condom among U.S. abstinence educators, evangelicals in Africa (including American evangelicals who are working on AIDS efforts in Africa) tend to view the condom as a necessary part of AIDS prevention efforts. Condom use is part of the comprehensive ABC strategy. This acronym, which stands for abstinence, be faithful, and use condoms, not only suggests the simplicity of the approach ("as easy as ABC") but also provides a hierarchy and order to the prevention methods, placing condoms as a device of last resort. The inclusion of the condom, however limited, in evangelicals' AIDS prevention efforts in Africa remains controversial, not least because many of the same evangelicals who view the condom as a tool for promiscuity in the United States constitute the current or potential donors for AIDS projects in Africa.

In light of this constraint, how do evangelical abstinence educators in Africa rhetorically construct the condom? In this chapter I argue that they construct the condom as (1) a tool for marital fidelity, (2) a tool for saving lives, (3) part of holistic community-based development, and (4) a tool for female empowerment. After demonstrating the prevalence of these four themes, I turn to an analysis of an evangelical statement of conscience on the AIDS crisis as an example of how these constructions of the condom affect public discourse about AIDS prevention. Although evangelicals tend to view the condom as a tool for promiscuity, in Africa the potential to save lives trumps the potential for increased promiscuity. The perceived lack of choices presented by the dire health situation in Africa provides rhetorical space for a positive construction of the condom as lifesaving. This medical focus echoes U.S. evangelicals' construction of abstinence as the healthy choice. The condom restores personal agency in a context of structural oppression. But if oppressive social and economic structures in Africa are to blame for individual promiscuity, the solution of abstinence as an individual choice will have weak resonance.

CONDOM AS A TOOL FOR MARITAL FIDELITY

A key argument for the evangelical abstinence movement in the United States is abstinence until marriage and faithfulness within marriage. This corresponds with the A and B points (abstinence and be faithful) of the ABC approach to curbing HIV/AIDS transmissions in Africa. In handling the controversial point C (use condoms) of the ABC approach, U.S.-based evangelical abstinence educators define C in terms of B. In effect, they portray condoms as a tool for enabling and preserving faithfulness within marriage.

In nearly all my interviews with evangelical leaders, respondents described each organization's condom policy primarily in terms of helping married couples to remain married in cases where one spouse is HIV-positive: "So there is a very critical place for the condom, especially in situations that are very common in Africa, where the only risk for HIV is being faithful to an unfaithful spouse. So we definitely discuss the condom." Here Deborah Dortzbach, international director of HIV/AIDS programs for World Relief, identifies the source of the presence of HIV in the marriage relationship: an unfaithful spouse. The condom is not described as promoting this promiscuous behavior; instead, the condom is portrayed as allowing the HIV-negative spouse to uphold the marriage vows while protecting his or her health. (According to most of my interview respondents, the spouse to be protected by condoms is typically female.) At the same time, *unfaithfulness* can refer to past or current infidelity on the part of the unfaithful spouse. The condom may promote disease-free marital fidelity on the part of the already-faithful spouse, but it does not address the possibility of continued promiscuity on the part of the unfaithful spouse. Protecting married couples is a primary focus of Global Care's condom policy: "We think there's definitely a need and a role for condoms. Condoms are needed by married people who wish to space their births. They're needed by married couples who are discordant, with HIV discordance. They're needed by married couples who don't know their status, which most people don't. . . . So, condoms need to be available."[3] The respondent refers to married couples for all three examples, two of which are directly related to HIV/AIDS protection.

CONDOM AS A TOOL FOR SAVING LIVES

Implicit in the description of the condom as a tool for preserving marital fidelity is an emphasis on protecting the faithful HIV-negative spouse from the unfaithful HIV-positive spouse. The underlying definition of the condom by abstinence educators in Africa is as a tool for saving lives. Variations on the key words *life* and *lifesaving* are repeated in the interviewees' responses about the role of the condom:

> We don't want to be unrealistic, and we want ultimately for *lives to be saved* and preserved.[4]

> But we definitely engage in dialogue about the condom and try to discuss the facts that it is effective when it's used properly with every sexual act and that there are many situations in which it is *lifesaving,* and as Christians that is our primary and superseding [goal], that overrides all of our concerns about sexuality. . . . [We] *promote life* so that we can then have a fulfilling life the way God wants us to have.[5]

> [A] condom itself is not an evil thing. They really do *save lives.*[6]

Interview respondents portray the condom as a medical device that prevents disease, not a license for promiscuity. The condom itself is not viewed as an evil thing. It is a tool that can be used for good or bad behavior (which the respondents would define as nonmarital sexual activity). For the organizations' staff members, however, the condom's potential for good as a medical device overcomes the risk that it will be used for evil. Tim Ziemer, then-CEO of World Relief, repeatedly articulated this focus on disease in his explanation of the organization's condom policy: "But we are very comfortable embracing the C [condom] as part of the overall opportunity to prevent the spread of AIDS. You have to understand it in a context of the disease, not promiscuity."

One World Relief respondent explicitly contrasts the culture of promiscuity in the United States with the culture of death in Africa: "If we're in the U.S. it kind of becomes a morality of whether or not this is going to influence kids to have sex, but the morality in the global sense is more, 'Is this going to keep someone alive or not?' And I think it's a totally different set of issues."[7] Abstinence educators working in Africa generally acknowledge the risk that condoms will do more than just prevent disease transmission: "So, does promoting the condom promote promiscuity? Possibly," acknowledges World Relief's Deborah Dortzbach. However, in the African context the risk of promiscuity is ranked as a lesser concern than the risk of transmitting disease and death.

Dortzbach explains that World Relief includes discussion of condoms in its curriculum and training but does not promote their use: "So we don't ignore or completely dismiss the use of the condom in some situations, but we don't promote its use among youth. We promote abstinence." If an African young person persists in sexual activity even after hearing the abstinence message, Dortzbach insists that it is important that the young person know about the condom: "So that begins to demystify how we might address the condom as a potentially lifesaving instrument, but it still emphasizes *the* lifesaving action, which is abstinence."

A Global Care staff member defends the organization's condom policy—which extends beyond married couples to include "high-risk populations," such as commercial sex workers and long-haul truck drivers—in terms of the biblical demand to value life: "We agree that abstinence and be faithful are critical, but because of scripture's valuing life . . . [there is] the need to protect it for high-risk populations. So there are certain truck drivers or prostitutes as well to protect life on using that." The biblical view of valuing life is described as a moral order that transcends the ABC approach. The activities of ABC are held to this higher standard, which justifies the use of condoms based on their lifesaving ability.

If condoms save lives, then withholding condoms kills. A biblical view that values life also holds murder as sin. One respondent portrays Christians who are unwilling to use condoms in their approach to HIV/AIDS prevention in Africa as equivalent to murderers: "Despite our goals for abstinence and faithfulness, there are people who engage in high-risk sex for many, many reasons. . . . We believe that their lives are sacred, that God cares about them, wants them to live. We believe that killing is as great a sin as adultery. Murder is as great a sin as adultery, and therefore we want them to protect their lives and the lives of their partners even if they decide to engage in the activity. So we believe that condoms should be available to them." Referring to the Ten Commandments, the respondent points out that both adultery and murder are sin. The sinful behavior of the promiscuous African man who brings HIV home to his faithful wife is equated with the behavior of a Christian relief and development worker who avoids discussing condoms as a means of HIV/AIDS prevention. In effect, withholding protection is viewed as the moral equivalent of infecting with disease.

CONDOM AS A PART OF HOLISTIC DEVELOPMENT

Closely linked to the portrayal of the condom as a tool for saving lives is the portrayal of the condom as a tool for holistic development. The rationale for the condom's role in saving lives is found in an overarching view of international community-based development that goes beyond merely encouraging sexual abstinence to promoting structural changes that eliminate the need for unhealthy sexual activity. U.S.-based evangelical abstinence educators focus on the individual sin of a sexually active teenager, whereas those working in Africa focus on the structural sin of an oppressive social, political, and economic system that forces individuals to engage in unhealthy sexual activity. In the United States the teenager is portrayed as possessing agency and therefore responsible for controlling his or her sexual desires and remaining abstinent. In Africa the social, political, and economic systems are deemed corrupt, rendering individual Africans not responsible for their actions. Instead, evangelical Christian rhetoric places the agency for change on evangelical Christians, not individual Africans, holding the church accountable to respond to the crisis created by structural sin.

The African context for abstinence is a far-reaching humanitarian crisis in which any and all methods (A, B, and C) are needed to curb the tide of deaths. One respondent points out that with disagreements in the U.S. evangelical community about the role of the condom, a sure way to achieve unity on the topic of AIDS in Africa is to focus on saving lives. "There are differing nuance positions on condom uses, but there is agreement on the importance of 'abstinence and be faithful,'" acknowledges a Global Care staff member. "[It's] a humanitarian tragedy with eight thousand people dying a day, with fourteen million orphans. There's an area to get agreement that there's a humanitarian tragedy going on and that you need to respond as a Christian. . . . There's more that unites us than divides us." The situation is urgent—a "humanitarian tragedy," in the words of this respondent—with countless numbers of innocent victims dying every day. A response is needed immediately. The immediacy of the need holds the possibility of tabling disagreements about condom use, and the focus on innocent victims raises the stakes of moral action. For evangelicals, innocent African orphans are a more compelling image in support of the condom than hormone-saturated American teenagers.

Global Care staff members articulate a holistic approach to encouraging both condom use and sexual abstinence. They discuss their HIV/AIDS work as part of a larger development program: "The developmental approach focuses on the fact that you have eight thousand people dying a day and that that's causing all sorts of issues. Many of them are schoolteachers, farmers. You've got child-headed households, both parents have died off. You have parents with children caring for dying parents. And of course they're not farming. The parents are not teaching the children. The children are not in school because children are doing the work on the farms, trying to keep the family going. It creates a developmental crisis."[8] The developmental crisis implies that an urgent response is needed. The focus is not reducing teenage pregnancy or achieving the ideal of sexual purity. The sexual transmission of HIV is seen as the stone in the pond that creates many ripples. In this case the ripples—"child-headed household," "dying parents"—have become large waves that require immediate attention.

In addition to acknowledging the scope of unchecked HIV/AIDS transmission and the urgency of finding a solution, the development approach acknowledges the complexities of causes in the African context. The ABC approach is viewed as a simple method for standardizing efforts for curbing HIV/AIDS transmission, but it does not account for the complex structural reasons for sexual behavior. Poverty and its effects are among the complex causes and are a key focus of the development approach. Antiretroviral drugs are expensive and a lower financial priority than buying food; many Africans view a future death from AIDS as a lesser threat when death from malnutrition is a constant and immediate concern. "Remember that most of the people are living in the developmental crisis on a dollar a day at $365 a year. . . . Some of that [medication] can be cost prohibitive," reminds a Global Care staff member. "So some people ask why give tests if they can't get drugs. There's no hope. And some people don't want to know. So you have to provide the hope of testing and medicine, but you also need to change behavior so people are not spreading it. You have the issue of care for the dying, the child. And so you need a holistic approach." A holistic approach is needed because changing behavior through sexual abstinence is not enough to solve the complex system of problems associated with HIV/AIDS.

An example of this complexity is the commercial sex worker. The development approach acknowledges that to encourage abstinence among prostitutes is foolhardy (and perhaps immoral) without eliminating the economic reasons for their sexual activity. Commercial sex workers are one of the high-risk populations that evangelical groups have identified as a target for the condom. The oppressiveness of structural poverty and the immediacy of the health crisis justify use of the condom as lifesaving for prostitutes. Global Care tries to find alternatives for the commercial sex worker, typically through economic development and microenterprise programs. "They're not in the business because it's their first choice," says a staff member. "They usually have economic pressures that are basically life—food on the table, education for their children or sometimes for themselves. And so they need economical alternatives, so we usually try to bring those alongside. But at the same time, we will counsel them that, as long as they're in this business, to use condoms."

Here the condom is contextualized within structural poverty and used alongside other programs to help reduce the economic factors that promote unhealthy sexual activity. This holistic approach provides options, thus restoring the agency of the commercial sex worker and her ability to choose among alternatives. The structural sin of poverty weakens the prostitute's agency: until she has other options for feeding herself and her family, my respondents apparently do not hold her responsible for her behavior. The respondents hold the evangelical aid worker (supported by the financial contributions of other evangelicals) responsible for creating other choices that eliminate the need for promiscuity.

The evangelical relief and development aid workers with whom I spoke are well aware of the tensions within the evangelical community between the abstinence-until-marriage advocates in the United States and the development workers in sub-Saharan Africa. As one respondent points out, the problem comes when a Western value for abstinence is transported to a different cultural context: "Focus on the Family doesn't understand the drivers of poverty, of powerlessness of women, gender and equity, the fact that girls aren't in school, the fact that girls are married when they're twelve, thirteen, fourteen years old, that girls are sold in many Asian and even African countries into marriage. I frankly think they take a very Western American, white suburban [view] . . . that's what they're concerned about for their daughters and sons here in America, and that's my feeling. I think they're reflecting that onto a very different situation."[9] The respondent singles out a high-profile conservative evangelical nonprofit—Focus on the Family—as representative of an evangelical approach that does not understand the complexities of the African context for abstinence. The respondent continues:

> What do the evangelicals really think or hope to achieve through a marital/abstinence-only or abstinence-until-marriage approach, especially in resource-poor countries, developing countries, given the taboos, the stigma about sex, the role of women? How does that help all of the other issues—the pressures of poverty? The fact that [in] some of these countries 25 percent of the population is already infected? You've got to protect them and the other 75 percent. They're in marriages, and they don't know. The other thing is that they don't know they're infected because there's absence of testing, and there's stigma, and they don't want to know. There are many, many reasons.

The reason for the lack of understanding of African complexities on the part of American evangelicals is found in the difference between idealism and pragmatism. The advocates in the United States have the luxury of dwelling on the idealism of sexual abstinence, but the aid workers in Africa must be pragmatic because they are faced each day with implementing AIDS prevention programs. "Some advocacy groups in the United States, who are Christian-based, [are] more focused on the moral values in relation to sexuality, like abstinence, be faithful. There's nothing wrong with that because it is needed," says a Global Care staff member. "But because we are operational, . . . we're doing the abstinence program, but we're also doing a lot of the care issues to see the need for the holistic treatment." Moral sexuality loses its influence as those trying to put the ideals into practice run into the complex structures of poverty.

CONDOM AS A TOOL FOR FEMALE EMPOWERMENT

Another portrayal of the condom that is implicit in the other portrayals—as a tool for marital fidelity, saving lives, and holistic development—is the condom as a tool for the empowerment of women. Within the focus on marital fidelity is a rhetoric of female empowerment that views the condom as a tool for a wife to save her own life. The holistic development approach, particularly in the example of commercial sex workers, highlights the role of the condom in saving the lives of women until the economic forces that necessitate their harmful sexual practices are abated.

"The woman is the one who's more vulnerable, and it's just often the man's prerogative and the man's decision," says World Relief's Rebecca Heidkamp. "So I think a lot of it has to do with the situation and the kind of powerlessness of women." Women are portrayed as trapped in a male-dominated society. They are vulnerable to HIV because of their powerlessness, as seen in their faithfulness to unfaithful husbands and their coerced positions as commercial sex workers.

The person most at risk for HIV/AIDS in Africa today is a married woman. "They're being faithful to their husbands, but they're still getting HIV/AIDS, and they don't have the authority to say their husbands should use condoms," says a Global Care staff member. Another staff member points out that a significant percentage of HIV-positive women had their first and only sexual relationship with their husband. The ABC approach, according to the respondent, is too simplistic. "It doesn't address the full range of the underlying issues of poverty and gender relations." The issue is the powerlessness of women, their lack of rights, and their lack of ability to negotiate for sex, according to the respondent. It is not uncommon for the first sexual encounter to be coerced. "So how is A, B, or C going to help them?" the Global Care staff member asks.

In the cases of women as prostitutes and faithful wives, the women are powerless to avoid HIV without the power to force condom use on their partners. The condom at the center of the controversy is the male condom, not the female condom. Men may control their marriages, and structures of poverty may control women's prostitution, but the condom is portrayed as holding the possibility for restoring power and agency to African women. However, it is a dim possibility if women do not already possess the power to influence their husbands.

STATEMENT OF CONSCIENCE ON HIV/AIDS

On June 11, 2003, fifty-four evangelical leaders signed the Statement of Conscience of the Evangelical Church Concerning the Global HIV/AIDS Crisis. The leaders were in Washington, D.C., as part of a forum on AIDS organized by World Vision, a large Christian humanitarian aid agency, and cosponsored by World Relief, the National Association of Evangelicals, and MAP International. The names and logos of the organizations appear at the top of the Statement of Conscience. As a position statement on AIDS and the evangelical church's response to it, the document briefly addresses the issue of the condom, which renders it controversial. An open letter to forum attendees from Concerned Women for America (CWA), also dated June 11, 2003, takes issue with what is perceived as a permissive attitude toward condom use in the Statement of Conscience. A close reading of both the Statement of Conscience and the letter from CWA finds two conflicting evangelical portrayals of the condom. The documents crystalize key differences in matters of agency—who is portrayed as responsible for spreading or stopping the disease—and audience—whether the message is directed at Americans or Africans.

The Statement of Conscience begins by establishing the size and scope of the problem and by defining the problem as a humanitarian one: "AIDS is the greatest humanitarian crisis of our time; it may be the greatest humanitarian crisis of *all* time." The opening paragraph goes on to use an extended metaphor of fire, highlighting the speed of transmission and the all-consuming devastation of the disease: "The flames of this pandemic are leaping across continents, consuming all they touch with no regard for race, culture, religion or economic status. In sub-Saharan Africa, where the contagion burns the hottest, entire communities have been consumed by the disease. Asia and Eastern Europe, particularly India, China and Russia, are the next front in this firefight."[10]

The choice of the fire metaphor is particularly interesting since sexual passion and desire—contributors to HIV transmission—are often described with the same metaphor (e.g., a "burning passion"). Fire is also used to describe sin and hell more generally, from Dante's *Inferno* to the hellfire and brimstone sermons of Great Awakening preachers and their descendants. In the opening lines of the Statement of Conscience, the sexual behavior of passionate individuals is not connected to the transmission of the disease. The greatest agency lies with the fire of the disease—it burns and consumes its helpless African victims, "with no regard for race, culture, religion or economic status." The behavior of Africans is not held responsible for the spread of the fire.

The next section of the document describes the extent of the crisis. The document uses startling statistics to create a sense of urgency: "Today, five people die every minute from the complications of this preventable disease." Five bullet points outline other "equally daunting" statistics. Two points focus on the number of deaths caused by AIDS. One point each focuses on orphans, women, and the global scope of the crisis.[11] The points do not discuss how transmission occurs; instead, they focus on the deadly outcomes of the disease. The fire of disease is leaving charred remains in its path of destruction. The victims are faceless numbers with no role in causing or preventing the disease.

The "Christian Church in America" has a role, however, as described in a section entitled "Christians as Agents of Change." As the subhead suggests, evangelical Christians possess the agency to douse the flames of HIV/AIDS. Christians have both the "opportunity to demonstrate their faith in action" and "the responsibility to bring the hope of Christ to those whose lives are seemingly hopeless." How the church in America is to articulate its faith through the curbing of disease transmission is outlined as "the promotion of sexual abstinence before marriage and faithfulness to one's spouse after marriage, reduction of stigma, as well as compassionate care for orphans, widows, and those already infected." In a new paragraph within the same section the document offers its position on the condom: "We realize that there is a divergence of opinion regarding the use of condoms as one strategy to slow the spread of the disease. We, therefore, respect the right of all signatories to hold to their own convictions on this issue."[12]

In the section that describes Christians as "agents of change," the document portrays condoms as "one strategy" to curb disease transmission and emphasizes the "right of all signatories" to decide whether they want to use this strategy. The statement regarding condoms is significant in that it decentralizes the decision making to individual organizations, effectively removing disagreements about the condom from the unifying document. In addition, the location of the statement on condoms is significant in that the condom is portrayed as one of the tools for the "agents of change" to use in their fight against AIDS, instead of one of the causes of the spread of the disease as a promoter of promiscuity, as Concerned Women for America argues.

The letter to evangelical AIDS forum attendees from Concerned Women for America, signed by Sandy Rios, then the organization's president, focuses on "three major points [that] will cause problems for many Evangelicals thinking of becoming a signatory." The first bullet point calls for the Statement of Conscience to "state unequivocally that while not all AIDS cases are a direct result of sinful behavior, the HIV/AIDS pandemic is rooted in disobedience to God's commandments and only Christ can transform lives so that AIDS can be eradicated."[13] This point roots the spread of disease in the behavior of individuals, locating the agency for the spread of disease in its victims. The sinful behavior is located in people, not oppressive structures. The solution for eradicating AIDS is not abstinence, marital faithfulness, or condoms but the transformative power of Jesus Christ.

The second point takes issue with the Statement of Conscience's "approval to any Christian organization choosing to hand out condoms," stating that "we strongly object." The letter argues for a specifically Christian solution to "a problem that has steadily become worse through the world's panaceas of compromise and condoms." Here the condom is portrayed as part of the problem of the spread of HIV/AIDS, not its solution. The letter goes on to request "stronger language" on the following condom-related issues: "The Christian imperative for abstinence before marriage and fidelity afterwards as the best (and probably only) deterrent to HIV/AIDS; behavior in conflict with Christian principles (promiscuity, prostitution and infidelity) being root causes and major factors in the spread of HIV/AIDS; the recognition that reliance on condoms has failed to stem the spread of HIV/AIDS; and acknowledgement that condom distribution encourages a false sense of safety and promotes behavior that violates Christian principles."[14] Again, individual behavior that contributes to the spread of HIV/AIDS is at the center of the argument. Here the letter focuses on the role of the condom as promoting "behavior that violates Christian principles," which was identified previously as "promiscuity, prostitution, and infidelity." The condom itself is not portrayed as evil but as a tool that promotes sinful behavior.

The Statement of Conscience and the letter from CWA illustrate two different evangelical portrayals of the condom in the context of HIV/AIDS. The Statement of Conscience describes the condom as "one strategy to slow the spread of the disease." The letter from CWA describes the condom as promoting behavior that "violates Christian principles," which is a "root cause" of the spread of HIV/AIDS.[15] In this way, the Statement of Conscience portrays the condom as a tool for curbing HIV/AIDS transmission, whereas the letter from CWA portrays the condom as contributing to HIV/AIDS transmission.

The CWA letter blames sinful individuals who engage in behaviors like sexual promiscuity that contravene Christian principles. The Statement of Conscience does not address the behavior of these individuals; instead, it uses statistics to portray them as individuals with limited agency to stop the flames of disease from spreading. It describes the fire of disease as a powerful force, able to consume entire communities. It does not address the fire of the community members' sexual desire and potentially promiscuous behavior. Instead of placing blame on promiscuous individuals, the Statement of Conscience places blame on American Christians for not responding to the humanitarian crisis: "Regrettably, the response to the cries of those infected with and affected by HIV/AIDS has been largely silence. The Church was not the first to the frontlines of this conflagration." The agency is placed solidly on Christians to respond to the need through a "loving and non-judgmental response to those infected with the virus and those affected by AIDS." The document offers five actions for signatories to take in order to pledge responsibility, including praying for those infected with the disease, providing financial resources, speaking out to remove the stigma of AIDS, advocating with government leaders, and promoting abstinence.[16] The letter from CWA places agency on individuals in AIDS-affected countries to stop their sinful behavior.

MATTERS OF AGENCY AND AUDIENCE

The interview data from World Relief and Global Care suggest that evangelicals portray the condom as a tool for encouraging marital fidelity, a tool for saving lives, part of holistic community-based development, and a tool for female empowerment. In the African context, evangelical abstinence educators see a role for the condom because they give greater importance to saving lives than the risk of promoting sexual promiscuity. In a twist on the evangelical focus on traditional marriage and marital faithfulness, evangelicals in Africa emphasize the condom's role in keeping couples together when one spouse is HIV-positive. Sinful behavior such as sexual promiscuity is defined in terms of holistic development, where the oppressive structures that perpetuate hunger and poverty are to blame, not prostitutes who are doing what they can to feed their children. The condom is also portrayed as empowering to women: although they still may have to endure coerced sex, women have a tool (if they can convince their partner to wear it) to protect their lives, if not their virginity.

The case of the Statement of Conscience and the letter from Concerned Women for America distills the tensions in the evangelical community about the condom and its uses. CWA portrays the condom as helping to spread AIDS, instead of helping to stop it. Blame is on the promiscuous individual, not the oppressive structure that forces individuals to be promiscuous. This view may be indicative of CWA's role as a U.S-focused abstinence advocate. In this case an American advocate is making a U.S.-centered argument (e.g., focus on the individual) and placing it in the African context. The other abstinence educators and organization staff members cited in this chapter are actively involved in Africa doing relief and development work; abstinence is part of their overall strategy to fight AIDS.

Global Care and World Relief take a more nuanced view of the complex context for AIDS, but CWA constructs agency as an effect of an individual agent. This focus on the individual could facilitate the case for abstinence, which argues for the individual to stop promiscuous behavior. The individual must possess some degree of agency to be able to exercise self-control and commit to abstinence. Blaming promiscuous behavior on societal structures weakens individual agency, and in this context the argument for abstinence appears strained. To put it another way, a call for condom-free abstinence might be made most successfully in a societal structure in which individuals possess a high degree of agency. Abstinence seems like a tough sell if individuals are portrayed as having little power to choose it.

The American evangelical abstinence message constructs promiscuous behavior (and the consequences of STDs and unwanted pregnancy) as essentially an individual problem; thus young people are positioned as individual agents with the power to exercise agency and control their bodies. In this way, the rhetorical strategy—crafting young people as agents—is a fitting response to the exigence of individual promiscuous behavior. In African countries, conversely, constructing individual Africans as agents who can control their own bodies does not appear to be a fitting response to the exigence of structural oppression. However, as the Statement of Conscience suggests, this qualifies as a suitable response when one considers the audience: here, the audience is American evangelicals, not Africans. If the problem of AIDS in Africa is to be constructed merely as a problem of individual sexual promiscuity, then the solution—an individual choice for abstinence—resides in Africans, not American evangelicals. Instead, constructing the problem of AIDS as essentially structural weakens the agency of individual Africans while strengthening the collective agency of American evangelicals to act as the benevolent saviors.

This example demonstrates another aspect of rhetorical agency: the rhetorical construction of nonagency as a precursor to reclaiming agency can function as a persuasive strategy whether the nonagent is oneself or someone else. The U.S. example in this study shows how evangelicals construct themselves (and the receivers of their abstinence message) as being without agency in order to make the triumphant move of reclaiming agency.[17] A similar move occurs in the African case; however, American evangelicals portray Africans as without agency in order to strengthen the agency of Americans who have both the power and the desire to act. The "victims" are either Africans (in the African context) or evangelicals (in the American context), but in both cases evangelicals successfully (re)construct themselves as agents with the agency to modify the exigence.

CHAPTER 8

What's Not So Great about Great Sex

The camera pans behind the South African studio audience as the American evangelical pastor and best-selling author Bruce Wilkinson walks across the stage to the glass-topped podium. "Welcome to Hope for Africa, a faith-based response to the HIV/AIDS epidemic," Wilkinson says to the camera. The session is one in a six-part video series hosted by Wilkinson and broadcast across South Africa to equip church leaders in HIV/AIDS prevention and care.

A striking feature of the studio set for the program is the stage, which is in the shape of a large red AIDS ribbon. Significantly, the ribbon is turned on its side. As Wilkinson explains to the audience, "Just as we've turned this red ribbon into a red fish, the symbol of Christ and our Christian fight against HIV/AIDS, together we can turn the tide of this deadly disease."[1]

As I described at the beginning of chapter 6, Bruce Wilkinson is an example of an entrepreneurial American evangelical who is exporting a message of abstinence to Africa as a method of AIDS prevention. The stage shaped as an AIDS-ribbon-turned-ichthus neatly typifies a characteristic of the evangelical sexual abstinence campaigns: the reclamation and manipulation of rhetorical strategies for evangelicals' moral and religious ends. Just as the AIDS ribbon turned on its side becomes a sign of Christ, so the desire for great sex (often communicated through the borrowed forms of a sexualized culture) becomes a reward of the sexual abstinence movement. The message is certainly persuasive, convincing millions of young people to pledge abstinence. But, as I have argued here, the message succeeds only in making abstinence all about sex. The evangelical abstinence campaigns are unwittingly raising a generation of young people with false expectations about the role of sex in marriage and about the sacrifice and commitment of marriage in general. By tying the abstinence commitment to one's religious commitment, the argument for abstinence threatens to weaken the religious faith of young people if the reward for choosing abstinence is never realized, whether because of singleness or the failure of marital sex to live up to expectations of greatness.

SO THIS IS GREAT SEX?

When I first met Jonathan Ebersol in 2004 during his sophomore year of college, he wasn't dating anyone. Weeks before graduation he met Claire at an event on sexuality at his church. It was a "cheesy, conservative Christian, culture wars kind of thing," Jonathan recalls, and he and Claire bonded instantly over their mutual disdain for the heavy-handed approach to the issue. Claire had just broken up with her boyfriend, and she and Jonathan talked about how they were enjoying being single.

They began to spend more time together, engaging in deep conversations. Jonathan was attracted to Claire's sharpness of mind and depth of character. Two months later they decided to begin dating. Both were committed to abstinence, and they talked about appropriate physical boundaries in their relationship. Jonathan respected Claire, and although he had strong feelings for her, he did not go as far physically with her as he had with girlfriends in high school. Fourteen months after they met, Jonathan and Claire were married. Claire gave Jonathan her purity ring after their wedding ceremony. They both had waited to have sex, and they were ready to receive their reward.

But the honeymoon did not deliver the great sex that they had been promised. "We thought it would be something intimate, something comforting that we could share. The whole 'one flesh' idea," Jonathan tells me. "It's become a complicated thing . . . more painful and divisive. It wasn't what we thought it would be." A month before their wedding Claire discovered through sharing memories with a family member that she had been sexually abused in early childhood. Looking back, Jonathan suspects that he saw warning signs of the emotional toll that this abuse had taken on Claire. Sometimes, when they were making dinner together before they were married, Jonathan would playfully touch Claire and she would flinch or pull away. Both Jonathan and Claire would be confused by her reaction. As they discovered on their honeymoon, sexual activity had become a vivid reminder of past pain.

"You have this ideal of what people have told you sex would be," Jonathan says, swiveling in his chair. When he tries to initiate sex, Jonathan feels as if he is hurting his wife. When she rebuffs his advances, Jonathan says that Claire feels as if she is depriving him. More often, they avoid sex altogether. The emotional pain is not worth it. Jonathan says he feels betrayed by all the people who told him that sex would be great. "You get all these winks and nudges at your wedding," he says. "[Sex is] supposed to be something very special, but it's also very complicated." Having grown up in an evangelical church, where he was steeped in the abstinence message, Jonathan says that he is frustrated that the campaigns teach boys that they are "ravenous sexual beings" and that if they wait for marital sex, it will be this "fun, greatest-thing-ever. It doesn't prepare you for the complexity of it all."

As Jonathan and Claire approach their first wedding anniversary, sex is still not what they thought it would be. Claire has sought counseling, and together they have read books dealing with overcoming abuse. Despite their challenges they remain committed to each other.

Jonathan recalls how his engaged friends would talk about how they were going to have sex all the time once they were married. Now Jonathan feels compelled to set them straight. What if you become paralyzed and can't have sex? he asks. What if you are unable to have children? It's okay to talk about the ideal of great sex in marriage, he says, but also the reality. "You can still be a godly Christian without an awesome sex life or without four kids and a minivan."

Jonathan's story points to one of the weaknesses in the abstinence campaigns. He and Claire were committed to abstinence and waited for sex until they got married but became disillusioned with marriage when they discovered that sex was not what they thought it would be. Although the primary goal of the campaigns is to prevent nonmarital sex, it seems that the campaigns could do more to portray a realistic image of marriage—both the moments of Hollywood-style romance and the mundane challenges of everyday life. Although evangelicals are promarriage, their marriages tend to reflect cultural trends, not biblical injunctions. According to a 2008 survey by the Barna Group, evangelical and other "born-again" Christians divorce at the same statistical rate as other Americans: among adults who have been married, one-third have experienced at least one divorce.[2] Evangelical abstinence campaigns can do more to strengthen future marriages, not just promise them as rewards.

GETTING WHAT I WANT

Another potential weakness of the abstinence campaigns is that the message of great sex may resonate more strongly with evangelical youths than the message about waiting for it. If sex is so great, why wait? According to Mark Regnerus, author of *Forbidden Fruit: Sex and Religion in the Lives of American Teenagers,* evangelical adolescents are having nonmarital sex at rates similar to adolescents with no religious affiliation (and at rates higher than mainline Protestant, Jewish, and Catholic teens).[3] Still, evangelical youth are much more likely to say that they support waiting for sex until marriage (and more likely to anticipate feeling guilt if they don't). As Regnerus points out, evangelical teens "don't always practice what they preach."[4] Religion plays a role in influencing decisions for delaying sex, but family structure and social class play a role, too. As for the evangelicals who may talk about abstinence but are actually having sex, religious affiliation does not equal religiosity. The high percentage of evangelical teens having sex could be attributed to a high percentage of lukewarm believers whose attendance at church on Sunday morning has little impact on their behavior Saturday night. Many young people with whom I spoke are dealing with their own fractured fairy tales; they were raised in Christian homes, but they acknowledge that their depth of religious commitment was shallow.

For Regnerus the most compelling explanation for the high rates of evangelical teen sex lies in what he sees as a clash of cultures: "The culture of traditionalist, evangelical religion, with its family-centered ideals and norms, and the culture of postmodern, consumption-oriented, media-saturated, self-focused, individualist capitalism."[5] Evangelical teenagers must negotiate cultures of sexual abstinence and permissiveness. They know that they are not supposed to have sex, but sex eventually "happens" to most.

The clash-of-cultures explanation is on the right track, but it leaves me unconvinced. Compromise or co-opting rings more true than clash. As I've pointed out here, God is hip when accompanied by loud music and laser lights. But the church, in its accommodation of secular strategies to make abstinence sexy, may have traded the power of transcendence for the power of persuasion. The producers of the evangelical abstinence campaigns are not unaffected by the same clash of cultures; in negotiating the two cultures they have used the forms of one to communicate the content of the other.

This leads to another weakness of the persuasive "great sex" message of the abstinence campaigns: it places the emphasis of marriage on personal fulfillment instead of sacrificial giving. Buried beneath the statistics is a disturbing story of risks and rewards. Regnerus identifies a "middle-class sexual morality" among religious youth, where the higher rewards of vaginal sex are bypassed in favor of lower-risk substitutes such as oral sex, masturbation, and pornography: "They are interested in remaining free from the burden of teenage pregnancy and the sorrows and embarrassments of STDs. They perceive a bright future for themselves, one with college, advanced degrees, a career, and a family. Simply put, too much seems at stake. Sexual intercourse is not worth the risks."[6] For religious youth, avoiding nonmarital sex may have less to do with religious commandments and more to do with career aspirations. In the case of evangelicals, the promise of great sex as a reward for sexual abstinence represents more than a clash between MTV and Sunday school. It changes the goal from pleasing God to pleasing oneself.

Risk-avoidance arguments (such as unwanted pregnancy and STDs) can still be found in abstinence rhetoric. They may have worked too well. Recently, a female Christian college student shared with me and her classmates that a close friend—a recent college graduate and newlywed—had just learned that she was pregnant. The news was recounted with shock and disbelief. What about graduate school? What about her career? What about uninterrupted great sex? Getting married young was an understandable, if not acceptable, choice in the student's view, but an unplanned pregnancy was viewed as a tragedy. According to the abstinence campaigns, this student did everything right: she waited to have sex until she got married. But her desire to have sex may have prompted an earlier marriage, before she had a chance to finish graduate school and launch her career. Judging by her friends' responses, getting pregnant while married (a natural consequence of sex, and one that prolife evangelicals would heartily endorse) was going to carry as much negative emotional baggage as getting pregnant while unmarried.

If waiting for sex is unrealistic, to borrow Bristol Palin's declaration, and evangelical teens are supposed to wait for sex until marriage, then it seems as though the logical solution is the promotion of marriage at younger ages. Researchers acknowledge (perhaps more readily than abstinence campaign producers) that a looming problem is a growing maturity gap, which is the lag between sexual maturity (about fourteen for boys and younger than thirteen for girls) and marriage (about twenty-six for men and twenty-four for women). Regnerus supports this solution: "Having to wait until age 25 or 30 to have sex *is* unreasonable. Yet if religious organizations and their adherents are going to continue advocating for Christian chastity, and I have no reason to suggest they won't or shouldn't, they must work more creatively to support younger marriages."[7] This proposition will set off warning sirens for feminists of all stripes, conjuring images of child brides, homebound and pregnant, their vocational callings growing as stale as this stereotype. Feminists aside, the solution is logical: if the religious admonition is to wait until you are married to have sex, and you want to have sex, then get married. But the promotion of younger marriages may create other problems: it may increase the success of abstinence pledges and reduce the number of pregnancies to unwed mothers (and perhaps reduce the number of abortions in the process), but it also may increase the number of divorces if the marital education of young people does not move much beyond the joy of sex. Just as the role of a supportive community—whether mature adults, family members, or a church community—is crucial for the success of abstinence pledges, so too the Christian community must see its role in supporting and developing healthy marriages. It is not enough for the evangelical church to promote sexual abstinence among teens and then ignore the role of chastity in marriage. It may take a village to raise a child, but it takes a church to raise a marriage.

Younger, church-supported marriages may solve the problem of abstinence as unrealistic, but this solution sidesteps a more critical issue. Younger marriages still make the problem all about sex and meeting *my* needs.[8] Marriage (and the "great sex" that comes with it) becomes merely the reward for abstinence or the escape hatch if you fear you may break your abstinence vow. The same impulse of self-fulfillment that propels younger marriages as a solution for the desire to have sex is the same impulse behind the college student's lament at her married friend's pregnancy. Evangelicals are widely in favor of contraception, which can be helpful in balancing multiple callings of marriage, parenthood, and vocation.[9] But when the choices become all about me, evangelicals have a problem, arguably one more significant than nonmarital sex.

As one of my interview respondents shared with me in a follow-up e-mail six years after we first met, sex is no longer important to her, because she does not think that it is important to God:

> I'm still single. Still a virgin. 25 years old. I haven't dated anyone recently and it's not because I haven't found the "right one" or because abstinence and virginity is important to me. It's because it's not important to me. I've spent these last years doing some amazing things. Traveling to Africa, doing service work with the poor, counseling and teaching recovering alcoholics and drug addicts, painting, reading, laughing, and loving being alive. I haven't had time for dating or sex; it just hasn't been a priority. It seems so important to the world, to the entertainment and advertising community, to most of my friends, and still to [the abstinence campaigns]. And that's great for them. But I don't feel like it's that important to God. Jesus' life was an amazing one. He spent what little time he had here on earth loving, healing, teaching, and saving people. NOT on getting them to keep their pants on through high school. Over time, as I've grown as a person and my faith has matured, I think that it's much more important how we love each other, that we take care of the broken and abused in this world, and share the grace and mercy we've received from God with others—rather than who we have sex with or when we have it.[10]

For this young person, the campaigns' focus on abstinence makes the Christian life more about sex and self-fulfillment and less about sacrifice and serving others.

ABSTINENCE IS A PROCESS

Despite the drawbacks of the abstinence campaigns' persuasive focus on sex, marriage, and pleasing oneself, the campaigns get a number of things right. For starters, the campaigns are forcing the church to talk about sex. It may be difficult for the soft voice of religion to be heard against the blaring megaphone of mediated culture, but the campaigns are cranking up the volume, and teens are listening. The campaigns are empowering young people—particularly young women—to respect their bodies and to make wise, healthy choices. Sex is a physical act of communication, and, as such, it is deeply connected to one's sense of self. The campaigns are wise to address issues of body image and self-esteem, helping young people to embrace their sexuality with confidence. The abstinence message is inclusive and does not differentiate between virgins and nonvirgins. The campaigns draw on a key element of evangelical theology—God's unconditional forgiveness—to make abstinence available to all, whether the teen is making the pledge for the first time or the fifth. The campaigns remind adolescents that, despite the insecurities and doubts and temptations they face, they are not alone. Winsome peer testimonies and encouragement to seek accountability mentors—not to mention the towering stacks of pledge cards, and stadiums and sanctuaries filled with hundreds of abstinent teens—can encourage abstinent teens during a turbulent period of life when virginity may be only one of many targets for peer ridicule and isolation.

What impressed me most was the dozens of young people with whom I spoke. My study quickly became about more than just how well the young people were receiving the sexy message of abstinence. My interview respondents showed me that sexual maturation is a process, whether one supports teenage sexual activity or sexual abstinence. Evangelical young people, like all young people, are doing their best to negotiate their sexual identities in a sexualized culture. Just because a young person has pledged abstinence doesn't mean that she is suppressing her sexuality. The abstinent young people I met are left with the challenge of disciplining their own sexuality and enacting their abstinence commitment while still growing and maturing as sexual beings, whether that means doing everything but sexual intercourse or saving their first kiss until their wedding day. My interview respondents showed me that abstinence is not an either-or proposition. The stories I have shared here illustrate the diversity of abstinence commitments, from the abstinent couple that struggles with sexual temptation to the nonvirgin couple for whom the road to abstinence has been rocky, from the attractive teen who is waiting for her prince charming to the lonely twentysomething who uses her abstinent commitment as a cover for her singleness. I met teens who flaunt their abstinence like some teens flaunt their sexuality. And I met teens for whom their abstinence commitment is a daily struggle, one that they know they will not win. Abstinence, much like sexuality itself, is a process as well as a source of identity. One strength of the campaigns is their ability to offer young people a sexual identity grounded in a lack of sexual activity. One strength of the young people's response to the campaigns is their ability to negotiate this identity within a culture of sex.

TOO MUCH OF A GOOD THING

The ominous red and black cover of a 2009 issue of *Newsweek* announces "the decline and fall of Christian America."[11] Paradoxically, this should be good news to evangelicals. Cultural saturation may be the point of evangelism, but becoming the status quo reduces the rhetorical power of the outsider.

In the case of the evangelical sexual abstinence campaigns, their success in the United States may prove to be part of their eventual decline. Once the movement has reached a saturation point with its audience and becomes part of mainstream culture, the choice for abstinence loses its outsider stance of cultural critique. This is one hazard of borrowing forms of popular culture for the purposes of persuasion: the more the campaigns try to look like the rest of popular culture, the less they will be able to present an alternative to popular culture. Data from the National Longitudinal Study of Adolescent Health support this analysis, suggesting that when the abstinence pledge becomes normative (which is calculated at more than 30 percent of a school's student body), it "ceases to have an effect."[12] Minority status as abstinence pledgers in a culture of sex fosters group identity and community, which participates in delaying sexual debut. In light of this, it becomes critical for abstinence educators to continue to portray popular culture as sex driven in order to maintain the abstinence movement's minority outsider status and hence its success.[13]

Whereas the Bearman and Brückner study identifies the limit of the abstinence movement's effectiveness as a calculable percentage of students who are abstinent, the study does not acknowledge that persistent effectiveness can be considered a result of rhetorical construction. That is, the actual number of abstinent students is less important than the rhetorically constructed perception that most students are having nonmarital sex. Non-normative or minority status is constructed within rhetoric. Even if a majority of a student body was practicing abstinence, the pledge could continue to have an effect by changing the reference group: the campaigns' rhetoric would need to portray the rest of the schools in the town or country as sex saturated, reinforcing a minority identity for the majority abstinence pledgers.

This paradox is similar to the one faced by the counterpublic of U.S. evangelicals. Just as the abstinence movement maintains its persuasive force if it continues to function as non-normative, so too American evangelicals maintain their persuasive force by portraying themselves as a minority in opposition to the rest of society. Evangelicals may constitute a majority of Americans, although their rhetoric constitutes them as a minority.[14] I have suggested that this marginalized position functions as a precursor to persuasion, in that it facilitates reclamation of agency that is used as a resource for persuasion. Power comes from the perceived periphery.

SECULAR ACCOMMODATION AS RHETORICAL STRATEGY

A rhetorical approach to the changed nature of a religious argument such as sexual abstinence in the public sphere focuses both on the ethos of the rhetor and the rhetor's ability to analyze his audience. In the present case the ethos of evangelicals as "evangels" of the "good news" of salvation through Jesus Christ offers a built-in agenda of persuasion, but the astute attention to audience explains the packaging of the religious message in the form of idioms of teen culture and the content of individual agency. In essence, the apparent secularization of religious arguments in the public sphere can be understood as part of a rhetorical strategy, not a triumph of dominant culture.

Here, rhetorical agency functions in both the inventional strategy of the rhetors and the use of that strategy through a construction of their audience as choice-making individuals. The rhetors use their communicative power to construct their audience as agents who can control their bodies and wait to have sex. The audience, or receivers, contributes to the sexual abstinence rhetoric, as well. For example, Jennifer Bartell, who is engaged to be married, articulates a secular defense for her abstinence commitment before she offers a religious defense. When asked why she didn't go ahead and have sex with her fiancé as she wanted to, Jennifer replies, "It's just not worth it. You never know what tomorrow's going to bring. Also, like, God's word says that sex is for marriage, and that doesn't mean that sex is for when you are engaged." Her first response is that breaking her abstinence commitment is not worth it because of its potentially harmful consequences. Her second response is that God prohibits nonmarital sex.

One can speculate that if the emphasis on effectiveness can dull the transcendence of religion, it can also alter the collective identity of a religious group. If evangelicals sharpen their distinct identity through their engagement and conflict with secular society, what happens to that identity when the symbolic boundaries between the in-group (evangelicals) and out-group (secular society) become blurred?[15] Appeals to the individual self and the effectiveness of religion may be rhetorical strategies on the part of the evangelical rhetors, but they may come back to shape and reshape the ethos of the rhetors themselves. As

Bearman and Brückner's study of virginity pledges suggests, when abstinence becomes mainstream, it loses its effectiveness. In public sphere theory, when a counterpublic such as evangelicalism becomes the public, it may lose its distinctiveness. Evangelicals' reappropriation of an individualistic rhetoric of choice may be persuasive, but it also reproduces an autonomous self within a religious tradition that purports to value community.[16]

The counterfinding is, of course, in the case of sub-Saharan Africa. Abstinence educators in Kenya and Rwanda offer a mixed abstinence message of benefits for the individual and obedience to God. African young people too talk about abstinence in terms of fearing God. American evangelicalism and its persuasive arguments about agency and benefits for the individual fit with a society that does not need God for daily survival, where a diagnosis of AIDS means treatment, not certain death. The message of individualism strikes a chord of dissonance in sub-Saharan Africa, where the belief that evil spirits cause AIDS is on the increase among youth.[17] Agency resides in the community and God is feared, not befriended. The difference in findings between the United States and sub-Saharan Africa reveals the impact of society on religious culture: In an individualist and consumerist society such as the United States, abstinence must have personal benefits. In a society of fragile social institutions and agency-poor individuals, abstinence must please God.

SPEAKING OF THE TRANSCENDENT

The women at a church in an AIDS-ravaged village in southern Mozambique know something about agency. During a visit, the *New York Times* columnist David Brooks asked the women and their pastor how they help prevent AIDS. They tell people about condoms was the first reply. But then they began talking in a "different language," Brooks writes, about how God changes human behavior. They pray for a man who beats his HIV-positive wife. They tell polygamists in their church that "God loves monogamy best."[18]

In his travels through southern Africa, Brooks says that he has become aware that the treatment of AIDS is a technical problem, for which there are technical solutions, but the prevention of AIDS requires changed behavior. The deeper problems of AIDS prevention, Brooks suggests, "can be addressed only by the language of ought, by fixing behavior into some relevant set of transcendent ideals and faiths. . . .

It's a language that has to be spoken by people who connect words like 'faithful' and 'abstinent' to some larger creed."[19]

Connecting sexual abstinence to a transcendent language of ought should be a critical factor in the success of the evangelical abstinence campaigns. In Kenya and Rwanda, where death itself is only a mild deterrent from risky sexual behavior, transcendent language of obeying and fearing God may be the only hope for changed behavior. In comparison, in the United States risky sexual behavior resulting in disease or unwanted pregnancy is not so much an end of life but an end of a future where one controls the outcome. Yes, so the argument goes, abstinence is God's plan, but it will bring personal benefits if one follows the plan. In the United States, a choice for abstinence is a choice for a better, more fulfilling tomorrow through a good marriage and great sex. In Kenya or Rwanda, a choice for abstinence may not bring a better tomorrow, but as a way of pleasing God the benefits are believed to be eternal.

In these cases, rhetorical agency as persuasion runs the risk of reducing transcendent language not to a technical language but to a language of the individual. Rhetorical agency as persuasion seems to best fit a cultural context in which the individual already has a range of choices and societal structures make self-determinism possible. However, rhetorical agency may be most needed in a cultural context where choices are few and death is at the door. The language of the individual, combined with a language of the transcendent, may bring the most persuasive power to a social campaign that relies on lasting changed behavior. As Brooks writes, "This is a mysterious task."[20]

A commitment to sexual abstinence—whether as AIDS prevention, pregnancy avoidance, or religious conviction—requires changed behavior. But perhaps Brooks has it backward; perhaps the changed behavior comes first and the changed belief follows. An abstinence leader once told me that a commitment to abstinence doesn't make sense without a commitment to Jesus Christ. One could also argue that a commitment to Jesus Christ doesn't make sense without a commitment to abstinence; in effect, belief in God should necessarily manifest itself in the outward expression of changed behavior. The daily act of practicing an abstinent lifestyle may provide today's evangelical youth with a tangible, bodily opportunity to perform their faith and to grow more faithful in the process. This potentially shifts the standard of the campaigns' effectiveness from the numbers of youth who maintain their abstinence pledges to the numbers of youth who are making religious commitments, making the campaigns less about sex and more about evangelism. The call to a life of purity is not just a positive spin on the negative prohibition of abstinence; it can also be understood as a new asceticism, a call to pious living. For evangelical young people, practicing abstinence allows them to inhabit their faith commitments in a practical way, training and disciplining their bodies to be more Christ-like. As the feminist scholar Saba Mahmood writes, "Instead of innate human desires eliciting outward forms of conduct, it is the sequence of practices and actions one is engaged in that determines one's desire and emotions."[21]

Returning the practice of abstinence to its roots as a spiritual discipline may offer the campaigns a strategy for changing a new generation of young people in both body and soul.[22] To this end, the campaigns are already persuading young people to consider abstinence through the rhetorical techniques described in this study. Now the campaigns need to take the next step and connect the dots between sexuality as good and God given and abstinence as the sacrifice of sexuality for the purpose of worship of God. In this sense, the evangelical abstinence campaigns would not merely be making chastity sexy. They would be making evangelicalism—and Christianity—sexy in the process.

List of Campaign Leaders

Real names of respondents are provided; all interviewed by author.

U.S. ABSTINENCE CAMPAIGN LEADERS

Booz, Laura (Pure Freedom). August 21, 2004. Milwaukee, Wis.

Burtt, Jason (Silver Ring Thing). September 21, 2008. Pittsburgh, Pa.

Crouse, Janice (Beverly LaHaye Institute, Concerned Women for America). September 14, 2004. Washington, D.C.

Etheridge, Albert (STAND/True Love Waits). June 26, 2004. Dallas.

Gresh, Dannah (Pure Freedom). October 16, 2004. Chicago.

Hayes, Kristi (Abstinence Clearinghouse). September 14, 2004. Washington, D.C.

Hester, Jimmy (True Love Waits). June 23, 2004. Nashville, Tenn.

McGarry, Joe (Silver Ring Thing). September 27, 2004. Boston.

Ross, Richard (True Love Waits). June 26, 2004. Dallas.

St. James, Rebecca (True Love Waits). June 26, 2004. Dallas.

Touchstone, Bob (STAND/True Love Waits). June 26, 2004. Dallas.

Weibel, Suzy (Pure Freedom). August 21, 2004. Milwaukee, Wis.

Wright, Wendy (Concerned Women for America). September 14, 2004. Washington, D.C.

AFRICAN ABSTINENCE CAMPAIGN LEADERS

Chandler, Rebecca (World Relief). November 22, 2004. Kigali, Rwanda.

Cunningham, Colette (World Relief). November 25, 2004. Kigali, Rwanda.

Dortzbach, Deborah (World Relief). September 16, 2004. Baltimore.

Global Care respondent A. September 15, 2004. Washington, D.C.

Global Care respondent B. September 15, 2004. Washington, D.C.

Habimana, Jean-Paul (World Relief). November 25, 2004. Kigali, Rwanda.

Heidkamp, Rebecca (World Relief). September 16, 2004. Baltimore.

Makona, Edgar (True Love Waits/Baptist AIDS Response Agency). November 19, 2004. Nairobi.

Muchemi, Sheila (Crisis Pregnancy Ministries). November 16, 2004. Nairobi.

Musya, Anne (Crisis Pregnancy Ministries). November 16, 2004. Nairobi.

Mwangi, John (Scripture Union). November 17, 2004. Nairobi.

Ngoga, Emmanuel (World Relief). November 25, 2004. Kigali, Rwanda.

Njeremani, Joy (Scripture Union). November 17, 2004. Nairobi.

Ogango, Tabitha (Focus on the Family). November 18, 2004. Nairobi.

Oloo, Tina (World Relief). November 18, 2004. Nairobi.

van Vuuren, Laura (World Relief). September 16, 2004. Baltimore.

Ziemer, Tim (World Relief). September 16, 2004. Baltimore.

Notes

INTRODUCTION

1. This is a pseudonym. I use pseudonyms for all teenage and young adult interview respondents. I also use pseudonyms for young people featured in abstinence events. I have omitted or changed some identifying features to protect identities. Real names are used for organizational leaders, except where noted.

2. Guttmacher Institute, "Facts on American Teens' Sexual and Reproductive Health."

3. See Luker, *When Sex Goes to School,* for a detailed account of the history of the competing views on sex education in public schools. See Carpenter, *Virginity Lost,* 178–81, for a quick overview.

4. In his State of the Union address in 2004, President Bush described what he considers a "fact of life": "Abstinence for young people is the only certain way to avoid sexually transmitted disease."

5. For a helpful overview of the history of federal funding for abstinence education in the United States, see Kliff, "Future of Abstinence."

6. Hamilton, Martin, and Ventura, "Births: Preliminary Data for 2006"; Ventura et al., "Revised Pregnancy Rates, 1990–97"; Martin et al., "Births: Final Data for 2006."

7. National Abstinence Education Association, "Teen Pregnancy Rates Demand Honest Look."

8. The extent of the impact of abstinence on HIV prevention remains controversial. In the case of Uganda, Edward C. Green points to abstinence as a significant part of behavior change. See Green, *Rethinking AIDS Prevention,* 155–60. Helen Epstein, in her book *The Invisible Cure,* points to the role of partner reduction (or "zero grazing"), 185–201.

9. UNAIDS/WHO, "Uganda: Epidemiological Country Profile."

10. Green, "Faith-Based Organizations," 6.

11. Ibid., 7.

12. Both *prolife* and *prochoice* are biased terms. I use both in this book in deference to what the parties who hold those positions use to refer to themselves. As William Saletan writes in the introduction to *Bearing Right: How Conservatives Won the Abortion War,* "Every attempt at unbiased language—for example, reserving the term *anti-abortion* to describe those who would outlaw the practice, or calling them 'anti-abortion rights' instead of 'pro-right-to life'—adds a new bias. The least biased solution is to let each side choose its name" (4).

13. The logic here is that a ban on late-term abortions would reduce the overall number of abortions performed, and advancements in ultrasound technology would make the fetus appear more "real" and babylike to the pregnant woman, prompting an emotional attachment and discouraging abortion.

14. Evangelism and social activism are central to what it means to be an evangelical, along with an emphasis on a "born-again" moment of conversion, a high view of scripture, and a belief in the death and resurrection of Jesus Christ as central to personal salvation. See Bebbington, *Evangelicalism in Modern Britain.*

15. Martino, "Virginity Pledges Work for Some Teens."

16. Bearman and Brückner, "Promising the Future," 1, 2.

17. Rosenbaum, "Patient Teenagers?"

18. Martino et al., "Virginity Pledges among the Willing"; Rand Corporation, "Virginity Pledges May Help Postpone Intercourse."

19. Martino, "Virginity Pledges Work for Some Teens."

20. The phrase is from Geertz, *Interpretation of Cultures.*

21. "True Love Waits Launches Community-wide Initiative."

22. Museveni, untitled public address.

23. Beehler, "True Love Waits to Expand Anti-AIDS Initiative."

24. Cole, "With This Ring."

25. Some Silver Ring Thing events are free to the public if the costs are underwritten by a local sponsor.

26. Silver Ring Thing Web site, www.silverringthing.com.

27. Ibid. Nationally, teen pregnancy was decreasing during this period; however, in 1996, when the Pattyns started Silver Ring Thing in Yuma, Arizona, the state recorded its highest number of cases of teen pregnancy ever. See Arizona Bureau of Vital Statistics, "Teenage Pregnancy, Arizona, 1986–1996."

28. John Guest is senior pastor of Christ Church in Grove Farm. His ministry organization hosts evangelistic crusades and supports his appearances as a frequent speaker at Promise Keepers events. Silver Ring Thing is listed on the Web site of Christ Church as a partner in ministry.

29. Connolly, "ACLU Sues HHS"; American Civil Liberties Union, "ACLU Announces Settlement."

30. Author's field notes from Silver Ring Thing events, September 19, 2008, Pittsburgh; November 8, 2008, Grand Rapids, Mich.; March 22, 2009, Chicago.

31. Author's field notes, Pure Freedom event, October 16, 2004, Chicago.

32. Struck, "Planned Purity," 32.

33. Pure Freedom Web site, www.purefreedom.org.

34. Eileen King, Pure Freedom, personal communication with author, May 18, 2009; Pure Freedom Web site.

35. My use of the terms *producers* and *receivers* is drawn from cultural sociology and Wendy Griswold's cultural diamond. See Griswold, *Cultures and Societies in a Changing World*. A cultural object, which Griswold defines as "shared significance embodied in form" (Griswold, *Renaissance Revivals*, 5), is both produced and received within a specific cultural and social context. In my study the cultural object of abstinence can function as an analytic tool to help explore the culture of evangelicalism.

36. Specifically, I interviewed thirteen U.S. evangelical abstinence leaders, seventeen evangelical abstinence leaders working in Africa, and thirty-five American young people older than eighteen. Of the thirteen American abstinence leaders, ten are paid staff, volunteers, or official representatives for one of the three abstinence organizations or one of their partner organizations. I held three additional interviews with staff members from the Abstinence Clearinghouse, a national resource for abstinence educators, and Concerned Women for America, a politically conservative Christian public policy organization. Both organizations promote abstinence; the interviews are included to provide context and perspective on the abstinence movement and the three organizations under consideration. The interviews with organizational leaders were conducted in person in Boston, Chicago, Dallas, Milwaukee, Nashville, and Washington, D.C. (or their surrounding metropolitan areas) between June 2004 and October 2004. I conducted an additional interview in September 2008 in Pittsburgh. See the appendix for more details. The shortest interview lasted twenty minutes; the longest interview was ninety minutes; the average interview was forty-six minutes. Of the thirty-five young people older than eighteen whom I interviewed, thirteen were male and twenty-two were female. The ages of the respondents ranged from eighteen to twenty-nine. At the time of the interviews, twelve of the respondents were single, eleven were dating, five were married, four were engaged, two were in courtship relationships, and one was divorced. The interviews were conducted between June 2004 and May 2005 and between September 2008 and April 2009. I interviewed three individuals in both the first and second waves of interviews. The sample is purposive, with a mix of respondents who made abstinence pledges at events sponsored by Pure Freedom, Silver Ring Thing, or True Love Waits. Twenty-six interviews were conducted in person; eight were conducted over the phone, and one was conducted by e-mail. The interviews ranged in length from twenty minutes to ninety minutes; the average length was forty-two minutes. The respondents were recruited through recommendations from organization leaders and evangelical church youth leaders. Using a snowball sampling method, I also asked respondents to suggest other young people to include in the study. The interviews were recorded and transcribed, then analyzed for key themes. Pseudonyms are used for all teenage interview respondents and individuals featured in the performance of abstinence events. Some identifying

characteristics have been withheld or changed to protect identities. Information about the seventeen interviews with sub-Saharan African abstinence leaders is included in chapter 6.

37. In some cases the event occurred in a suburb or small town near one of the cities. See the appendix for location details.

38. These methods of data collection and analysis are informed by a grounded theory approach to qualitative research. See Glaser and Strauss, *Discovery of Grounded Theory*. Grounded theory develops the research problem with close attention to respondents' concerns, allows coding categories to emerge from the data instead of imposing preexisting structures, and aims to build theory instead of testing existing theory. A grounded theory approach is particularly suited to rhetorical analysis because of its focus on words, phrases, and sentences as units of analysis. See Strauss and Corbin, *Basics of Qualitative Research*, 92.

39. I am grateful to the students in my Theology of the Body mentoring course for their candid discussion of many of the ideas presented here: Amanda Adams, Sarah Barlett, Hannah Sutherland, Elizabeth Wilhoit, and Sunita Yee. I also wish to thank my teaching and research assistants for their contributions to this study: Ryan Ellis, Abigail Gunderson, Marissa Lowe, Catherine Paquette, Abigail Perl, and William Stell.

40. The disciplines of rhetoric and sociology both deal with symbolic meaning embodied in text, including such "texts" as spoken or written discourse, body language, and visual images. See Wuthnow, *Vocabularies of Public Life*, 6. Text does not include that which is inside someone's head; the methodological significance here is that meaning making is empirically observable. Indeed, what transforms an individual into a rhetor is the public utterance of speech, not just the cognitive awareness of a rhetorical situation. Although similar in focus and aim, the fields of rhetoric and cultural sociology maintain their distinct disciplinary traditions. Communication studies (which can include the study of rhetoric) may focus on the "performative aspects of a public utterance," whereas a more sociological focus may focus on the ways in which the public utterance—both its form and content—communicates social understanding (9). Also, a communication studies approach tends to emphasize key themes and arguments in public discourse, whereas cultural sociology considers the "complex codes, distinctions, rules, and interplay between form and content that permit a public utterance to articulate with its social environment" (9).

41. Rhetoric is not merely concerned with identifying textual themes and arguments and exploring how they work but interpreting the invention and function of texts in order to understand how they *mean*. A full understanding of the rhetorical situation allows for a rich "thick description" approach to rhetorical analysis that examines the speaker's invention of the message, the audience's reception of the message, as well as the mitigating cultural factors of exigence, constraints, and opportunities. See Bitzer, "Rhetorical Situation," and Geertz, *Interpretation of Cultures*. A study of rhetoric that is informed by cultural sociology is reflexive, considering the constraints and opportunities that the rhetorical situation imposes on the text, as well as how the text means and alters the rhetorical situation. In this way, a rhetorical approach to under-

standing a cultural artifact such as a religious or social movement can provide rich interpretive data of groups, messages, and meanings.

42. Edward Schiappa distinguishes between definitions of essence and usage. Instead of asking "What is abstinence?" Schiappa would claim one should ask "How ought we use the word *abstinence?*" Posing it as a question of usage brings one closer to understanding how a word like *abstinence* functions to shape reality and make meaning. See Schiappa, *Defining Reality,* xi, 3–10.

43. Sociologists examine message resonance in terms of mobilization and participation in social movements. See Gamson, "Constructing Social Protest"; Benford, "An Insider's Critique"; Snow et al., "Frame Alignment Processes." Words and images can frame social movements in ways that encourage movement participation. For more on frame analysis, see Entman, "Framing"; Goffman, *Frame Analysis.*

44. Rhetorical analysis considers the structure, organization, and form of discourse, but it also examines the specific figures and tropes used by the rhetor, along with the broader rhetorical situation of speaker, audience, exigence, constraints, and opportunities. See Bitzer, "Rhetorical Situation."

45. Scholars in the humanities have sought to reestablish the primacy of rhetorical agency as a response to a postmodern critique that decenters the subject and reduces rhetors to mere "points of articulation" with diminished agency for rhetorical invention (Gaonkar, "Idea of Rhetoric," 25–85). Broadly speaking, rhetorical agency involves the capacity to act (Geisler, "How Ought We to Understand," 12). Upon further investigation, however, scholars have defined this slippery term in a variety of ways, including rhetorical agency as ideology (Gaonkar, "Idea of Rhetoric"); agency as power (Blithefield, position paper; Brouwer, position paper); agency as responsibility (Geisler, "How Ought We to Understand"); agency as human potential (Gunn, position paper); agency as a resource (Geisler, "How Ought We to Understand"); agency as performance (Lucaites, position paper); and agency as illusion (Condit and Gunn, position papers). Karlyn Kohrs Campbell captures the essence of the plurality of views of agency by defining *agency* as "polysemic and ambiguous, a term that can refer to invention, strategies, authorship, institutional power, identity, subjectivity, and subject positions, among others." In her five-part definition of agency, Campbell negotiates the rhetor's dual nature as both inventor and point of articulation. See Campbell, "Agency: Promiscuous and Protean," 1, 3. The communal aspect of agency, including the situatedness of agents in culture and the linguistic constraints that it imposes, renders rhetors as points of articulation. At the same time, rhetors are inventors, linking past and present: "In this sense, agency is invention, including the invention, however temporary, of *personae,* subject-positions, and collectivities" (9; emphasis in original). Here, Campbell moves the discussion on the concept of rhetorical agency from debates about the autonomous subject to suggest that agency is itself rhetorical—that is, invented and constructed. Agency that is rhetorical can be used as a tool for persuasion. This understanding of agency as constructed and discovered in and through rhetoric motivates my study.

46. Two recent books consider the connection between religion and sexuality: see Regnerus, *Forbidden Fruit,* and Freitas, *Sex and the Soul.* The books

are similar in aim but different in method and approach. Regnerus analyzes national surveys of teens and sexuality to examine the impact of religion on sexual behavior decisions. Freitas interviews college students at secular, Catholic, and evangelical institutions to understand the impact of religion and spirituality on choices about sex. My study focuses on the actual abstinence campaigns—the events, organizers, and attendees—in order to understand how evangelicals are persuading young people to wait for sex.

47. For a thoughtful study on how strategies of all kinds of abstinence (not just sexual) relate to personal identity, see Mullaney, *Everyone Is Not Doing It*.

48. That "my body, my choice" framings existed before the use of choice rhetoric in the contemporary evangelical sexual abstinence campaigns suggests a subsequent circulation of choice rhetoric among feminists and evangelicals; however, any stronger claim of causation invites a post hoc fallacy. Indeed, one could argue that feminists reappropriated choice rhetoric from American evangelicals, who have historically focused on salvation as a personal choice. The direction of the discourse is less important than the observation that feminist discourse and evangelical discourse come from self-constructed positions as counterpublics.

49. "New Abortion Rhetoric."

50. Although *Roe v. Wade*, the 1973 Supreme Court decision legalizing abortion, was based on a right to privacy, it was rhetorically constructed in public discourse as a right to choice. See Condit, *Decoding Abortion Rhetoric*.

51. See Fraser, "Rethinking the Public Sphere," for a discussion of subaltern counterpublics. She defines *subaltern counterpublics* as "parallel discursive arenas where members of subordinated social groups invent and circulate counterdiscourses to formulate oppositional interpretations of their identities, interests, and needs" (123). Fraser cites the U.S. feminist subaltern counterpublic as a prototypical example, with its various festivals, book stores, journals, and conferences.

52. Numerous studies chart the history of evangelicalism. A few noteworthy texts include Balmer, *Making of Evangelicalism*; Balmer, *Blessed Assurance*; Marsden, *Understanding Fundamentalism and Evangelicalism*. See also Noll, *American Evangelical Christianity*, and *Rise of Evangelicalism*.

53. The Habermasian public sphere relies on a conception of rhetorical agency in which individual autonomous agents bracket inequalities and engage in rational debate about public matters for the common good. See Habermas, *Structural Transformation*. Feminist critiques of this model point out that the public sphere is anything but accessible to all; historically, gender and class exclusions support the distinction of the bourgeois by separating them from the private sphere, in effect weakening the agency of women and members of lower classes. See Eley, "Nations, Publics, and Political Cultures"; Fraser, "Rethinking the Public Sphere"; Landes, *Women and the Public Sphere*. Indeed, one of the aims of feminist critiques of the bourgeois public sphere is to liberate the private realm—both the issues and women who have been relegated there—into the public. See Benhabib, "Models of Public Space."

54. Fraser, "Rethinking the Public Sphere," 115.

55. Princeton Survey Research/Newsweek, "Would you describe yourself as a born-again or Evangelical Christian, or not?"

56. Beinart, "Morally Correct," 6.

57. For a recent collection of essays on the variety of choices facing women in the areas of sexuality and reproduction, see Hayden and Hallstein, *Contemplating Maternity.*

58. Feminist critiques of the Habermasian bourgeois public sphere suggest that women's issues have been privatized. A central focus of women's struggles is to "make these issues public" (Benhabib, "Models of Public Space," 90). Public sphere models have created sharp distinctions between "justice and the good life, public matters of norms as opposed to private matters of value, public interests versus private needs" (89). These distinctions have "served to confine women and typically female spheres of activity like housework; reproduction; nurture and care for the young, the sick, and the elderly to the 'private' domain" (89–90). These have been considered matters of the "good life" and unavailable for public discourse: "As with any modern liberation movement, the contemporary women's movement is making what were hitherto considered private matters of the good life into public issues of justice" (92). I suggest here that once the private issues are liberated into the public, they focus on justice for the individual, not justice for the common good.

59. For a discussion of the impact of rights talk in public life, see Glendon, *Rights Talk.* For a discussion of the impact of individualism, see Elshtain, *Democracy on Trial.* See also Lasch, *Culture of Narcissism,* and Sennett, *Fall of Public Man.*

60. In my study of media framing of reproduction from 1983 to 2003, I discovered that the rhetoric of choice has migrated from the issue of abortion to other issues of reproduction, including infertility and in vitro fertilization, RU-486, late-term abortion, and sexual abstinence. See Gardner, "My Body, My Choice."

61. Bellah et al., *Habits of the Heart.*

62. Ibid.

63. See Bellah, "Civil Religion in America"; Hart, *Political Pulpit;* Wuthnow, *Restructuring of American Religion.*

64. Audi, "Religious Values, Political Action"; Rorty, "Religion as Conversation-Stopper."

65. Audi, "Religious Values, Political Action," 287.

66. Rorty, "Religion as Conversation-Stopper," 172.

67. Audi and Wolterstorff, *Religion in the Public Square;* Williams, "Language of God."

68. Audi and Wolterstorff, *Religion in the Public Square,* 112–13.

69. Williams, "Language of God," 173.

70. Hunter, *American Evangelicalism,* 75, 87, 95.

71. See Finke and Stark, *Churching of America.* Mark Shibley views secular accommodations as providing churches (institutions that are embedded in secular pluralist society) with the "cultural currency" they need for adaptive strength and growth. See Shibley, *Resurgent Evangelicalism.*

72. Taylor, *A Secular Age*. See Jakobsen and Pellegrini, *Secularisms*, for a collection of essays challenging the idea that secularization has forced religion to remain in the private sphere.

73. Smith, *American Evangelicalism*.

74. John Schmalzbauer's study of the symbolic boundaries between the sacred and secular reveals that Catholic and evangelical journalists and academics translate their sacred beliefs into secular language. He conjectures this could negatively affect religion by increasing the secularization of public discourse. See Schmalzbauer, *People of Faith*, 202.

75. As Marsha Witten points out in her rhetorical analysis of American Protestant sermons, the religious discourse contains elements of cultural accommodation as well as cultural resistance. Persuasive engagement with culture leaves the rhetor open for persuasion by culture, as well. See Witten, *All Is Forgiven*.

76. Hauerwas, "On Being a Christian," 233–34; emphasis in original.

CHAPTER 1

1. For a transcript of the interview, see Van Susteren, "Exclusive: A Visit with the Palins."

2. Others have observed the feminist overtones of Bristol's responses. See Traister, "Bristol Palin Stammers the Truth."

3. Mohler, "Palin Parable."

4. See Turner, *Ritual Process*, 94–130. See also Turner, *Forest of Symbols*, 93–111, for more on liminality.

5. Smith, *American Evangelicalism*, 89.

6. Joe McGarry, interview by author, September 27, 2004, Boston.

7. Brake, *True Love Waits Goes Home*, 66.

8. Author's field notes, Silver Ring Thing event, September 25, 2004, Boston.

9. Douglas, *Purity and Danger*, 9, 44. I thank Robert Wuthnow for recommending this classic text. For more on Douglas and an application of her theories to evangelicals and purity, see Freitas, *Sex and the Soul*, 78–79.

10. I use the term *nonmarital* to describe sexual activity that occurs apart from the marital relationship. The more commonly used phrase "premarital sex" refers to sexual activity that is both outside and before marriage, implying stages of intimacy or a progression that leads to marriage. See Nathanson, *Dangerous Passage*, 33–34. While evangelical abstinence campaigns largely assume that adolescents will one day be married, I do not make a similar assumption.

11. D. Gresh, *And the Bride Wore White*, 77, 146.

12. This shift to purity is evident in the titles of evangelical sexual abstinence resources. Alcorn, *Purity Principle*; Elliot, *Passion and Purity*; D. Gresh, *And the Bride Wore White*; and St. James, *Wait for Me*, are a few examples.

13. For a discussion of the connection between abstinence and purity, see Mullaney, *Everyone Is Not Doing It*, 75–80. Mullaney identifies three definitions of purity in relation to abstinence: a lack of contamination, a contrast to innocence, and a strategy of order.

14. B. Gresh, *Who Moved the Goalpost?* 87.

15. *Silver Ring Thing Sexual Abstinence Study Bible,* 14; emphasis in original.

16. True Love Waits Pledge Card, published by LifeWay Christian Resources of the Southern Baptist Convention, Nashville, Tenn., 1993; emphasis in original.

17. Emphasis added.

18. True Love Waits Web site, www.lifeway.com/tlw/.

19. D. Gresh, *And the Bride Wore White.*

20. McDowell, *Why True Love Waits,* 457.

21. St. James, "Wait for Me."

22. True Love Waits Web site; author's field notes, Silver Ring Thing event, September 25, 2004, Boston.

23. Researchers perpetuate this mixed metaphor, as well. In her 2001 study of interpretations of virginity loss, the sociologist Laura Carpenter writes about how an individual chooses a new personal and social identity when she "decides to lose her virginity." See Carpenter, *Virginity Lost,* 137.

24. Carpenter, in her study of metaphors of virginity loss, notes the disagreement among some of her interview respondents as to whether to classify nonconsensual sex as virginity loss. Technically, the victims of coerced sex may no longer be virgins, but some respondents were reluctant to classify them as such because the virginity was not freely given. All nine respondents who had been victims of rape or another form of nonconsensual sex agreed that coerced sex does not count as lost virginity (Carpenter, *Virginity Lost,* 132).

25. Rankin and Ross, *When True Love Doesn't Wait,* 16–17.

26. Ibid., 17.

27. Indeed, the gift of virginity should be reciprocated with a gift of virginity. The giving of one's virginity establishes solidarity and obligates the receiver to return the favor. For a classic study of the complicated rituals of gift giving and receiving, see Mauss, *Gift.*

28. This medicalizing of a moral problem is not new. Constance Nathanson, in her book *Dangerous Passage,* traces the rise of adolescent pregnancy as a social problem. She identifies the birth control pill and legalized abortion as contributing to adolescent pregnancy as a medical problem. For prolife evangelicals, pregnancy is not the problem; the problem is the sexually promiscuous public culture that results from the availability of contraception and abortion.

29. Author's field notes, Silver Ring Thing event, September 25, 2004, Boston.

30. See Douglas, *Purity and Danger;* Smith-Rosenberg, "Sex as Symbol in Victorian Purity."

31. Smith-Rosenberg, "Sex as Symbol in Victorian Purity," S229.

CHAPTER 2

1. Feldt, *War on Choice,* 62.

2. See Douglas, *Purity and Danger.*

3. Regnerus, a sociologist, claims that the current debate about sex education is irrelevant because of the powerful impact of new media technologies such as the Internet, which give teenagers access to information about sex. It doesn't matter whether sex education in public schools includes such controversial topics as oral sex and condom use, because young people can easily find graphic information about both on the Web. See Regnerus, *Forbidden Fruit*, 58–59.

4. See Balmer, *Blessed Assurance*.

5. Ironically, evangelicals' use of the products of popular culture also served to distance them from popular culture. Evangelicals formed media enterprises—radio and television stations, publishing houses, record companies—with the ostensible purpose of reaching secular culture but with the practical result of reinforcing an enclaved culture of evangelicalism. Evangelicals now had "safe, family-friendly" books, music, and radio and television programs that protected evangelicals from the evils of secular culture. What began as an enterprise to bring new people into the church ended up as a case of preaching to the choir. However, the evangelistic impulse remained. These enclaved cultural products set an example—a "city on the hill"-style of evangelism—that attempted to win souls for Christ by highlighting the difference between secular and religious culture. For a fascinating study of contemporary Christian media, see Hendershot, *Shaking the World for Jesus*.

6. Author's field notes, Pure Freedom event, October 16, 2004, Chicago.

7. True Love Waits Web site, www.lifeway.com/tlw.

8. I explicate the "virginity as a gift" metaphor in greater detail in chapter 1.

9. I am grateful to my teenage and young adult interview respondents for the candor with which they shared their stories. I have changed their names to protect their identities and have changed or withheld other identifying characteristics.

10. In the nonrepresentative sample of this study, Kevin Brooks's response is common among evangelical teenagers. However, this view may not be common across all teenagers. Laura Carpenter found that just more than one-third of her interview respondents discussed virginity as stigma. See Carpenter, *Virginity Lost*.

11. Donna Freitas describes the skit a bit differently. She asserts that "the volunteer whose heart is 'ripped apart' is almost always female." In my participant-observation of four Silver Ring Thing events, the volunteer was always male. See Freitas, *Sex and the Soul*, 83–84.

12. See Winner, *Real Sex*. Winner addresses this as one of the myths of the church regarding nonmarital sex, that somehow it will be less enjoyable because it does not occur within marriage.

13. My finding, that great sex in marriage is promised to those who wait, expands on the virginity pledge study of the National Longitudinal Study of Adolescent Health, which found that those who support abstinence programs do not focus on the negative consequences of sex, because it would appear to legitimize sex if the consequences were good: "Instead, they stress moral systems that justify saying no thank you to sex in and of itself." See Bearman and

Brückner, "Promising the Future," 861. While this is partly true, producers of the evangelical abstinence rhetoric also emphasize great sex as a goal of abstinence—saying no to sex now may be part of an evangelical Christian moral system, but it also is a strategy to preserve the potential for great sex later.

14. For the original article see Mattox, "Aha!"

15. The rings used by Silver Ring Thing are engraved with the scripture reference for First Thessalonians 4:3, 4: "It is God's will that you should be sanctified: that you should avoid sexual immorality; that each of you should learn to control his own body in a way that is holy and honorable" (New International Version).

16. Brake, *True Love Waits Goes Home*, 46, 47.

17. Author's field notes, True Love Waits event, June 26, 2004, Dallas.

18. Even MTV unwittingly helped the abstinence campaigns. At the 2008 MTV Video Music Awards, the comedic host Russell Brand publicly teased the Jonas Brothers for wearing purity rings. Jordin Sparks, an award presenter, shot back, "It's not bad to wear a promise ring, because not everybody, guy or girl, wants to be a slut." See Kaufman, "Russell Brand/Jonas Brothers VMA Flap."

19. Gerard A. Hauser writes that the claim that bodies can argue is problematic because "the body is an ambiguous form of signification." Bodies are both biological and symbolic. Thus, Hauser claims, bodies need contextual framing because "the meaning we attribute to unvarnished bodily display is not necessarily the assertion being advanced" (Hauser, "Incongruous Bodies," 5). In the present case I suggest that the discourse of the testimony provides the context, but the body of the abstinent testifier advances the claim that abstinence is appealing.

20. In her exploration of the role of personal testimony in prochoice films, Barbara A. Pickering suggests that identification goes beyond discourse and includes the visual impact of the rhetor, implicating "the power of the human body as argument" (Pickering, "Women's Voices as Evidence," 19).

21. Physical bodies too function as arguments in contemporary public advocacy. Homosexual bodies kissing in public "kiss-ins" function as social protest of homophobia in the context of HIV/AIDS. Bodies in trees scheduled to be cut down by loggers argue for an ecocentrism that affirms the interconnectedness of humans and nature. See DeLuca, "Unruly Arguments."

22. Tyler, *Freedom's Ferment*, 338–39.

23. Ibid., 339.

24. Furnas, *Life and Times of the Late Demon Rum*, 89; emphasis in original.

25. I discuss the implications of a rhetorical construction of virginity in chapter 1.

26. Conversion testimonies form a unique genre of personal narrative, testing the boundaries of narrative fidelity through stories that emphasize dramatic personal change. For a rhetorical analysis of Charles Colson's dramatic religious conversion following his involvement in the Watergate scandal, see Griffin, "Rhetoric of Form in Conversion Narratives."

CHAPTER 3

1. Author's field notes, True Love Waits event, June 26, 2004, Dallas.

2. Craven, "Beauty and the Belles," 124. See also Bottigheimer, *Fairy Tales and Society*; Do Rozario, "Princess and the Magic Kingdom."

3. Zipes, "Breaking the Disney Spell," 22, 23; see also Zipes, *Fairy Tales and the Art of Subversion*.

4. Warner, *From the Beast to the Blonde*.

5. See Bell, Haas, and Sells, *From Mouse to Mermaid*; Wasko, *Understanding Disney*.

6. Warner, *From the Beast to the Blonde*, 314.

7. St. James, *Wait for Me*, 3.

8. Ibid., 3–4. It is worth noting that the writer does not clearly identify the gender of the protagonist, instead using the generic pronoun *you* to establish a close identification between the reader and the story. St. James uses the same technique in the second story, but the *you* is described as a knight who has "lost his life in pursuit of the beautiful damsel" (5). However, St. James provides numerous clues that the protagonist in the first story is assumed to be female. The feminine descriptions of the protagonist as lost, alone, and afraid in a dark woods and the subsequent rescue by a male on horseback match descriptions of stock female characters in traditional fairy tales. An argument could be made that the story allows for a homosexual reading of the reward of waiting for true love, but this is not plausible in light of the author's publicly stated support of traditional heterosexual marriage and biblical narratives that depict Jesus Christ as the bridegroom returning to rescue and claim his bride, the church. Additional evidence for a female protagonist lies in the story's presentation as part of a binary with the second story in which a clearly identified male protagonist saves the day. The generic *you* in both stories attempts to create strong reader identification between the protagonists and both male and female readers.

9. St. James, *Wait for Me*, 7–8, 10.

10. Zipes, "Breaking the Disney Spell," 37.

11. Bishop, *Princess and the Kiss*, 8.

12. Ibid., 16–17, 19, 28.

13. St. James, *Wait for Me*, 4.

14. Ibid., 4, 5.

15. Bishop, *Squire and the Scroll*, 1, 4.

16. Ibid., 7, 14, 25, 30.

17. Arterburn and Stoeker, *Every Young Man's Battle*, 137–52.

18. Author's field notes, True Love Waits, June 26, 2004, Dallas.

19. B. Gresh, *Who Moved the Goalpost?*

20. Eldredge, *Wild at Heart*, 6, 7, 9, 79; emphasis in original.

21. E. Ludy, *God's Gift to Women*, 44, 217; emphasis in original.

22. "Kiss a Toad," bookmark, Heritage House '76, Snowflake, Arizona, 2003.

23. Jana Spicka, "Okay, let me spell it out for you . . ." bookmark, Life Cycle Books, Niagara Falls, New York, 2002.

24. Jana Spicka, "Do I look like a prince to you?" bookmark, Life Cycle Books, Niagara Falls, New York, 2002.

25. Spicka, "Do I look like a prince to you?" and "Okay, let me spell it out for you."

26. Spicka, *Locket and the Mask*, 9.

27. Ibid., 19, 21, 25, 30–31.

28. Author's field notes, Pure Freedom event, October 16, 2004, Chicago; Gresh, *And the Bride Wore White*, 13–14. The scene of the tea party has been replicated at other Pure Freedom events as recently as 2008. The Styrofoam cup message has been repackaged as a type of storybook fable and presented on stage as part of the Secret Keeper Girl Tour (author's field notes, Pure Freedom, April 3, 2009, Chicago).

29. D. Gresh, *And the Bride Wore White*, 79, 84–88.

30. Author's field notes, Pure Freedom event, October 16, 2004, Chicago; Gresh, *Secret Keeper*, 34, 44.

31. Ibid., 12, 19, 23.

32. Ibid., 20.

33. Ibid., 43–44; emphasis in original.

34. Ibid., 46 (emphasis in original), 47–48, 46, 47, 48.

35. See Boddy, *Wombs and Alien Spirits*. Boddy's study of an Islamic women's healing cult in northern Sudan offers a detailed example of women using the tools of their oppression to resist domination. Saba Mahmood (2005) describes this type of agency as "the capacity to realize one's own interests against the weight of custom, tradition, transcendental will, or other obstacles (whether individual or collective)" (Mahmood, *Politics of Piety*, 8).

36. These testimonies function as embodied arguments, which I describe at length in chapter 2.

37. One leader told me that my presence in the room would make the men uncomfortable as they shared their stories. We agreed that I would sit on a bench outside the room, blocked by the open door, so that I could hear the session, but the presenters could not see me and I could not see them. The names I use here are pseudonyms.

38. Travers, *In Search of the Hero*, 9.

39. Bearman and Brückner, "Promising the Future," 2.

40. A similar claim about the support and subversion of traditional gender roles is made about Disney fairy tales, which encourage conformity and reaffirm a patriarchal status quo while opening up possibilities for feminist readings that reverse traditional conceptions of gendered power. See Downey, "Feminine Empowerment in Disney's 'Beauty and the Beast.'" Alternatively, Disney fairy tales may be merely a "cunning domestication of feminism itself" (Warner, *From the Beast to the Blonde*, 313).

41. Donna Freitas observes the use of the fairy-tale narrative among the evangelical respondents in her study of sexuality and religion on college campuses. See *Sex and the Soul*, 75–92. Her analysis confirms the maintenance of traditional gender roles (active men, passive women) within the abstinence movement: "Women . . . *submit* to their guardian, and they *wait* for their prince to come along and for their purity to *be taken* on their wedding day" (92;

emphasis in original). My analysis agrees with Freitas's to a point: I suggest that the fairy narrative functions both to support and subvert traditional gender roles.

42. Smith-Rosenberg, "Sex as Symbol in Victorian Purity," S221, S222, S242, S243.

43. Bartkowski and Read, "Veiled Submission," 80.

44. Ibid., 79.

45. Griffith, *God's Daughters,* 181, 179.

46. For a scathing critique of aggressive masculinity and the negative impact of a culture of purity on young men and women, see Valenti, *Purity Myth.*

47. For a recent exploration of the creative balance of leadership and submission maintained by many evangelical women, see Worthen, "Housewives of God."

48. See Mahmood, *Politics of Piety.* Mahmood provides a sharp critique of feminist scholarship that assumes women's agency is defined by women's ability to resist patriarchal domination. She identifies the tension in feminist scholarship's dual aims as an *"analytical* and a *politically prescriptive* project" that assumes freedom as normative to feminism (10; emphasis in original).

49. Mahmood, *Politics of Piety,* 15.

50. Indeed, one could make the claim that the evangelical abstinence campaigns are designed specifically for young women. While Pure Freedom holds coed events, most of its publications and events are designed for young women.

CHAPTER 4

1. Dannelly, *Saved!*

2. Ibid.

3. Evangelical abstinence campaigns have been satirized on television and in print, as well. An episode of the animated series *The Family Guy* features the "Opal Ring Crusade," a Christian abstinence campaign that distributes misinformation about sex, such as condoms fail 100 percent of the time, and anyone who has sex outside marriage is automatically in Al Qaeda. See Chevapravatdumrong, "Prick Up Your Ears." Tom Perotta's novel *The Abstinence Teacher* centers on the relationship between a high school human sexuality teacher and an evangelical Christian.

4. This widely quoted statistic is from the National Longitudinal Study of Adolescent Health. See Bearman and Brückner, "Promising the Future," for their analysis of the effectiveness of virginity pledges.

5. Mark Regnerus, using results from the National Longitudinal Study of Adolescent Health, points out that abstinence pledge movements are successful at increasing the age of lost virginity, reducing the number of sexual partners, and reducing the likelihood of partners who cheat. See Regnerus, *Forbidden Fruit,* 100–101.

6. Ibid., 161–62.

7. See chapter 2 for a definition and discussion of embodied argument.

8. This perspective differs from those of the respondents in Donna Freitas's 2008 study of sexuality and religion on college campuses. See Freitas, *Sex and*

the Soul. She writes that a number of her female respondents "complained of being nothing more than 'ladies in waiting,' of not being allowed [by their religious culture] to do anything to get guys to notice them or ask them out" (92). They chafed at the passive role thrust upon them. In contrast, my female respondents described their commitment to abstinence as empowering.

9. I explore the different messages to males and females as part of an analysis of the fairy-tale narrative in chapter 3.

10. Most of those who had had consensual sex did so before they had made an abstinence pledge.

11. The presence of sexual boundaries among evangelical youths has been observed elsewhere. See Freitas, *Sex and the Soul,* 88–92. Her interview respondent Mark Johnson worries about how far he can go sexually with a young woman without damaging his spiritual life. What is noteworthy about my findings is that the interview respondents reveal a diversity of views on where the boundaries should lie.

12. The Christian author Joshua Harris is widely credited with starting the contemporary courtship movement among young evangelicals. See Harris, *I Kissed Dating Goodbye* and *Boy Meets Girl.*

13. I discuss the campaigns' tropological shift from abstinence to purity in chapter 1.

CHAPTER 5

1. See Ludy and Ludy, *When God Writes Your Love Story.*

2. When I interviewed them, ten young adults self-reported that they had not been abstinent, either before or after making an abstinence pledge.

3. Neal, *Romancing God,* 159, 172.

4. Carpenter, *Virginity Lost,* 194–95.

5. Lauren Winner dispels this myth in her book *Real Sex,* 85–90.

6. My study suggests that Carpenter's "act of worship" metaphor is underrepresented. Each of my respondents views his or her virginity as a gift from God and her or his corresponding commitment to abstinence as an act of worship.

7. Carpenter, *Virginity Lost,* 205.

8. Ibid., 207.

9. I introduce the rhetoric of second virginity in chapter 2.

10. Maken, *Getting Serious about Getting Married,* 28, 22; emphasis in original. See also Watters, *Get Married.*

11. Maken, *Getting Serious about Getting Married,* 16, 130.

12. Ibid., 129, 182.

13. "If a woman wants to be a lawyer, she can go to law school, take the Bar Exam, send out resumes to employers, and practice law. If a woman wants to run for office, she can put her name in the hat, run a good election campaign, and win the race. If a woman wants to travel to Australia, she can buy airline tickets, pack her bags, and go. In other words she can do something to accomplish her goals. But if she wants to get married, she's told to sit like a bump

on a log until the right Christian man finds her. I don't think so," Maken writes (*Getting Serious about Getting Married*, 165).

14. In this section I use *homosexual* as an umbrella term to include all gays, lesbians, bisexuals, and transgendered people.

15. The events are not the only site where there is silence on homosexuality: few Christian books on sexual abstinence address the topic. See Speck, "Homosexuality: Is There Hope?" in *Sex: It's Worth Waiting For*, 165–88; B. Gresh, "On Homosexuality," in *Who Moved the Goalpost?* 205–207.

16. Evangelical views on the morality of homosexuality may be growing increasingly at odds with the rest of American society. A 2008 Gallup poll showed Americans evenly divided on the issue of "homosexual relations," with 48 percent believing it to be "morally acceptable" and 48 percent considering it to be "morally wrong." See Saad, "Americans Evenly Divided." Two years later, a 2010 Gallup poll showed an increase in support for the morality of homosexuality: "Americans' support for the moral acceptability of gay and lesbian relations crossed the symbolic 50% threshold in 2010. At the same time, the percentage calling these relations 'morally wrong' dropped to 43%, the lowest in Gallup's decade-long trend." See Saad, "Americans' Acceptance of Gay Relations." A majority of Americans may believe homosexuality to be moral, but interestingly they don't want its morality taught to their children. In a 2004 poll about sex education in the public schools, only a small percentage of Americans believe homosexuality should be taught as "acceptable": "Fifty-two percent said schools should teach 'only what homosexuality is, without discussing whether it is wrong or acceptable,' compared with 18 percent who said schools should teach that homosexuality is wrong and 8 percent who said schools should teach that homosexuality is acceptable." See NPR/Kaiser/Kennedy School Poll, "Sex Education in America."

17. Denny Pattyn, e-mail to author, April 27, 2010.

18. Ibid.

19. See Grenz, *Welcoming but Not Affirming*, 122. Grenz bases his separation of disposition from acts on biblical definitions of sin: "Christian theology maintains that the present world is fallen, that is, creation does not yet correspond to the fullness of God's intention" (119). He writes that God will both redeem and judge: "As the great physician, God will heal our fallen sinfulness in the new creation, and as our judge, God will condemn our sinful actions. Hence, our fallen disposition is sinful in that it is foundational to our sinning. But it is our sinful acts—which bring God's condemnation upon us—that are what marks us as guilty before God" (120).

20. B. Gresh, *Who Moved the Goalpost?* 206–207. For an insightful ethnography of the ex-gay movement, see Erzen, *Straight to Jesus*.

21. The psychologist Stanton L. Jones writes that "what the Bible treats as an isolated *act* to be condemned (namely, people of the same gender having sex), our society treats as a fundamental element of personal *identity*" (Jones, "Loving Opposition," 24; emphasis in original). He asserts that true Christian identity, whether for the homosexual or heterosexual, is to be found in Christ, not in sexual desires. He paraphrases the apostle Paul in Romans 6:16 to suggest that while Christian identities may be secure, human choices to act on sexual

desires make a person become more a slave to sin or more a slave to Christ: "If what you mean by saying you are a homosexual is that your identity is defined by your gayness and that living out those sexual leanings is essential to your very nature, then your identity is misplaced; you are trying to build an identity on shifting sand" (24).

22. Lifelong sexual abstinence is not the same as celibacy, as Stanley Grenz points out: "Unlike celibacy, abstinence in singleness is not a particular calling for certain persons, but an ethical ideal for all who are not married. And unlike celibacy, which is a chosen, permanent (or semi-permanent) response to a sensed call from God, the commitment to abstinence in singleness is a particular, and for many people temporary, outworking of the overarching call to a life of sexual chastity that comes to all" (Grenz, *Welcoming but Not Affirming*, 126–27).

23. The political philosopher and pastor Dale Kuehne disagrees with those who claim that the Bible supports monogamous homosexual relationships but condemns promiscuous ones. See Kuehne, *Sex and the iWorld*. He argues that the logic on which this claim is based—that sex is essential to personal fulfillment—is faulty. On the contrary, Kuehne asserts that humans were created for an intimate love relationship with God, from which we are given the ability to love others (164). Deemphasizing sex and marriage, he claims, reinvigorates biblical sexual boundaries without unfairly punishing homosexuals and unmarried heterosexuals: "If this is true, then prohibiting sexual relations between unmarried people does not rob them of the ability to enjoy true love and intimacy now or for a lifetime because sex is not a necessary stop on the pathway to true love and intimacy. If this is true, then the prohibition against homosexual relations does not deny people who are so inclined the experience of true love and happiness" (161). See also Jones, "Loving Opposition."

24. McMinn, *Sexuality and Holy Longing*, 129.

CHAPTER 6

1. Morgan, "Mr. Jabez Goes to Africa."

2. Caldwell, "Where Jabez Doesn't Cut It"; Morgan, "Mr. Jabez Goes to Africa."

3. Morgan, "Purpose-driven in Rwanda," 2, 7.

4. "Remarks by the President"; "Bush Signs Initiative"; Office of U.S. Global AIDS Coordinator and the Bureau of Public Affairs, U.S. State Department, "The United States President's Emergency Plan for AIDS Relief: A Commitment Renewed."

5. UNAIDS, "Report on the Global AIDS Epidemic," 5, 9, 13; Global Coalition on Women and AIDS Web site, http://womenandaids.unaids.org.

6. See AMFAR, "Gender-Based Violence."

7. For a fascinating account of the potential impact of behavior change such as abstinence in the AIDS epidemic in Africa, see Epstein, *Invisible Cure*.

8. Beehler, "True Love Waits to Expand"; Silver Ring Thing Web site, www.silverringthing.com; Pure Freedom Web site, www.purefreedom.org; Office of

the U.S. Global AIDS Coordinator, U.S. Department of State, "Critical Interventions."

9. See Shilts, *And the Band Played On;* Treichler, *How to Have Theory.*

10. Bartlett and Curran, *World Vision International's AIDS Initiative,* 11.

11. "World Relief Journals," 11.

12. U.S. Agency for International Development, "USAID Announces First Round"; "World Relief Journals," 6; "Mobilizing for Life."

13. "World Relief Annual Report."

14. I interviewed in person seventeen people from six evangelical organizations that are involved in producing abstinence rhetoric. The interviews were conducted at field offices in Kenya and Rwanda, and at World Relief's international headquarters in Baltimore between September 15 and November 25, 2004. The interviewees are staff members of World Relief (World Relief Kenya; World Relief Rwanda); one of World Relief's abstinence partner agencies (Crisis Pregnancy Ministries; Scripture Union); or an evangelical organization that is based in the United States and involved in abstinence education in both Africa and the United States (True Love Waits; Focus on the Family; Global Care). Both True Love Waits and Focus on the Family have an informal partnership with World Relief in its abstinence work. At the request of the two interview respondents from Global Care, I use pseudonyms for both the respondents and the organization. The shortest interview lasted thirty minutes; the longest was two hours.

I chose Kenya and Rwanda as sites for this study because of their location in sub-Saharan Africa and their inclusion in World Relief's USAID grant for abstinence education. Using two countries, rather than one, provides variance, as well: Nairobi, considered the most "Western" city of East Africa in terms of economic infrastructure, contrasts with Kigali, which is little more than an assemblage of villages on neighboring hills. In addition to living with the specter of AIDS, Rwanda's remaining 8.4 million inhabitants in many ways are still recovering from the 1994 genocide, in which more than one million Tutsis and moderate Hutus died.

Ten years after the genocide it was estimated that 101,000 children were heading roughly 42,000 households. In many cases their parents had died, either from AIDS or the genocide, or were imprisoned for genocide-related crimes. See UNICEF, "Ten Years after Genocide." Kenya, in contrast, is a relatively healthier country, with an HIV-transmission rate that seems to have stabilized. As in Uganda, HIV transmission rates in Kenya have dropped in recent years, from 13.6 percent median HIV prevalence in 1997–98 to 9.4 percent in 2002. See UNAIDS/WHO, "AIDS Epidemic Update 2004," 26. A 2007 study noted a slight increase in HIV prevalence since 2003, although prevalence among adults in urban areas decreased in 2007. See UNAIDS/WHO, "AIDS Epidemic Update 2009," 29.

15. I visited four World Relief youth abstinence clubs in Kigali between November 22 and 24, 2004. The first group (group 1) met on Monday, November 22, 2004, from 10:00 A.M. to 12:30 P.M. at an evangelical church in the Kimihurura district of Kigali. Ten youths and one pastor were in attendance.

The second club (group 2) met on Monday, November 22, 2004, from 4:00 P.M. to 6:30 P.M. at an evangelical church in the Kabeza district of Kigali. About one hundred youths were in attendance. The third club (group 3) met on Tuesday, November 23, 2004, from 10:00 A.M. to 12:30 P.M. at an evangelical church in the Nyarutarama district of Kigali. About sixty young people and· two pastors were in attendance.

The fourth club (group 4) met on Wednesday, November 24, 2004, from 5:00 P.M. to 7:15 P.M. at an evangelical church in the Nyamirambo district of Kigali. The group consisted of fourteen youths, two pastors, and a few other youths who joined the meeting late. I am withholding specific names of churches to protect the identities of participants.

Participant-observation and group interviews were conducted with each abstinence club. The abstinence trainers and I asked questions of the group as part of the regular club meeting. Individual group members were encouraged to respond. The interviews were conducted in English with the assistance of an interpreter.

16. Pumpelly et al., *True Love Waits Leaders' Manual* (Nairobi, 2002), 34–35.

17. Pumpelly et al., *True Love Waits Leaders' Manual* (Kampala, Uganda, 1998), 51.

18. Focus on the Family, "No Apologies," 11.

19. Heidkamp, Dortzbach, and Njoroge, "Choose Life," 3, 6; Khamadi et al., *Worth the Wait Manual,* i.

20. Bertolet et al., "Mobilizing for Life," 20.

21. Abstinence certainly has played a role in reducing HIV transmission rates in sub-Saharan Africa, although to what extent is hotly debated. In the case of Uganda, some credit abstinence as a crucial factor in decreased HIV transmission rates. See Green, *Rethinking AIDS Prevention,* 155–60. Others emphasize the role of "zero grazing" or partner reduction. See Epstein, *Invisible Cure,* 185–201.

22. Sheila Muchemi, interview by author, November 16, 2004, Nairobi.

23. Pumpelly et al., *True Love Waits Leaders' Manual* (Kampala, Uganda, 1998; Nairobi, 2002).

24. The woman was speaking Kinyarwanda, which was translated into English for me.

25. Bertolet et al., "Mobilizing for Life."

CHAPTER 7

1. Neff and Morgan, "Jesus Freak."

2. Ibid.

3. "Global Care" is a pseudonym for a Christian relief and development organization. The respondents from this organization requested that their names, position, and affiliation not be used in this study.

4. Rebecca Heidkamp, interview by author, September 16, 2004, Baltimore; emphasis added.

5. Deborah Dortzbach, interview by author, September 16, 2004, Baltimore; emphasis added.

6. Heidkamp interview; emphasis added.

7. Ibid.

8. Global Care respondent A, interview by author, September 15, 2004.

9. Global Care respondent B, interview by author, September 15, 2004.

10. MAP International et al., Statement of Conscience, 1; emphasis in original.

11. Ibid., 1, 2.

12. Ibid., 2.

13. Rios, letter to evangelical AIDS forum attendees, 1.

14. Ibid., 1.

15. MAP International et al., Statement of Conscience, 2; Rios, letter to evangelical AIDS forum attendees, 1.

16. MAP International et al., Statement of Conscience, 1, 2, 3.

17. I discuss this strategy of reclaiming agency in chapter 1.

CHAPTER 8

1. WorldTeach USA, *Hope for Africa.*

2. Barna Group, "New Marriage and Divorce Statistics Revealed."

3. See Regnerus, *Forbidden Fruit.* The study draws on two main sources of data: the National Longitudinal Study of Adolescent Health and the National Survey of Youth and Religion (NSYR). Regnerus is a coinvestigator of the NSYR.

4. Regnerus, *Forbidden Fruit,* 161.

5. Ibid., 157.

6. Ibid., 180. Also see pp. 163–82 for a more complete description of this middle-class morality.

7. Regnerus, *Forbidden Fruit,* 85, 213. Elsewhere, Regnerus amplifies his case for young marriage. See Regnerus, "Say Yes," and Regnerus, "The Case for Early Marriage."

8. The evangelical promise of great sex in marriage reinforces a modern notion of marriage as a space where two individuals come together to get their individual needs met. In contrast, Lauren Winner (2005), drawing on Wendell Berry, suggests that marital sex is great because it is "an embodied way of entering into community with one's spouse and of enacting God's love." See Winner, *Real Sex,* 55. Far from being merely a personal relationship, marriage is a communal relationship with specific responsibilities to the community as a model of "God's love actualized among God's people," Winner says (144).

9. For a brief history of evangelical views on contraception and their connection to the abstinence campaigns, see Gardner, "God's Protection."

10. Anonymous source, e-mail to author, January 20, 2010.

11. Meacham, "End of Christian America."

12. Bearman and Brückner, "Promising the Future," 891.

13. The perpetuation of the abstinence campaigns as marginalized could manifest itself in opposition to a sex-saturated society or it could create minority

groups within the abstinence movement itself. It is conceivable that if the evangelical sexual abstinence campaigns continue to gain in popularity and become part of mainstream culture, adolescents may find other ways to distinguish themselves from the group. This could explain the increased popularity of more conservative views of heterosexual relationships among evangelical youths, including courtship models of dating and commitments to delay first kisses as part of an overall commitment to abstinence.

14. In a 2005 poll 54 percent of American adults self-identified as born-again or evangelical Christians. See Princeton Survey Research/Newsweek, "Would you describe yourself as a born-again or Evangelical Christian, or not?"

15. Smith, *American Evangelicalism*.

16. A similar critique is made of feminist efforts to reclaim agency. See McKerrow, "Corporeality and Cultural Rhetoric."

In McKerrow's discussion of a corporeal rhetoric and the need to "write women into history" (316), he acknowledges Michelle Ballif's critique of attempts to reappropriate feminist agency: "Are we not, then, merely making Woman into a *legitimate* coin, a *proper* currency, a *respectable* asset, but without questioning the very stand—the phallogocentric standard of Truth—that finds her lacking, that is responsible for her devaluation?" (quoted in McKerrow, "Corporeality and Cultural Rhetoric," 316; emphasis in original). Without questioning the standard by which women are silenced, the standard becomes reproduced in their voice: "Our attempts to (re)read women, to (re)cover women, to (re)present women, and to therefore (re)cast history, are insidious acts of (re)appropriation" (316). A similar argument can be made regarding American evangelicals' strategic use of victimization to enable the reappropriation of agency for the purpose of persuasion. Arguing from the periphery by constructing oneself as a victim may strengthen persuasive power, but it reinstates the oppressive structures—in this case, the triumph of the individual—in the rhetoric.

17. Bertolet et al., "Mobilizing for Life."

18. Brooks, "Wisdom We Need to Fight AIDS."

19. Ibid.

20. Ibid.

21. Mahmood, *Politics of Piety,* 157. In the context of her study of the women's piety movement in Egypt, she writes that bodily acts such as wearing the veil constitute "*critical markers* of piety as well as the *ineluctable means* by which one trains oneself to be pious" (158; emphasis in the original).

22. Spiritual disciplines such as fasting, meditation, and chastity demonstrate one's control over one's bodily desires while recognizing one's dependence on God. See Foster, *Celebration of Discipline;* Willard, *Spirit of the Disciplines;* Winner, *Real Sex.*

Bibliography

Alcorn, Randy. *The Purity Principle*. Sisters, Ore.: Multnomah, 2003.

Ali, Lorraine. "Choosing Virginity." *Newsweek,* December 9, 2002, 60–66.

American Civil Liberties Union. "ACLU Announces Settlement in Challenge to Government-Funded Religion in the Abstinence-Only-Until-Marriage Program the 'Silver Ring Thing.'" Press release, February 23, 2006. www .aclu.org/reproductiverights/sexed/24246prs20060223.html.

AMFAR (The Foundation for AIDS Research). "Gender-Based Violence and HIV among Women: Assessing the Evidence." AMFAR Issue brief no. 3, June 2005. www.amfar.org/uploadedFiles/In_the_Community/Publications/ Gender%20BAsed%20Violence%20and%20HIV%20Among%20Women .pdf.

Anderson, Benedict. *Imagined Communities: Reflections on the Origin and Spread of Nationalism*. London: Verso, 1991.

Arizona Bureau of Vital Statistics. "Teenage Pregnancy, Arizona, 1986–1996." www.azdhs.gov/plan/report/tp/teen96/index.htm.

Arterburn, Stephen, and Fred Stoeker. *Every Young Man's Battle: Strategies for Victory in the Real World of Sexual Temptation*. Colorado Springs, Colo.: WaterBrook, 2002.

Audi, Robert. "Religious Values, Political Action, and Civic Discourse." *Indiana Law Journal* 75, no. 273 (2000): 273–94.

Audi, Robert, and Nicholas Wolterstorff. *Religion in the Public Square: The Place of Religious Convictions in Political Debate*. Lanham, Md.: Rowman and Littlefield, 1997.

Balmer, Randall. *Blessed Assurance: A History of Evangelicalism in America*. Boston: Beacon, 1999.

———. *The Making of Evangelicalism: From Revivalism to Politics and Beyond*. Waco, Tex.: Baylor University Press, 2010.

Barlett, Christopher A., and Daniel F. Curran. *World Vision International's AIDS Initiative: Challenging a Global Partnership.* Boston: Harvard Business School, 2004.

Barna Group. "New Marriage and Divorce Statistics Revealed," March 31, 2008. www.barna.org/barna-update/article/15-familykids/42-new-marriage-and-divorce-statistics-released.

Bartkowski, John P., and Jen'nan Ghazal Read. "Veiled Submission: Gender, Power, and Identity among Evangelical and Muslim Women in the United States." *Qualitative Sociology* 26, no. 1 (2003): 71–92.

Bearman, Peter, and Hannah Brückner. "Promising the Future: Virginity Pledges and First Intercourse." *American Journal of Sociology* 106 (2001): 859–912.

Bebbington, David W. *Evangelicalism in Modern Britain: A History from the 1730s to the 1980s.* London: Routledge, 1989.

Beehler, Don. "True Love Waits to Expand Anti-AIDS Initiative in Africa." *Baptist Press,* April 12, 2007. www.bpnews.net/BPnews.asp?ID=25373.

Beinart, Peter. "Morally Correct." *New Republic.* November 29, 2004. www.tnr.com/article/morally-correct.

Bell, Elizabeth, Lynda Haas, and Laura Sells. *From Mouse to Mermaid: The Politics of Film, Gender, and Culture.* Bloomington: Indiana University Press, 1995.

Bellah, Robert. "Civil Religion in America." *Daedalus* 96, no. 1 (1967): 1–21.

Bellah, Robert et al. *Habits of the Heart: Individualism and Commitment in American Life.* New York: Harper and Row, 1985.

Benford, Robert D. "An Insider's Critique of the Social Movement Framing Perspective." *Sociological Inquiry* 67 (1997): 409–30.

Benhabib, Seyla. "Models of Public Space: Hannah Arendt, the Liberal Tradition and Jürgen Habermas." In Craig Calhoun, ed., *Habermas and the Public Sphere,* 73–98. Cambridge, Mass.: MIT Press, 1992.

Berger, Peter L., and Thomas Luckmann. *The Social Construction of Reality.* New York: Doubleday, 1966.

Bertolet, K., R. Chandler, Z. Mukakibibi, E. Ngoga, and R. Reichenbach. "Mobilizing for Life: A Knowledge, Attitudes and Practices Final Survey 2003." World Relief, Kigali, Rwanda, 2003.

Bevere, Lisa. *Kissed the Girls and Made Them Cry.* Nashville, Tenn.: Thomas Nelson, 2002.

Bishop, Jennie. *The Princess and the Kiss.* Anderson, Ind.: Warner Press, 1999.
———. *The Squire and the Scroll.* Anderson, Ind.: Warner Press, 2004.

Bitzer, Lloyd. "The Rhetorical Situation." *Philosophy and Rhetoric* 1 (1968): 1–14.

Blithefield, J. Position paper presented to the Rhetorical Agency working group at the meeting of the Alliance of Rhetoric Societies, Evanston, Ill., September 2003.

Boddy, Janice. *Wombs and Alien Spirits.* Madison: University of Wisconsin Press, 1989.

Boehmer, Nancy. *True Love Waits: Seize the Net Manual, 2001–2002.* Nashville, Tenn.: LifeWay Press, 2000.

Bottigheimer, Ruth, ed. *Fairy Tales and Society: Illusion, Allusion and Paradigm*. Philadelphia: University of Pennsylvania Press, 1986.

Brake, Barbara. "AIDS/HIV Rate Slashed in Uganda after 10 Years of True Love Waits." *Baptist Press*, February 25, 2003.

———. *True Love Waits Goes Home, Manual 2003–2004*. Nashville, Tenn.: LifeWay Press, 2002.

Brooks, David. "The Wisdom We Need to Fight AIDS." *New York Times*, June 12, 2005, A14.

Brouwer, Daniel C. Position paper presented to the Rhetorical Agency working group at the meeting of the Alliance of Rhetoric Societies, Evanston, Ill., September 2003.

Bush, George W. "State of the Union Address," January 20, 2004. www.cnn.com/2004/ALLPOLITICS/01/20/sotu.transcript.1/.

"Bush Signs Initiative to Fight AIDS Abroad." White House press release, May 27, 2003. www.usembassy.it/file2003_05/alia/A3052701.htm.

Caldwell, Deborah. "Where Jabez Doesn't Cut It." *Beliefnet*, November 13, 2003. www.beliefnet.com/Inspiration/2003/11/Where-Jabez-Doesnt-Cut-It.aspx.

Campbell, Karlyn Kohrs. "Agency: Promiscuous and Protean." Paper presented at the Alliance of Rhetoric Societies meeting, Evanston, Ill., September 2003. www.rhetoricsociety.org/ARS/pdf/campbellonagency.pdf.

Carey, James W. *Communication as Culture*. Boston: Unwin Hyman, 1989.

Carpenter, Laura. *Virginity Lost*. New York: New York University Press, 2005.

Chapman, Gary, and Tony Rankin. *A Student's Guide to the Five Love Languages: True Love Waits*. Nashville, Tenn.: LifeWay Press, 2003.

Chevapravatdumrong, Cherry. "Prick Up Your Ears," television episode of *The Family Guy* directed by James Purdom. New York: Twentieth Century Fox, November 19, 2006.

Cole, Sean. "With This Ring: Pledging Abstinence." Radio broadcast on *Inside Out*, Anna Bensted, executive producer. Boston: WBUR, 2004. www.insideout.org/documentaries/withthisring/.

Condit, Celeste. *Decoding Abortion Rhetoric*. Urbana: University of Illinois Press, 1990.

———. Position paper presented to the Rhetorical Agency working group at the meeting of the Alliance of Rhetoric Societies, Evanston, Ill., September 2003.

Connolly, Ceci. "ACLU Sues HHS over Abstinence Aid," *Washington Post*, May 17, 2005, A10.

Craven, Allison. "Beauty and the Belles: Discourses of Feminism and Femininity in Disneyland." *European Journal of Women's Studies* 9, no. 2 (2002): 123–42.

Crowley, Sharon. "Response to Karlyn Kohrs Campbell, 'Agency.'" Paper presented at the meeting of the Alliance of Rhetoric Societies, Evanston, Ill., September 2003.

Cunningham, D., and J. Cunningham. *Adventure Unlimited: Growing Up in Today's World*. Kijabe, Kenya: Scripture Union—Aid for AIDS, 1994.

Daniels, Robert. *The War Within*. Wheaton, Ill.: Crossway Books, 1997.

Dannelly, Brian, dir. *Saved!* Film produced by William Vince, Michael Stipe, Sandy Stern, and Michael Ohoven. Los Angeles: MGM Home Entertainment, 2003.

DeLuca, Kevin M. "Unruly Arguments: The Body Rhetoric of Earth First!, ACT UP, and Queer Nation." *Argumentation and Advocacy* 36 (1999): 9–21.

DeVreis, M., comp. *True Love Waits.* Nashville, Tenn.: Broadman and Holman, 1997.

DeVries, M., and S. Shellenberger. *True Love Waits: Bible for Youth, New International Version.* Nashville, Tenn.: Broadman and Holman, 1996.

Do Rozario, Rebecca-Anne C. "The Princess and the Magic Kingdom: Beyond Nostalgia, the Function of the Disney Princess." *Women's Studies in Communication* 27 (2004): 34–59.

Douglas, Mary. *Purity and Danger: An Analysis of the Concepts of Pollution and Taboo.* New York: Routledge and Kegan Paul, 1966.

Downey, S. D. "Feminine Empowerment in Disney's 'Beauty and the Beast.'" *Women's Studies in Communication* 19, no. 2 (1996): 185–212.

Eden, Dawn. *The Thrill of the Chaste.* Nashville, Tenn.: W Publishing, 2006.

Eldredge, John. *Wild at Heart.* Nashville, Tenn.: Nelson Books, 2001.

Eldredge, John, and Staci Eldredge. *Captivating.* Nashville, Tenn.: Nelson Books, 2005.

Eley, Geoff. "Nations, Publics, and Political Cultures: Placing Habermas in the Nineteenth Century." In Craig Calhoun, ed., *Habermas and the Public Sphere*, 289–339. Cambridge, Mass.: MIT Press, 1992.

Elliot, Elisabeth. *Passion and Purity: Learning to Bring Your Love Life under Christ's Control.* Grand Rapids, Mich.: Revell, 2002.

Elmer-Dewitt, Philip. "Making the Case for Abstinence." *Time,* May 24, 1993, 64–65.

Elshtain, Jean Bethke. *Democracy on Trial.* New York: Basic, 1995.

Entman, Robert M. "Framing: Toward Clarification of a Fractured Paradigm." *Journal of Communication* 43, no. 3 (1993): 51–58.

Epstein, Helen. *The Invisible Cure: Africa, the West, and the Fight against AIDS.* New York: Farrar, Straus and Giroux, 2007.

Erzen, Tanya. *Straight to Jesus.* Berkeley: University of California Press, 2006.

Ethridge, Shannon, and Stephen Arterburn. *Every Young Woman's Battle.* Colorado Springs, Colo.: WaterBrook Press, 2004.

Feldt, Gloria. *The War on Choice: The Right-Wing Attack on Women's Rights and How to Fight Back.* New York: Bantam, 2004.

Finke, Roger, and Rodney Stark. *The Churching of America, 1776–1990: Winners and Losers in Our Religious Economy.* New Brunswick, N.J.: Rutgers University Press, 1992.

Focus on the Family. "No Apologies: The Truth about Life, Love and Sex." Nairobi, Kenya, n.d.

Foster, Richard. *Celebration of Discipline.* 3d ed. San Francisco: HarperSanFrancisco, 1998.

Fraser, Nancy. "Rethinking the Public Sphere: A Contribution to the Critique of Actually Existing Democracy." In Calhoun, ed., *Habermas and the Public Sphere*, 109–42. Cambridge, Mass.: MIT Press, 1992.

Freitas, Donna. *Sex and the Soul: Juggling Sexuality, Spirituality, Romance, and Religion on America's College Campuses.* New York: Oxford University Press, 2008.

Furnas, J.C. *The Life and Times of the Late Demon Rum.* New York: G.P. Putnam's Sons, 1965.

Gamson, William A. "Constructing Social Protest." In Hank Johnston and Bert Klandermans, eds., *Social Movement and Culture,* 85–106. Minneapolis: University of Minnesota Press, 1995.

Gaonkar, Dilip Parameshwar. "The Idea of Rhetoric in the Rhetoric of Science." In Alan G. Gross and William M. Keith, eds., *Rhetorical Hermeneutics: Invention and Interpretation in the Age of Science,* 25–85. Albany: State University of New York Press, 1997.

Gardner, Christine J. "God's Protection." *Wall Street Journal,* August 18, 2006. http://online.wsj.com/article/SB115586774753539078.html.

———. "My Body, My Choice: Media Framing of Reproduction, 1980–2003." Paper presented at the Mass Communication Division of the National Communication Association annual meeting, Boston, November 2005.

Garth, L., and J. Velasquez. *True Love Waits.* CD. Franklin, Tenn.: Everyday Records, 1999.

Geertz, Clifford. *The Interpretation of Cultures.* New York: Basic, 1973.

Geisler, Cheryl. "How Ought We to Understand the Concept of Rhetorical Agency? Report from the ARS." *Rhetoric Society Quarterly* 34, no. 3 (2004): 9–17.

———. "Teaching the Post-Modern Rhetor: Continuing the Conversation on Rhetorical Agency." *Rhetoric Society Quarterly* 35, no. 4 (2005): 107–13.

Gerson, Michael J. "For Key Abortion Foes, A Sudden Pragmatism." *U.S. News and World Report,* June 1, 1998, 25–26.

Glaser, Barney G., and Anselm L. Strauss. *The Discovery of Grounded Theory.* New York: Aldine de Gruyter, 1967.

Glendon, Mary Ann. *Rights Talk.* New York: Free Press, 1991.

Goffman, Erving. *Frame Analysis.* Cambridge, Mass.: Harvard University Press, 1974.

Green, Edward C. "Faith-Based Organizations: Contributions to HIV Prevention." Cambridge, Mass.: Harvard Center for Population and Development Studies, September 2003.

———. *Rethinking AIDS Prevention: Learning from Successes in Developing Countries.* Westport, Conn.: Praeger, 2003.

Grenz, Stanley J. *Welcoming but Not Affirming: An Evangelical Response to Homosexuality.* Louisville, Ky.: Westminster John Knox Press, 1998.

Gresh, Bob. *Who Moved the Goalpost? Seven Winning Strategies in the Sexual Integrity Gameplan.* Chicago: Moody Press, 2001.

Gresh, Dannah. *And the Bride Wore White: Seven Secrets to Sexual Purity.* Chicago: Moody Press, 2004.

———. *Secret Keeper: The Delicate Power of Modesty.* Chicago: Moody Press, 2002.

———. *Seven Secrets to Sexual Purity: A Ten-Session Retreat or Bible Study Based on the Book.* State College, Pa.: Pure Freedom, 2000.

Griffin, Charles J. G. "The Rhetoric of Form in Conversion Narratives." *Quarterly Journal of Speech* 76 (1990): 152–63.

Griffith, R. Marie. *Born Again Bodies*. Berkeley: University of California Press, 2004.

———. *God's Daughters: Evangelical Women and the Power of Submission*. Berkeley: University of California Press, 1997.

Griswold, Wendy. *Cultures and Societies in a Changing World*. Thousand Oaks, Calif.: Pine Forge Press, 1994.

———. *Renaissance Revivals: City Comedy and Revenge Tragedy in the London Theatre, 1576–1980*. Chicago: University of Chicago Press, 1986.

Gunn, Joshua. Position paper presented to the Rhetorical Agency working group at the meeting of the Alliance of Rhetoric Societies, Evanston, Ill., September 2003.

Guttmacher Institute. "Facts on American Teens' Sexual and Reproductive Health." January 2010. www.guttmacher.org/pubs/fb_ATSRH.html.

Habermas, Jürgen. *The Structural Transformation of the Public Sphere*, translated by Thomas Burger. Cambridge, Mass.: MIT Press, 1989.

Hall, Amy Laura. *Conceiving Parenthood*. Grand Rapids, Mich.: William B. Eerdmans, 2008.

Hamilton, Brady E., Joyce A. Martin, and Stephanie J. Ventura. "Births: Preliminary Data for 2006," *National Vital Statistics Report* 56, no. 7 (December 5, 2007). www.cdc.gov/nchs/data/nvsr/nvsr56/nvsr56_07.pdf.

Harris, Joshua. *Boy Meets Girl: Say Hello to Courtship*. Sisters, Ore.: Multnomah, 2000.

———. *I Kissed Dating Goodbye*. Sisters, Ore.: Multnomah, 1997.

Hart, Roderick P. *The Political Pulpit*. West Lafayette, Ind.: Purdue University Press, 1977.

Hauerwas, Stanley. "On Being a Christian and an American." In Robert Madsen et al., eds., *Meaning and Modernity: Religion, Polity, and Self*, 224–35. Berkeley: University of California Press, 2002.

Hauser, Gerard A. "Incongruous Bodies: Arguments for Personal Sufficiency and Public Insufficiency." *Argumentation and Advocacy* 36 (summer 1999): 1–8.

———. *Vernacular Voices*. Columbia: University of South Carolina Press, 1999.

Hayden, Sara, and D. Lynn O'Brien Hallstein, eds. *Contemplating Maternity in an Era of Choice: Explorations into Discourses of Reproduction*. Plymouth, U.K.: Lexington, 2010.

Heidkamp, Rebecca, Deborah Dortzbach, and Lucy Njoroge. "Choose Life: Helping Youth Make Wise Choices." World Relief, Nairobi, Kenya, 2002.

Hendershot, Heather. *Shaking the World for Jesus*. Chicago: University of Chicago Press, 2004.

Hunter, James Davison. *American Evangelicalism: Conservative Religion and the Quandary of Modernity*. New Brunswick, N.J.: Rutgers University Press, 1983.

———. *Evangelicalism: The Coming Generation*. Chicago: University of Chicago Press, 1987.

Iannaccone, Laurence R. "Why Strict Churches Are Strong." *American Journal of Sociology* 99 (1994): 1180–1211.

Ingrassia, Michele. "Virgin Cool." *Newsweek,* October 17, 1994, 58–69.

Irvine, Janice M. *Talk about Sex: The Battles over Sex Education in the United States.* Berkeley: University of California Press, 2004.

Jakobsen, Janet, and Ann Pellegrini. *Love the Sin.* Boston: Beacon, 2004.

———, eds. *Secularisms.* Durham, N.C.: Duke University Press, 2008.

Jones, Stanton L. "The Loving Opposition." *Christianity Today,* July 19, 1993, 19–25.

Kaufman, Gil. "Russell Brand/Jonas Brothers VMA Flap Spurs Abstinence Group's Leader to Send Purity Ring to Palin's Daughter." MTV.com, September 9, 2008. www.mtv.com/news/articles/1594447/20080909/jonas_brothers.jhtml.

Khamadi, J., V. Kahuko, A. Njoroge, G. Ojiambo, and V. Reczek. *Worth the Wait Manual.* Nairobi: Crisis Pregnancy Ministries Kenya, 2000.

Klein, J. "Learning How to Say No: Clinton's New Teen-Pregnancy Program Will Counsel Abstinence." *Newsweek,* June 13, 1994, 29.

Kliff, Sarah. "The Future of Abstinence." *Newsweek,* October 27, 2009. www.newsweek.com/id/219818/page/1.

Kristof, Nicholas. "Following God Abroad." *New York Times,* May 21, 2002, A21.

Kuehne, Dale S. *Sex and the iWorld.* Grand Rapids, Mich.: Baker Academic, 2009.

Landes, Joan B. *Women and the Public Sphere in the Age of the French Revolution.* Ithaca, N.Y.: Cornell University Press, 1988.

Lasch, Christopher. *The Culture of Narcissism.* New York: W.W. Norton, 1979.

Lucaites, John L. Position paper presented to the Rhetorical Agency working group at the meeting of the Alliance of Rhetoric Societies, Evanston, Ill., September 2003.

Ludy, Eric. *God's Gift to Women: Discovering the Lost Greatness of Masculinity.* Sisters, Ore.: Multnomah, 2003.

Ludy, Eric, and Leslie Ludy. *When God Writes Your Love Story.* Sisters, Ore.: Multnomah, 1999.

Ludy, Leslie. *Authentic Beauty.* Sisters, Ore.: Multnomah, 2003.

Luker, Kristin. *Abortion and the Politics of Motherhood.* Berkeley: University of California Press, 1984.

———. *When Sex Goes to School.* New York: W.W. Norton, 2006.

Mahmood, Saba. *Politics of Piety.* Princeton, N.J.: Princeton University Press, 2005.

Maken, Debbie. *Getting Serious about Getting Married.* Wheaton, Ill.: Crossway Books, 2006.

MAP International, National Association of Evangelicals, World Relief, World Vision. "Statement of Conscience of the Evangelical Church Concerning the Global HIV/AIDS Crisis." Washington, D.C., June 11, 2003.

Marsden, George. *Understanding Fundamentalism and Evangelicalism.* Grand Rapids, Mich.: W.B. Eerdmans, 1991.

Martin, Joyce A. et al. "Births: Final Data for 2006." *National Vital Statistics Reports* 57, no. 7 (January 7, 2009). www.cdc.gov/nchs/data/nvsr/nvsr57/nvsr57_07.pdf.

Martino, Steven C. "Virginity Pledges Work for Some Teens." *Providence Journal*, April 1, 2009. www.projo.com/opinion/contributors/content/CT_sex1_04–01–09_1SDNCE9_v24.3e664cd.html.

Martino, Steven C. et al. "Virginity Pledges among the Willing: Delays in First Intercourse and Consistency of Condom Use." *Journal of Adolescent Health* 43, no. 4 (2008): 341–48. www.region8ipp.com/Docs/Articles/Martino.pdf.

Mattox, William R. "Aha! Call It the Revenge of the Church Ladies." *USA Today*, February 11, 1999, 15A.

Mauss, Marcel. *The Gift: The Form and Reason for Exchange in Archaic Societies,* trans. W. D. Hall. New York: W. W. Norton, 2000.

McDowell, Josh. *Why True Love Waits: The Definitive Book on How to Help Your Kids Resist Sexual Pressure.* Wheaton, Ill.: Tyndale House, 2002.

McKerrow, Raymie. "Corporeality and Cultural Rhetoric: A Site for Rhetoric's Future." *Southern Communication Journal* 63, no. 3 (1998): 315–28.

McMinn, Lisa Graham. *Sexuality and Holy Longing.* San Francisco: Jossey-Bass, 2004.

Meacham, Jon. "The End of Christian America." *Newsweek,* April 13, 2009, 34–38.

"Mobilizing for Life: World Relief's Comprehensive AIDS Ministry." Undated World Relief brochure. Available: 7 East Baltimore Street, Baltimore, Md. 21202.

Mohler, Albert. "The Palin Parable—Bristol Says Abstinence 'Not Realistic At All,'" February 19, 2009. www.albertmohler.com.

Morgan, Timothy C. "Mr. Jabez Goes to Africa." *Christianity Today,* October 17, 2003. www.christianitytoday.com/ct/2003/november/1.44.html.

———. "Purpose-Driven in Rwanda." *Christianity Today,* September 23, 2005. www.christianitytoday.com/ct/2005/october/17.32.html.

Morrow, Lance. "Fifteen Cheers for Abstinence." *Time,* October 2, 1995, 90.

Mullaney, Jamie L. *Everyone Is Not Doing It: Abstinence and Personal Identity.* Chicago: University of Chicago Press, 2006.

Museveni, Janet. Untitled public address at "Common Ground: A Shared Vision for Health" conference, Medical Institute for Sexual Health, Washington, D.C., June 2004. www.medinstitute.org/medical/index.

Nathanson, Constance A. *Dangerous Passage: The Social Control of Sexuality in Women's Adolescence* (Philadelphia: Temple University Press, 1991), 33–34.

National Abstinence Education Association. "Teen Pregnancy Rates Demand Honest Look." Press release, January 7, 2009. www.abstinenceassociation.org/newsroom/032409_teen_pregnancy_rates_demand.html.

Neal, Lynn S. *Romancing God.* Chapel Hill: University of North Carolina Press, 2006.

Neff, David, and Timothy C. Morgan. "Jesus Freak." *Christianity Today,* December 2, 2002. www.christianitytoday.com.

"The New Abortion Rhetoric." Editorial. *New York Times,* March 22, 1999. www.nytimes.com/1999/03/22/opinion/the-new-abortion-rhetoric.html.

Noll, Mark A. *American Evangelical Christianity: An Introduction.* Oxford, U.K.: Wiley-Blackwell, 2001.

———. *The Rise of Evangelicalism: The Age of Edwards, Whitefield, and the Wesleys.* Downers Grove, Ill.: InterVarsity Press, 2004.

NPR/Kaiser/Kennedy School Poll. "Sex Education in America." February 24, 2004. www.npr.org/templates/story/story.php?storyId=1622610&ps=rs.

Office of the U.S. Global AIDS Coordinator. U.S. Department of State. "Critical Interventions: Faith-Based Organizations." Washington, D.C.: 2005. www.state.gov/documents/organization/56966.pdf.

Office of U.S. Global AIDS Coordinator and the Bureau of Public Affairs. U.S. State Department. "The United States President's Emergency Plan for AIDS Relief: A Commitment Renewed." September 2009. www.pepfar.gov/press/107735.htm.

Perotta, Tom. *The Abstinence Teacher.* New York: St. Martin's, 2007.

Pickering, Barbara A. "Women's Voices as Evidence: Personal Testimony in Pro-Choice Films." *Argumentation and Advocacy* 40 (2003): 1–22.

Princeton Survey Research Associates International/Newsweek Poll. "Would you describe yourself as a born-again or Evangelical Christian, or not?" Public Opinion Online, November 30, 2005. Available through LexisNexis Academic. Item: 1638190.

Pumpelly, Sharon et al., eds. *True Love Waits Leaders' Manual.* Kampala: Magazine Consult, 1998. Available: True Love Waits, P.O. Box 1734, Kampala, Uganda.

———. *True Love Waits Leaders' Manual,* 2002. Available: True Love Waits Kenya, Baptist East Africa Region, P.O. Box 48390, Nairobi, Kenya.

Rand Corporation. "Virginity Pledges May Help Postpone Intercourse among Youth." Press release, June 10, 2008. Santa Monica, Calif. www.rand.org/news/press/2008/06/10/.

Rankin, D. Tony, and Richard Ross. *When True Love Doesn't Wait.* Nashville, Tenn.: LifeWay Press, 1998.

Regnerus, Mark. "The Case for Early Marriage." *Christianity Today,* July 31, 2009. www.christianitytoday.com/ct/2009/august/16.22.html.

———. *Forbidden Fruit: Sex and Religion in the Lives of American Teenagers.* New York: Oxford University Press, 2007.

———. "Say Yes. What Are You Waiting For?" *Washington Post,* April 26, 2009. www.washingtonpost.com/wp-dyn/content/article/2009/04/24/AR2009042402122.html.

"Remarks by the President on the Signing of H.R. 1298, the U.S. Leadership against HIV/AIDS, Tuberculosis and Malaria Act of 2003." White House press release, May 27, 2003. www.usembassy.it/file2003_05/alia/A3052701.htm.

Rios, Sandy. Letter to evangelical AIDS forum attendees. Concerned Women for America, Washington, D.C., June 11, 2003.

Rorty, Richard. "Religion as Conversation-Stopper." In *Philosophy and Social Hope,* 168–74. New York: Penguin, 1999.

Rosenbaum, Janet Elise E. "Patient Teenagers? A Comparison of the Sexual Behavior of Virginity Pledgers and Matched Nonpledgers." *Pediatrics* 123 (2009): 110–20. www.pediatrics.org/cgi/content/full/123/1/e110.

Ross, Deborah. "Escape from Wonderland: Disney and the Female Imagination." *Marvels and Tales* 18 (2004): 53–66.

Rowbotham, Judith. *Good Girls Make Good Wives: Guidance for Girls in Victorian Fiction.* Oxford: Basil Blackwell, 1989.

Saad, Lydia. "Americans' Acceptance of Gay Relations Crosses 50% Threshold." Gallup, May 25, 2010. www.gallup.com/poll/135764/Americans-Acceptance-Gay-Relations-Crosses-Threshold.aspx.

———. "Americans Evenly Divided on Morality of Homosexuality." Gallup, June 18, 2008. www.gallup.com/poll/108115/americans-evenly-divided-morality-homosexuality.aspx.

Saleton, William. *Bearing Right: How Conservatives Won the Abortion War.* Berkeley, Calif.: University of California Press, 2004.

Samson, Lisa. *Apples of Gold: A Parable of Purity.* Colorado Springs, Colo.: WaterBrook Press, 2006.

Schemo, Diana Jean. "Saving Themselves: What Teenagers Talk about When They Talk about Chastity." *New York Times,* January 28, 2001. www.nytimes.com/2001/01/28/weekinreview/28WORD.html.

Schiappa, Edward. *Defining Reality: Definitions and the Politics of Meaning.* Carbondale, Ill.: Southern Illinois University Press, 2003.

Schmalzbauer, John. *People of Faith: Religious Conviction in American Journalism and Higher Education.* Ithaca, N.Y.: Cornell University Press, 2003.

Sennett, Richard. *The Fall of Public Man.* New York: W. W. Norton, 1974.

Shapiro, Joseph P. "Teenage Sex: Just Say 'Wait.'" *U.S. News and World Report,* July 26, 1993, 56–59.

Shibley, Mark A. *Resurgent Evangelicalism in the United States: Mapping Cultural Change since 1970.* Columbia: University of South Carolina Press, 1996.

Shilts, Randy. *And the Band Played On.* New York: St. Martin's, 1987.

Silver, Marc. "Teenage Sex, after Magic." *U.S. News and World Report,* December 16, 1991, 90–93.

Silver Ring Thing Sexual Abstinence Study Bible. Corralitos, Calif.: Bible at Cost, 2002.

Smith, Christian. *American Evangelicalism: Embattled and Thriving.* Chicago: University of Chicago Press, 1998.

Smith, Michael W., and Lisa Bevill. *True Love Waits.* CD. Nashville, Tenn.: Genevox Music Group, 1994.

Smith-Rosenberg, Carroll. "Sex as Symbol in Victorian Purity: An Ethnohistorical Analysis of Jacksonian America." *American Journal of Sociology* 84 (1978): S212–47.

Snow, David A., E. Burke Rochford, Steven K. Worden, and Robert D. Benford. "Frame Alignment Processes, Micromobilization and Movement Participation." *American Sociological Review* 51 (1986): 464–81.

Speck, Greg. "Homosexuality: Is There Hope?" In *Sex: It's Worth Waiting For,* 165–88. Chicago: Moody Press, 1989.

Spicka, Jana. *The Locket and the Mask*. Heiskell, Tenn.: Jana Spicka, 2002.

St. James, Rebecca. "Wait for Me." *Transform*. CD. Franklin, Tenn.: Forefront B00004ZDMO, 2000.

St. James, Rebecca, with Dale Reeves. *Wait for Me: Rediscovering the Joy of Purity in Romance*. Nashville, Tenn.: Thomas Nelson, 2002.

Strack, Jay, and Diane Strack. *Until You Say I Do*. Nashville, Tenn.: LifeWay Press, 1997.

Strauss, Anselm L., and Juliet M. Corbin. *Basics of Qualitative Research*. Thousand Oaks, Calif.: Sage 1998.

Struck, Jane. "Planned Purity." *Christian Parenting Today* 17, no. 4, (summer 2005), 1–5. www.christianitytoday.com/momsense/2005/summer/plannedpurity.html?start=1.

Swidler, Ann. "Culture in Action: Symbols and Strategies." *American Sociological Review* 51 (1986): 273–86.

Swindoll, Charles. *Cultivating Purity in an Impure World*. Plano, Tex.: IFL, 2005.

"Taking the Pledge: Organization Urges Kids to Take Abstinence Promise." *60 Minutes Highlights,* May 22, 2005. http://cbs4.com/news60min/sixtyminutes_story_142195533.html.

Taylor, Charles. *A Secular Age*. Cambridge, Mass.: Belknap, 2007.

———. *Sources of the Self*. Cambridge, Mass.: Harvard University Press, 1989.

Traister, Rebecca. "Bristol Palin Stammers the Truth." *Salon*, February 18, 2009. www.salon.com/life/feature/2009/02/18/bristol_palin.

Travers, P. L. *In Search of the Hero: The Continuing Relevance of Myth and Fairy Tale*. Claremont, Calif.: Scripps College, 1970.

Treichler, Paula. *How to Have Theory in an Epidemic*. Durham, N.C.: Duke University Press, 1999.

True Love Waits: Crossing Bridges with Purity, Manual 1999–2000. Nashville, Tenn.: LifeWay Christian Resources of the Southern Baptist Convention, 1998.

"True Love Waits Launches Community-wide Initiative." *Baptist Press*, February 14, 2005. www.bpnews.net/bpnews.asp?ID=20143.

Turner, Victor. *The Forest of Symbols*. Ithaca, N.Y.: Cornell University Press, 1967.

———. *The Ritual Process*. Chicago: Aldine, 1969.

Tyler, Alice Felt. *Freedom's Ferment*. Minneapolis: University of Minnesota Press, 1944.

UNAIDS. "Report on the Global AIDS Epidemic, Executive Summary." UNAIDS, Washington, D.C., 2008. http://data.unaids.org/pub/Global Report/2008/JC1511_GR08_ExecutiveSummary_en.pdf.

UNAIDS/WHO. "AIDS Epidemic Update December 2004." www.reliefweb.int/rw/lib.nsf/db900sid/LHON-69TDCG/$file/AIDS_Update_UNAIDS_Dec_2004.pdf?openelement.

———. "AIDS Epidemic Update December 2009." http://data.unaids.org/pub/Report/2009/JC1700_Epi_Update_2009_en.pdf.

————. "Uganda: Epidemiological Country Profile on HIV and AIDS," 2008. http://apps.who.int/globalatlas/predefinedReports/EFS2008/short/EFSCountryProfiles2008_UG.pdf.

UNICEF. "Ten Years after Genocide, Rwandan Children Suffer Lasting Impact." Press release, April 6, 2004. www.unicef.org/media/media_20325.html.

U.S. Agency for International Development. "USAID Announces First Round of Grants for President Bush's Emergency Plan for AIDS Relief." Press release, April 13, 2004. Washington, D.C. www.usaid.gov/press/releases/2004/pr040413_1.html.

Valenti, Jessica. *The Purity Myth: How America's Obsession with Virginity Is Hurting Young Women.* Berkeley, Calif.: Seal Press, 2009.

Van Susteren, Greta. "Exclusive: A Visit with the Palins." *On the Record,* Fox News, February 18, 2009. www.foxnews.com/story/0,2933,494205,00.html.

Ventura, Stephanie J., Joyce C. Abma, William Mosher, and Stanley Henshaw. "Revised Pregnancy Rates, 1990–97, and New Rates for 1998–99: United States." *National Vital Statistics Report* 52, no. 7 (October 23, 2003). www.cdc.gov/nchs/data/nvsr/nvsr52/nvsr52_07.pdf.

Warner, Marina. *From the Beast to the Blonde: On Fairy Tales and Their Tellers.* New York: Noonday Press, 1995.

Wasko, Janet. *Understanding Disney: The Manufacture of Fantasy.* Cambridge: Polity, 2001.

Watters, Candice. *Get Married: What Women Can Do to Help It Happen.* Chicago: Moody, 2008.

Willard, Dallas. *The Spirit of the Disciplines.* San Francisco: HarperSanFrancisco, 1988.

Williams, Rhys. "The Language of God in the City of Man: Religious Discourse and Public Politics in America." In Corwin E. Smidt, ed., *Religion as Social Capital: Producing the Common Good,* 171–89. Waco, Tex.: Baylor University Press, 2003.

Winner, Lauren. *Real Sex.* Grand Rapids, Mich.: Brazos Press, 2005.

Witten, Marsha. *All Is Forgiven: The Secular Message in American Protestantism.* Princeton, N.J.: Princeton University Press, 1993.

Wolfe, Alan. *The Transformation of American Religion.* New York: Free Press, 2003.

Wood, Naomi. "Domesticating Dreams in Walt Disney's 'Cinderella.'" *Lion and the Unicorn* 20 (1996): 25–49.

"World Relief Annual Report." Baltimore, Md.: World Relief, 2007. www.wr.org/media/pdf/Annual_Report_2007.pdf.

"The World Relief Journals: Annual Report 2004." Baltimore, Md.: World Relief, 2004. http://worldrelief.org/Document.Doc?id=346.

WorldTeach USA. Hope for Africa. Atlanta: WorldTeachUSA, n.d. Videotape. Available: 4201 North Peachtree Road, Suite 200, Atlanta, GA 30341.

Worthen, Molly. "Housewives of God." *New York Times Magazine,* November 12, 2010. www.nytimes.com/2010/11/14/magazine/14evangelicals-t.html.

Wuthnow, Robert. *Christianity and Civil Society: The Contemporary Debate.* Valley Forge, Pa.: Trinity Press International, 1996.

———. *Producing the Sacred: An Essay on Public Religion*. Urbana: University of Illinois Press, 1994.

———. *The Restructuring of American Religion*. Princeton, N.J.: Princeton University Press, 1988.

———. *The Struggle for America's Soul: Evangelicals, Liberals, and Secularism*. Grand Rapids, Mich.: William B. Eerdmans, 1989.

———, ed. *Vocabularies of Public Life*. London: Routledge, 1992.

Zipes, Jack. "Breaking the Disney Spell." In Elizabeth Bell, Lynda Haas, and Laura Sells, eds. *From Mouse to Mermaid: The Politics of Film, Gender, and Culture*, 21–42. Bloomington: Indiana University Press, 1995.

———. *Fairy Tales and the Art of Subversion*. New York: Routledge, 2006.

Index

TEXT
10/13 Sabon Open Type

DISPLAY
Sabon Open Type

COMPOSITOR
Toppan Best-set Premedia Limited

INDEXER
Barbara Roos

PRINTER & BINDER
Maple-Vail Book Manufacturing Group